Henry James and the Father Question

The intellectual relationship between Henry James and his father, who was a philosopher and theologian, proved to be an influential resource for the novelist. Andrew Taylor explores how James's writing responds to James Senior's epistemological, thematic and narrative concerns, and relocates these concerns in a more secularised and cosmopolitan cultural milieu. Taylor examines the nature of both men's engagement with autobiographical strategies, issues of gender reform, and the language of religion. He argues for a reading of Henry James that is informed by an awareness of paternal inheritance. Taylor's study reveals the complex and at times antagonistic dialogue between the elder James and his peers, particularly Emerson and Whitman, in the vanguard of mid nineteenth-century American Romanticism. Through close readings of a wide range of novels and texts, he demonstrates how this dialogue anticipates James's own theories of fiction and selfhood.

ANDREW TAYLOR is College Lecturer in English and American Literature at University College Dublin.

Cambridge Studies in American Literature and Culture

Editor
Ross Posnock, New York University

Founding Editor
Albert Gelpi, Stanford University

Advisory Board
Sacvan Bercovitch, Harvard University
Ronald Bush, St. John's College, Oxford University
Wai Chee Dimock, Yale University
Albert Gelpi, Stanford University
Gordon Hutner, University of Kentucky
Kenneth Warren, University of Chicago
Walter Benn Michaels, University of Illinois, Chicago

Henry James and the Father Question

ANDREW TAYLOR

University College Dublin

PUBLISHED BY THE PRESS SYNDICATE OF THE UNIVERSITY OF CAMBRIDGE
The Pitt Building, Trumpington Street, Cambridge, United Kingdom

CAMBRIDGE UNIVERSITY PRESS
The Edinburgh Building, Cambridge CB2 2RU, UK
40 West 20th Street, New York, NY 10011-4211, USA
477 Williamstown Road, Port Melbourne, VIC 3207, Australia
Ruiz de Alarcón 13, 28014 Madrid, Spain
Dock House, The Waterfront, Cape Town 8001, South Africa

http://www.cambridge.org

First published 2002

Printed in the United Kingdom at the University Press, Cambridge

Typeface Bembo 11/12 pt.   *System* LATEX 2$_\varepsilon$ [TB]

A catalogue record for this book is available from the British Library

Library of Congress Cataloguing in Publication data

Taylor, Andrew, 1968–
Henry James and the father question / Andrew Taylor.
    p.   cm. (Cambridge Studies in American Literature and Culture 129)
Includes bibliographical references and index.
ISBN 0 521 80722 0
1. James, Henry, 1843–1916 – Philosophy.   2. James, Henry, 1811–1882 – Influence.
3. James, Henry, 1843–1916 – Family.   4. James, Henry, 1811–1882 – Family.
5. Fathers and sons – United States.   6. Fathers and sons in literature.   7. Fathers figures
in literature.   8. Autobiography in literature.   9. Philosophy in literature.   10. Fathers
in literature.   11. Self in literature.   I. Title.   II. Series.
PS2127.P5 T39 2002
813′.4 – dc21   2001043250

ISBN 0 521 80722 0 hardback

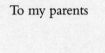

To my parents

Contents

Acknowledgements

Many people have helped me, knowingly or otherwise, in the writing of this book.

Tony Tanner's support and enthusiasm were fundamental in the project's genesis and its development. His untimely death deprived literary criticism of a distinctive and exuberant voice.

I am grateful too for the advice and comments of others familiar with aspects of my work: Alice Adams, Jean Chothia, David Cross, Paul Giles, Richard Gooder, Fiona Green, Philip Horne, Susan Manning, Adrian Poole, Ross Posnock and Brian Ridgers. The comments of Cambridge University Press's two anonymous readers were also helpful in shaping a stronger book. My editor at the Press, Ray Ryan, has been constantly positive and generous with his time. My colleagues in the English Department at University College Dublin have provided a supportive intellectual community, and I thank them for that. Thanks also are due to the librarians at the Houghton Library, Harvard University, the Massachusetts Historical Society, and the Swedenborg Society, London for their tireless work in assisting my research.

Philip West and Daniel Grimley have been sources of strength and friendship which I value greatly. Finally, I owe a debt of gratitude to Ellie Herrington. She knows why.

Note on the text and brief titles

I refer to the novelist as 'Henry James' and to his father as 'James Senior' or 'the elder James' throughout.

The following abbreviations are used throughout the book:

A	Henry James, *Autobiography*, edited by Frederick W. Dupee (London: W. H. Allen, 1956)
B	Henry James, *The Bostonians* (1886) (Harmondsworth: Penguin, 1988)
CWE	Ralph Waldo Emerson, *The Complete Works of Ralph Waldo Emerson*, Centenary Edition, edited by Edward E. Emerson, 12 vols. (Boston: Houghton Mifflin, 1903–4)
EAE	Henry James, *Literary Criticism: Essays on Literature, American and English Writers* (New York: Library of America, 1984)
EWP	Henry James, *Literary Criticism: French Writers, Other European Writers, The Prefaces to the New York Edition* (New York: Library of America, 1984)
JMN	Ralph Waldo Emerson, *The Journals and Miscellaneous Notebooks of Ralph Waldo Emerson*, edited by William H. Gilman, George P. Clark *et al.*, 16 vols. (Cambridge, MA: Harvard University Press, 1960–82)
James	James Family Papers, Houghton Library, Harvard University
Journals	Ralph Waldo Emerson, *Journals of Ralph Waldo Emerson*, edited by Edward Waldo Emerson and Waldo Emerson Forbes, 10 vols. (Boston: Houghton Mifflin Company, 1909–14)

LE   Ralph Waldo Emerson, *The Letters of Ralph Waldo
            Emerson*, edited by Ralph L. Rusk and Eleanor M. Tilton,
            10 vols. (New York: Columbia University Press, 1939–95)
Letters   Henry James, *The Letters of Henry James*, edited by Leon
            Edel, 4 vols. (Cambridge, MA: Harvard University Press,
            1974–84)
WJ   Ralph Barton Perry, *The Thought and Character of
            William James*, 2 vols. (Boston: Little, Brown, 1935)

Introduction

The nature of inheritance

The news in July 1915 that Henry James was contemplating becoming a British citizen was greeted by the *New York Times* with irritation that the writer should wish to make such a change and with certainty that he would decide, finally, to remain an American. Prior to any official announcement, the paper published an editorial under the title 'Are We To Lose Henry James?' There it lamented that although during the author's long exile in Europe 'he has become thoroughly Anglicized in his tastes and his point of view', it was nonetheless incredible that James should wish to perform such a public casting-off of what could now, after all, only be 'the empty symbol of allegiance'. Conceding to a degree the viability of James's dissatisfaction with his native land (America's lack of commitment in the First World War – she would not participate until April 1917), the *Times* suggested that he nevertheless ought to feel proud of the relief work being undertaken by other (significantly) 'real' Americans. It concluded by predicting, more in hope than expectation, that the pull of the novelist's New World roots would ultimately prove more powerful than any lengthy process of Europeanisation: 'he is, after all, of such American stock as few have cared to disown. We fancy the memories of his New England ancestry and its precious traditions will keep him with us, after all.'[1] When report of James's decision to transfer his citizenship reached New York, the *Times* printed a further, more critical piece, characterising the author as 'one of those agreeable cosmopolitans' that Americans, 'with their much more salient character, their genuineness', nevertheless all too foolishly rush to admire. The paper rather reluctantly concluded, in very Jamesian language, that 'to the literary man choice of his scene is to be granted'.[2] Others less cosseted, it implied, did not have such a luxury.

That James felt uncomfortable with any crude definition of patriotism – of nationality defined as the public and collective manifestation of

1

apparently stable and homogenous individual identity – is evident in his critique in the British magazine *Literature* of a collection of articles published in 1897 by the future American president Theodore Roosevelt. Roosevelt, the self-cultivated embodiment of the strenuous life and advocate of a vigorous policy of American expansionism, had been highly disparaging of James in an address delivered to the Brooklyn Young Republican Club some thirteen years earlier, in 1884. The *New York Times* had reported the speech the following day.

> Plenty of men were willing to complain of the evils of our system of politics, but were not willing to lift a finger to remedy them. Mr Roosevelt said that his hearers had read to their sorrow the works of Henry James. He bore the same relation to other literary men that a poodle did to other dogs. The poodle had his hair combed and was somewhat ornamental, but never useful. He was invariably ashamed to imitate the British lion.

Effete and decorative, Henry James and his kind 'were possessed of refinement and culture to see what was wrong' but yet displayed none of 'the robuster virtues that would enable them to come out and do . . . right'.[3] James at the time seems to have made no response to Roosevelt's attack, other than to write the following month to Grace Norton, the wife of his sometime editor Charles Eliot Norton, to request more details of its substance: 'I have heard nothing, & know nothing, of it. I never look at the American papers – I find them . . . intolerable.'[4] Whether this information from his correspondent was forthcoming is unknown. What is clear is that Roosevelt's 1897 collection, *American Ideals: And Other Essays Social and Political*, offered James the opportunity to respond in public to a political and cultural philosophy which he found deeply distasteful.

He was particularly interested in Roosevelt's essay 'True Americanism' (1894), the content of which, although not mentioning James specifically, elaborated on the ideas and imagery of the earlier criticism of him (and rehearsed the unfavourable publicity he would receive in 1915). For Roosevelt, Americanisation entailed a process of absolute redefinition of identity in which all trace of European inheritance was washed away. Of the ever-growing number of American immigrants he declared: 'We must Americanize them in every way, in speech, in political ideas and principles, and in their way of looking at relations between Church and State. We welcome the German or the Irishman who becomes an American. We have no such use for the German or Irishman who remains such.'[5] Such a conception of American identity was founded on recognisable Anglo-Saxon traits that had been most abundant during the Revolutionary period. The historian Jack Pole has argued that Roosevelt 'believed that the character of the American nationality was fixed in the period from 1776 to 1787', and that as a result 'all subsequent mingling was a process of continued assimilation into the original type'.[6] Americanness was conceived as something empirical and attainable, a single identity to be achieved once the 'spirit of colonial dependence' (23) had been expunged. As in the *Times* editorial following James's change of citizenship, cosmopolitanism was singled out for criticism, for it produced a 'flaccid habit of mind' which 'disqualif[ies] a man from doing good work in the world' (21). Roosevelt offered a sketch of one afflicted with such a disability that serves equally well as a more forceful variation on the 1915 judgement of James's apparently wavering patriotism:

> Thus it is with the undersized man of letters, who flees his country because he, with his delicate effeminate sensitiveness, finds the conditions of life on this side of the water crude and raw; in other words, because he finds that he cannot play a man's part among men, and so goes where he will be sheltered from the winds that harden stouter souls. This *emigré* may write graceful and pretty verses, essays, novels; but he will never do work to compare with that of his brother, who is strong enough to stand on his own feet, and do his work as an American.   (24–5)

Roosevelt's explicit agenda here is, in Martha Banta's neat phrase, to assail 'the scandal of failed masculinity'.[7] The expatriate writer, characteristically for Roosevelt always male, displays an unnatural femininity verging on total emasculation (he is sensitive and 'undersized'), far removed geographically and temperamentally from the rugged braveries of the New World exemplar. *This* figure, released from the enervating temptations of Europe, is proud 'to stand on his own feet... as an American'. Such an image of upright authoritativeness was one which Roosevelt went out of his way to promote. A contributor in 1917 to the socialist magazine *The Masses*, a publication generally unsympathetic to the now ex-president, described this strategy of self-fashioning and its embeddedness within an expansionist and nationalist ideology. Roosevelt's return to a kind of performative naturalness masked the triumph of 'civilised' American values:

> [Roosevelt] goes in for the strenuous life, and becomes our main apostle of virility. When occasion offers, he naturally assumes the role of the cowboy, because the cowboy is highly symbolic of the vital type... Next, in the Spanish War, he appears as a rough rider; a distinct promotion in the scale of virility, the rough rider being in essence the cowboy plus the added feature of participation in the virile game of war. Later on, as an explorer, playing with jungles and living among wild men and beasts, he approaches still nearer to the primitive male.[8]

'The Strenuous Life', a speech delivered in 1899, is Roosevelt's *locus classicus* of this potent combination of self-definition and national destiny. 'I wish to preach, not the doctrine of ignoble ease, but the doctrine of the strenuous life', it began, 'the life of toil and effort, of labor and strife.'[9]

America's new role in the world, one which it had to fulfil to become 'a really great people' (6), was to 'build up our power without our own borders', to 'enable us to have our say in deciding the destiny of the oceans of the East and West' (9). To achieve this would require the suppressing of 'the over-civilized man, who has lost the great fighting masterful virtues' (6) in favour of one in full possession of 'those virile qualities necessary to win in the stern strife of actual life' (2).

Henry James's relations with Roosevelt were complex and shifting. He could write to Edith Wharton in 1905, after a dinner at the White House, of his fascination with 'Theodore I' (as he titled him), whose energy and constant self-displaying he likened, not uncritically, to both 'a wonderful little machine . . . destined to be overstrained, perhaps, but not as yet, truly, betraying the least creak' and the brash spectacle of a shop-front window on Broadway.[10] To Wharton's sister-in-law, Mary Cadwalder Jones, James wrote about the same episode in more effusive terms, but again caught the note of presidential performativity: 'Theodore Rex is at any rate a really extraordinary creature for native intensity, veracity and *bonhomie* – he plays his part with the best will in the world and I recognise his amusing likeability' (*Letters*, IV, 337). Yet the imperial nature of Roosevelt's administration worried James, such that elsewhere he could refer to him as 'a dangerous and ominous Jingo' (*Letters*, IV, 202). James's critique of *American Ideals* is a variation on this anxiety. Roosevelt's assertion that 'it is "purely as an American" . . . that each of us must live and breathe' earns James's ridicule for its assumption that the 'American' name is a 'symbol revealed once for all in some book of Mormon dug up under a tree'. In an age in which peoples are no longer isolated or homogenous, in which so much effort has been made 'to multiplying contact and communication, to reducing separation and distance, to promoting, in short, an inter-penetration that would have been the wonder of our fathers', Roosevelt's belief in a superior and singular American type displays a reductive perception akin, for James, to wearing 'a pair of smart, patent blinders'. This is not to suggest that James is an advocate of the new technologies which had reduced the size of the globe; he is enough of a cultural conservative to fear that 'we may have been great fools to invent the post office, the newspaper and the railway, all manifestations of 'a Frankenstein monster at whom our simplicity can only gape'. But Roosevelt's solution in turn 'leaves us gaping' (*EAE*, 664). Whatever value Roosevelt's thoughts may have on the other issues with which his volume deals – civil service reform, the New York police department, political machinations at the highest levels – he is finally impaired 'by the puerility of his simplifications' (*EAE*, 665).

Writing to his brother William in 1888, James had famously declared his belief in 'a big AngloSaxon total' in which individual nationalities were

'destined to such an amount of melting together' that to argue for ghet-
toised difference and uniqueness would be an 'idle & pedantic' exercise
(*Letters*, III, 244). Although such a holistic approach to nationality would
later come under some pressure in the New York of *The American Scene*
(1907) (where melting becomes bleaching, and homogeneity rather than
inclusive difference is identified as the insidious national goal), here James
advocates a co-mingling of the individual and national identity, where
fusion does not undermine individuality but rather serves to enhance the
nation-state by its presence. Against Roosevelt, James's conception of
the patriotic impulse is regarded as a 'privilege' (*EAE*, 665); it becomes something inclusive, more comfortable in incorporating alternative and diverse allegiances than insisting upon a narrowly conceived
notion of 'national consciousness', the 'screws' of which Roosevelt had
attempted to tighten 'as they have never been tightened before' (*EAE*,
663). 'National consciousness' was a phrase which James had used twice
before – on these occasions in a positive context – to characterise the
sensibility of his friend James Russell Lowell.[11] With Lowell, James
writes, 'the national consciousness had never elsewhere been so cultivated' (*EAE*, 546). It was flexible and permeable enough to incorporate
alternatives: Lowell's 'main care for the New England . . . consciousness, as
he embodied it, was that it could be fed from as many sources as any other
in the world, and assimilate them with an ingenuity all its own: literature,
life, poetry, art, wit, all the growing experience of human intercourse'
(*EAE*, 547). This national consciousness, although unwaveringly 'intense',
nevertheless manifested itself as a form of patriotism which Lowell
'could play with'; he was able 'to make it various', such that he avoided
what James identified as the New England danger of provincialism –
'shutting himself up in his birth-chamber' (*EAE*, 518, 533).

Theodore Roosevelt's equating of his much more politicised ideal of
the New World citizen with images of sturdy self-reliance points to the
degree to which the American conception of individualism, as identified by Alexis de Tocqueville and celebrated by Ralph Waldo Emerson,
continued to influence hegemonic national self-definition. In addition to
the blunt topographical fact of American existence – the identification,
physical mapping and settlement of a previously uncharted land – the
concept of the country as embodying a vision of self-invention and democratic equality provided an eloquent and resonant vocabulary with which
the national history might be written. Daniel Walker Howe has remarked
that Thomas Jefferson's 'pursuit of happiness' sanctified the right of each
American to decide what kind of person he or she wished to become:
'that is, the belief that ordinary men and women have a dignity and value
in their own right, and that they are sufficiently trustworthy to be allowed
a measure of autonomy in their lives'.[12] Individualism was a constitutional

given, but as such was prone to the kind of adoption by institutional and capitalist America for ends which bore little resemblance to its formulation in Emersonian idealism. Seymour Martin Lipset, in his recent study of the continuing effects of enshrined individualism on American politics and culture, notes that 'the national classical liberal ideology' served to sustain an American economy 'characterized by more market freedom, more individual landownership, and a higher wage income structure . . . [I]t was the laissez-faire country par excellence . . . [in which] hard work and economic ambition were perceived as the proper activity of a moral person.'[13] As I shall show, this alliance of ideal with inevitably tarnished economic practice was one which Emerson had to carefully negotiate; for others it signified a fatal myopia inherent in the ideal of individualism itself.

Emerson had characterised Boston in 1861 as 'the town which was appointed in the destiny of nations to lead the civilization of North America'. Its pre-eminent position, he asserted, was founded on 'principles not of yesterday' but rather those which 'will always prevail over whatever material accumulations' (*CWE*, XII, 188, 209). That on a wider level New England still represented metonymically a repository of fine and defining American values too important to disown is evident in the 1915 *Times* editorial. There, if we recall, James's New England ancestry with its 'precious traditions' was cited as the decisive argument for his retaining his citizenship, ensuring his rejection, even if only symbolically, of the superficial 'material accumulations' of Europe. Of course, the simple biographical fact that James was born in New York, a city of such importance to him that he sought to memorialise it in his Edition, is ignored by the writer of the piece, who chooses to relocate James *culturally* in the native idealism of an Emersonian America rather than acknowledge his actual roots in, and continuing attachment to, the heterogeneous metropolis. James's immediate ancestor, his father the religious philosopher Henry James Senior, although an intimate of Emerson, Bronson Alcott and others in the vanguard of American Romanticism, rejected the lauding of the individual self characteristic of Emersonian transcendentalism. This asserted that in an America perceived as discovered by each person anew, each could possess the world in his or her own image, to the extent that the dialectic of self and 'other' is dissolved – everything is a manifestation of self and therefore potentially comprehensible to it. A characteristic instance of James Senior's repudiation of this privileging of the solitary can be found in a series of letters he wrote to the *New York Tribune* newspaper between November 1852 and January 1853. His principal adversary in the columns of the *Tribune*, Stephen Pearl Andrews, was a radical socialist who had established a utopian community on Long Island in 1851 and was now advocating the complete repeal of all marriage laws under the principle of the absolute 'Sovereignty of the Individual'. 'What is the limit up to which Man', Andrews asked, 'simply in virtue of being man, is entitled, of right, to the exercise of freedom, without the interference of Society, or – which is the same thing – of other individuals?'[14] His answer, reiterated throughout the correspondence, was unequivocal: democracy was 'the right of every individual to govern himself' (43). For that to be possible, each individual was obliged to establish 'the exact limits of encroachment' between himself and his neighbour, 'religiously refraining from passing those limits, and mildly or forcibly restraining [the neighbour] from doing so' (81).

This assertion was the secular – one might say tangible – extension of Emerson's spiritualised manifesto of self-reliance. Emerson's belief that only through the cultivation of 'the integrity of your own mind' can one hope for 'the suffrage of the world' (*CWE*, x, 50) becomes something more systematised and concrete in Andrews's image of absolute self-government: 'I claim individually to be my own nation. I take this opportunity to declare my National Independence, and to notify all other potentates, that they may respect my Sovereignty' (62). As Carl Guarneri has remarked in his study of the American utopian impulse, Andrews's theory 'rested on the conventional liberal faith that if left completely to themselves, individuals would prosper and the whole society benefit'.[15] Emerson would not have disagreed with that; indeed the self-proclaimed anarchic individualism of Andrews has been identified as existing at the heart of Emerson's philosophy too, especially by early Marxist readers of American literature such as V. F. Calverton and Granville Hicks. For such a politically inflected criticism, eloquent and elegant essays on self-reliance and personal independence could not hide the fact that Emerson was unprepared for the tangible results of his words, words which lent credence to a political and economic bias unwilling to promote social cohesion and communal responsibility.[16] Even more than Henry David Thoreau at Walden Pond, Andrews had taken the Concord writer's poetic philosophising to the point of actual implementation, to the point at which an unempirical belief (such as Emerson's) in individual progress was deemed to be insufficient. 'Vague notions of the natural goodness of man', Andrews warned, were 'no guarantee of right action' (44). What was needed was the recognition that reformers 'have a Science to study and a definite work to perform ... not a mere senseless, and endless, and aimless agitation to maintain' (12). Andrews represents the professionalisation of what he considered to be the ineffective, somewhat dilettante efforts of his reformist contemporaries. His unswerving belief in individualism as 'the profoundest, and most valuable, and most transcendentally important principle of political and social order' (41) achieved widespread expression in the pages of a popular New York newspaper and was acted out with fellow adherents on Long Island; Thoreau's embodiment of self-reliance, by contrast, had been practised in sylvan isolation and relative obscurity.

James Senior's response to Andrews's lionisation of the individual was to express his contrary belief that 'the best aspiration of the individual man is bound up with the progress of society' (60). Directly opposing the reification of the self, he declared: 'I can conceive of no "individual sovereignty" which precedes a man's perfect adjustment to nature and society' (57). Only through the development of a christianised community which recognised that individual selfhoods are transitory and inadequate could humankind hope to achieve spiritual redemption. James Senior hoped for men 'no longer visible or cognizable to God in their *atomic individualities*, but only as so many *social units*, each embracing and enveloping all in affection and thought'.[17] The philosophies of both Emerson and Andrews displayed, to his mind, an arrogant spiritual immaturity which mistakenly insisted upon the primacy of the individual, innocently cocooned in self-confident isolation from the potentially troublesome and conflicted realities of the wider community. John Jay Chapman, discussing Emerson in a volume of essays of 1898, focuses on just this sense of stasis and fixity in the Concord writer's thinking. Comparing him to the poetic genius of Robert Browning, who 'regards character as the result of experience and as ever changing growth', Chapman notes how Emerson conceives of it as 'rather an entity complete and eternal from the beginning. He is probably the last great writer to look at life from a stationary standpoint.'[18] James reviewed Chapman's book for the *Literature* magazine, considering the essay on Emerson to be 'the most effective critical attempt made in the United States, or I should suppose anywhere, really to get near the philosopher of Concord' (*EAE*, 687). Much as James himself had done in his *Hawthorne* (1879), Chapman argued that 'the New England spirit in prose and verse was, on a certain side, wanting in life' (*EAE*, 688). 'Life' in its present complexities and uncertainties was what Emerson's philosophy seemed to transcend. As Richard Poirier has described it, Emersonianism was characterised by its ceaseless *futurity*, an 'apparent obliviousness to the present circumstance, [a] living into the future', beyond the reach of the fetters of historical and social laws.[19] In discussing the relationship between both Henry Jameses and Emerson I want to illustrate the extent to which the certainties of the transcendental self were deemed inadequate for the spiritual reflections of the father and the fictional explorations of the son. For both men, it was the flawed individual, able to accept indeterminacy and error, who was best able to progress beyond the false sureties of the self.

The philosopher Charles Sanders Peirce, acquaintance of James Senior, William, and Henry, coined the term *fallibilism* for this attitude of radical uncertainty, describing it thus in 1887:

I used for myself to collect my ideas under the designation *fallibilism*; and indeed the first step toward *finding out* is to acknowledge you do not satisfactorily know already; so that no blight can so surely arrest all intellectual growth as the blight of cocksureness; . . . Indeed, out of a contrite fallibilism, combined with a high degree of faith in the reality of knowledge, and an intense desire to find things out, all my philosophy has always seemed to me to grow.[20]

The mystical self-confidence of American transcendentalism had earned Peirce's scorn – the Concord movement was a 'virus' against which the more academically rigorous 'atmosphere of Cambridge held many an antiseptic'.[21] Insistent doubt, he suggested, resisted the acquisition of such relaxed assurances, for '[w]e cannot be absolutely certain that our conclusions are even approximately true'.[22] Moreover, unlike the Emersonian credo of self-reliance, Peirce's understanding of individual growth depended upon the existence of a shared communality sensitive to expansion, one flexible (and indeed fallible) enough to incorporate alternative and discordant elements. Reality, Peirce argued, 'essentially involves the notion of a COMMUNITY, without definite limits, and capable of a definite increase of knowledge'.[23]

A close examination of James Senior's writings and sensitive readings of his son's fiction illustrate the extent to which, although Peirce may have formulated the concept, the embrace of fallibility was an essential stage in the epistemological process for both men.[24] Thus it is curious that what critical attention has been paid to the relationship between father and son has tended to gloss over the very considerable differences between James Senior and American transcendentalism, instead claiming both James and his father as fellow Emersonians. Quentin Anderson argued in his highly influential *The Imperial Self* (1971) that James, along with Emerson and Walt Whitman, displayed his representative Americanness through a 'profound extrasocial commitment' which 'ignores, elides, or transforms history, politics, . . . the hope for purposive change'.[25] The novelist's focus, Anderson suggested, was exclusively on 'the absolutism of the self' (ix), a solipsistic withdrawal from the complexities of the 'institutions and emotional dispositions of associated life' (3). Moreover responsibility for such a retreat lay with the fathers of this generation of writers, men who 'their sons did not accept . . . as successful in filling the role popularly assigned them' (15). The removal of the cultural authority of the father, Anderson claimed, directly, and detrimentally, affected the degree to which the fate of the son was 'bound up with the fate of the polity' (16). Anderson's concern for the apparently ahistorical strain in James sits uneasily with his analysis of the novelist in an earlier and much more eccentric book, *The American Henry James* (1957). There he went to extreme lengths to argue that James adopted wholesale his father's blend of transcendentalism and Swedenborgianism to produce an elaborate allegorical playing-out of James Senior's philosophical system. Choosing to ignore those novels which did not fit in with his thesis of seamless correspondence (*pace The Imperial Self*, texts such as *The Europeans*, *Washington Square*, and *The Bostonians* are rejected on the basis that they are *too* dependent upon 'the historically grounded attitudes of the time and place of the story'),[26] Anderson made some large claims for the degree of influence: 'Henry Junior . . . seems to have swallowed his father's psychology whole' (59); 'The younger son is, to my knowledge, the only man who has ever *used* the elder James's beliefs' (67). It soon becomes clear why many of the novelist's earlier works are discarded, for Anderson chooses to concentrate on James's late phase, which represents for him an allegorical trilogy depicting the phases of religious regeneration identified by James Senior. Thus the father's somewhat prejudiced understanding of Judaism is represented in *The Ambassadors* by Woollett's New England moralism; *The Wings of the Dove* embodies the Christian church with Milly Theale as its saviour; and *The Golden Bowl* illustrates the apotheosis of a Swedenborgian New Jerusalem, with the reconciliation of Maggie Verver and the Prince symbolising the harmonious joining of the world's contraries. Such a rigid and linear interpretation of highly complex and ambiguous narratives is flawed even before it begins its rather predictable trajectory if we remember that Henry James chose to place *The Ambassadors* second of the three novels in the New York edition, after *The Wings of the Dove*, thus disrupting Anderson's conceptual order.

More recent critics continue to locate James both as a novelist influenced by philosophical discourse and as one whose work is amenable to interpretation through certain later philosophical formulations. Richard A. Hocks's study of the relationship between Henry and his brother William suggested a striking congruity between the novelist's work and William's pragmatist thought, such that the latter's philosophy is 'literally *actualized* in the literary art and idiom of Henry'.[27] In his detailed and convincing commentary on the voluminous correspondence between the two brothers, Hocks summarises his project with the bold assertion that 'William does the naming, Henry the embodying' (225). Paul B. Armstrong offers a phenomenological reading of James, drawing on an eclectic range of theorists (Husserl, Heidegger, Merleau-Ponty) to discuss the novelist's structuring of experience and consciousness. He makes no reference to James Senior however, a surprising omission which is especially felt in his discussion of *The Portrait of a Lady* and the connection he makes between it and William James's ideas of freedom and necessity.[28] While his linking of the novel to William is useful and clarifying, Armstrong seems unaware that the same concepts which he finds in the brother's philosophy had also been discussed at length by James Senior. He illustrates what seems to be a reluctance amongst critics to grapple with the father's admittedly complex and often confusing ideas – it is as if Henry's philosophical inheritance is thought to begin and end with William. Merle Williams, a critic whose approach is similarly phenomenological, recognises the possibility of paternal influence, even if only to raise the topic without exploring it further. Dismissing Anderson's approach ('there are certainly no simple causal connections to be exposed'), she suggests that James Senior's rejection of a firmly established selfhood encouraged both a 'proclivity towards startling moral innovation' and 'the dizzying process of forging new moral categories',[29] transformations dramatised by James in his searching investigations into problems of subjectivity, truth and social intercourse.

The earliest sustained accounts of James Senior's life tended to skirt around the question of influence. Austin Warren had worked closely with William James's son, Henry III, using many of the family papers to produce a biography in 1934, *The Elder Henry James*; an earlier account, in C. Hartley Grattan's *The Three Jameses: A Family of Minds* (1932), had not had the benefit of access to such important sources, broaching the subject of paternal influence only in the broadest terms in the book's epilogue, where James's 'thinking' was deemed 'less comprehensive than that of his father and his brother [William], but in general tendency he came around to the same ends'.[30] Ralph Barton Perry's *The Thought and Character of William James* (1935) and F. O. Matthiessen's *The James Family* (1947) saw the publication of large portions of James Senior's writing (a project later continued by Giles Gunn in his 1974 selection of the elder James's works). Two books offering detailed interpretation and explanation of James Senior's philosophy also appeared: Frederic Harold Young's *The Philosophy of Henry James Senior* (1951); and Dwight W. Hoover's *Henry James, Sr and the Religion of Community* (1969). Both have been useful in assisting my understanding of the diffuse thought of their subject. But as if warned off by the severity of many of the appraisals of Anderson's book, more recent critical and biographical consideration of the father's influence on his children has swung away from considering the broader possibilities and characteristics of inheritance to the opposite extreme, so that what has become accentuated are the apparently disabling effects of James Senior's more illiberal tendencies. Howard Feinstein's fascinating 1985 biography, *Becoming William James*, delved more deeply into the James family dynamics than had any earlier interpreter, emphasising the oedipal battles in the male lineage running from William James of Albany through James Senior to his son William. For Feinstein, James Senior's forceful personality acted as a deeply inhibitive force which the eldest son particularly struggled to overcome. Jean Strouse, in her 1981 account of the life of Alice James, persuasively documented the difficulties of being an intelligent woman in a family so focused on the concerns of its three most articulate males, James Senior, William and Henry. Jane Maher, in her book *Biography of Broken Fortunes* (1986), similarly revealed the relative lack of paternal attention paid to the other two children, Wilkie and Robertson.

But it is the work of the critic Alfred Habegger, and his analysis of the relationship between James and his father, which has proved most useful and provocative for my study. To his credit, Habegger's three books, *Gender, Fantasy, and Realism in American Literature* (1982), *Henry James and the 'Woman Business'* (1989) and *The Father: A Life of Henry James, Sr* (1994), have been largely responsible for the resurrection of interest among James scholars in James Senior. Yet his approach (especially in the first two titles) has been highly polemical and his readings of the works of both novelist and philosopher often contentious. Like Anderson in *The Imperial Self*, Habegger blames James's apparent artistic limitations on the failure of James Senior to instil in his son any sense of conventional masculine identity or role. The renunciatory impulse of many of the novelist's characters, their escape (to Habegger's mind) from the realities of the surrounding society, is connected directly with James's life: '[James] never learned the things boys took for granted, never caught onto the language men actually spoke. Early in life he failed to earn masculinity in the ways that American boys and men had to earn it.'[31] James's painfully stunted emotional development ('One of the basic givens in Henry James's life,' Habegger writes, 'was a deep and humiliating anguish at his failure ever to become a proper man' (267)) invalidates any claims made on his behalf to being a writer of social interaction and experience. In short, he laments James's inability to create convincing realistic narratives in the manner of his contemporaries William Dean Howells, Theodore Dreiser and Frank Norris. Repeating Anderson's thesis that James's art was essentially extrasocial, he makes the extraordinary claim that 'James was in fact a very poor observer – that his fiction, rather than offering any sort of knowledge of men and manners, offers the pleasures of escape from a reality seen as secretly coarse, brutal, sinister, and exploiting' (274). Thus James's great legacy to literature resides in the modernist credentials of his late work, for where realism is 'a genuinely tribal literature', modernism 'cannot take seriously the social and historical milieu' (294); the novelist's skill is in depicting the workings of 'the searching but still *innocent* mind' (281; my emphasis).

This reading of James's apparent limitations represents a critique of the aesthetic 'world elsewhere' of Richard Poirier's now classic formulation, one which sought to argue that an Emersonian bias characterises the definitive qualities of American literature from the transcendentalists to the moderns. America's literary modernism is, according to Poirier, firmly grounded in an Emersonian discourse of thinking and being. 'Literature generates its substance, its excitements, its rhetoric, and its plots often with the implicit intention, paradoxically, to get free of them and to restore itself to some preferred state of naturalness, authenticity, and simplicity.'[32] The connection between transcendentalism and arch-modernism is established as Poirier traces this tradition from Emerson through William James to T. S. Eliot and Wallace Stevens, arguing that within this continuum from Emerson to Eliot was demonstrated the only effective political and social critique possible for the writer. In a country in which non-conformity could be seen as the embodiment of the hegemonic individualist credo, critique through linguistic innovation becomes the only legitimate means of articulating difference: 'we can most effectively register our dissent from our fate by means of troping, punning, parodistic echoings, and by letting vernacular idioms play against revered terminologies' (72). For Habegger, this argument represents an avoidance of actual social engagement; Poirier's tradition is no more than a form of dehistoricised aestheticism masquerading as a genuine critique of social reality. Narrative realism by contrast 'has more insight, for it knows that we are what we are because of complex social contracts and a long chain of events including our own prior choices'.[33]

Given Habegger's characterisation of James as a modernist precursor, unable to conceive of a language of reality other than that created by the shifting epistemologies of his characters, it is strange that the charge levelled against the novelist in the critic's next book, *Henry James and the 'Woman Business'*, focuses on the degree to which James appropriates the *social* ideology of his father. No longer the impaired social realist, James now becomes the mouthpiece of James Senior's reactionary ('reactionary' certainly when measured against twenty-first century criteria) but not uncommon thinking on sexual politics. I discuss this aspect of James Senior's philosophy and the nature of its connection to his son's novel *The Bostonians* in chapter 4, but the point I want to make here is simply that whether James is labelled as a damaged figure, an aesthete unable to describe social interaction, or as a partisan dramatiser of his father's social ideas, the focus for Habegger's criticism remains consistently on the elder James as the source of his son's apparent failings, both personal and artistic. Wanting to escape the critical trap of judgement based on ahistorical criteria and polemical biography, this present book is an unashamedly contextualist approach to Henry James and his work. Rather than simply offering readings of a number of the texts alone, I have sought to expand the ways we might think about James by examining aspects of American thought and culture which impinged upon both him and his father. The book is based upon the conviction that the biographical, literary, philosophical, religious and historical are emphatically linked, and that aspects other than the strictly literary are potentially fruitful *for* the examination of the literary. By this I do not wish to denigrate the critical approach which chooses to focus exclusively on the internal workings of the James *corpus*, to suggest that such methodology is without value. But the premise in these pages is that an analysis combining readings of various and competing discourses can offer greater potential for understanding than any single viewpoint. The annexation of writers from the historical and social milieus in which they lived and worked serves only to assign to a particular text a false independence from the rest of the culture, such that text and context have little, if anything, to say to each other. It is this misleading estrangement which I want to avoid, by suggesting ways in which the context can have a productive, even if sometimes problematic, relevance to the literary text under discussion. Of course debate over the critical validity of a contextualist reading of any individual or text continues. Derrideans eschew any context as a category useful for situating either the writer or the work. The playfulness of deconstructionism at its purest, a theory whose own paternity lies in the textual strategies of the New Critics, prefers to locate the text firmly within its own boundaries, although a narrow concession to the extra-textual is made when such boundaries are expanded to include other texts (*as* texts) and, of course, the context of language. The hazard inherent in contextualising, whether we read with an eye towards biographical intentionality, cultural location or social engagement, is that we will inevitably fail to find, as Dominick LaCapra has stated, '*the* context'. Sophisticated texts (such as Henry James's) have too many contexts to allow for individual interpretations which can rest comfortably in a sense of their own inclusiveness. Such texts direct our attention to 'a set of interacting contexts whose relations to one another are variable and problematic and whose relation to the text being investigated raises difficult issues in interpretation';[34] the danger in striving for a final context is the danger of asserting closure and exhaustive comprehension. ('Relations stop nowhere', James had warned.) Similarly, Paul Giles has recently reminded context-seekers that 'it is wrong to suppose a historical context can ever be a neutral foundation which needs simply to be made visible before the relationship between text and context ... can be appreciated in its true light'.[35] Ideological, non-empirical motivations are at work in the choice and application of even the most apparently transparent of contextual apparatus. But granting this statement does not render invalid or unnecessary a literary criticism sensitive to positioning a writer within his or her society, culture and politics. The test surely is how well this perspective is able to bring forth new insight and understanding of the text, without claiming that any resultant reading can be definitive.

The immediate context for Henry James, and for this book, is his family – specifically his father. But the kind of paternal inheritance I wish to uncover is not of the psychologised, Freudian kind so exhaustively played out in Leon Edel's classic, if at times overdetermined, biography, a work which, as Adeline Tintner has noted, continues to supplant for many the reading of James's texts themselves. Edel produced a compelling story in which 'the quintet of volumes turns into a five-act play in which the hero is James and the other characters are his novels and tales'.[36] His history of the James family becomes an epic and highly readable tale, but one which, at times, suffers too much from a desire to find patterns of behaviour and dynamics of motivation which too neatly explain the narrative of the life. Inheritance, for my purposes, is a less immediately graspable and more subtle concept than the model of repression and sublimation which structures Edel's chronology. It embraces the shifting currencies of intellectual ideas and of certain cultural dispositions as they are embodied and enacted across decades. My purpose is to rescue James Senior from the kind of blinkered and dehistoricised reading which both Quentin Anderson's and Alfred Habegger's theses have exhibited; to re-examine Henry James Senior's intellectual career in order to explore the ways in which it became distilled, often merely in the form of ancestral echoes, into the writing of his novelist son. While not wishing to deny that James Senior was an often infuriating and inhibiting figure for all of his children, his intellectual inheritance nevertheless provided James with both a productive narrative framework and subject matter for his own writing. That the nature of this inheritance must be more oblique than that suggested by Anderson's forced matching does not invalidate the project, but rather takes into account the markedly different cultural and social atmosphere in which James was working. One generation on from a New England still predominantly guided by religious authority (although one in the process of fragmentation and division), the novelist's concerns were more secular and cosmopolitan; instead of the freedoms for polemic offered by the philosophical treatise, his preference was for the competing demands of fictional narrative. Yet despite these very different emphases and genres, many of the millenarian religious preoccupations of James Senior continued to resonate in the more compromised and unresolved world of the novelist's characters.

In a tradition which includes Ludwig Feuerbach's *The Essence of Christianity* (1841), Max Weber's *The Protestant Ethic and the Spirit of Capitalism* (1904–5) and Emile Durkheim's *Elementary Forms of Religious Life* (1912), to cite just three of the prominent works which have sought to evaluate and revive the sacred in terms of its secular manifestations, Clifford Geertz formulated such a continuation of the religious sentiment in his essay 'Religion as a Cultural System' in terms which are apposite to my discussion of the Jamesian inheritance. 'Religious concepts spread beyond their specifically metaphysical contexts', Geertz writes, 'to provide a framework of general ideas in terms of which a wide range of experience – intellectual, emotional, moral – can be given meaningful form.' Religious tenets signify for the more secular age 'an historically transmitted pattern of meanings embodied in symbols, a system of inherited conceptions expressed in symbolic forms by means of which men communicate, perpetuate, and develop their knowledge about and attitudes toward life'. Although Geertz is outlining the case for residual inheritance in terms of its applicability to *his* field of cultural anthropology, such a critique of a too narrow, reductively doctrinal definition of the religious impulse retains a relevance for the literary critic.[37] For example, Susan L. Mizruchi has most recently exemplified the continuing pertinence of religious concepts in her examination of the reworking of the theological tradition of 'sacrifice' in a number of classic American texts of the late nineteenth and early twentieth centuries. Quoting the maxim of the nineteenth-century Professor of Greek at Oxford, Benjamin Jowett, that 'If religion is to be saved at all it must be through the laity and statesmen', Mizruchi argues persuasively that sacrificial ideas not only 'mediated the divide between secular and spiritual realms in this era' but that the significance of the word expanded, enabling it to incorporate a wider focus applicable to a growing interest in, and professionalisation of, social science.[38] Sacrifice, she shows, had a relevance to 'social thought and social action, supporting the most entrenched as well as innovative institutions (from charity to life insurance) and mediating the most complex developments (from the "invention" of homosexuality to the rise of racial segregation)' (23). As a result, now 'the principle of sacrificial exchange that animates every human relationship ... extends to a larger social policy of sacrificial alms or collective welfare' (198).For Charles Sanders Peirce, religious terminology (such as 'sacrifice') became most effective once it managed to liberate itself from concrete doctrinal particularities in this way. The *vagueness* of religious terms, Peirce explained, ensured their continued use and relevance, their adaptability to changing cultural contexts and moral systems. His example pulls no punches:

> 'God' is a vernacular word and, like all such words, but more than almost any, is *vague*. No words are so well understood as vernacular words, in one way; yet they are invariably vague; and of many of them it is true that, let the logician do his best to substitute precise equivalents in their places, still the vernacular words alone, for all their vagueness, answer the principal purposes. This is emphatically the case with the very vague word 'God,' which is not made less vague by saying that it imports 'infinity,' etc., since those attributions are at least as vague.[39]

The only vocabulary we have with which to discuss religious matters, Peirce suggests, is of an incorporeality that ensures its ability to sustain a currency in the language, and thus a relevance, however refracted and re-imagined, for the users of that language.

In 1897 William James had championed the continuing validity of the religious sensibility in an increasingly scientific world. In 'The Will to Believe' he asserted that religion remained 'a live hypothesis' with a significance that science had yet to invalidate.[40] Although the empirical mind, 'rugged and manly' in its 'submission to the icy laws of outer fact' (461), sought to deliver man from the blight of scepticism into the clean air of certitude and objective evidence, William doubted that such a trouble-free realm even existed. Echoing Peirce (to whom the essay is dedicated), he suggests that 'We find no proposition ever regarded by anyone as evidently certain that has not either been called a falsehood, or at least had its truth generally questioned by someone else' (467). A fear of not being in error, ensuring a dependence on scientific absoluteness as the standard of proof, has encouraged a shallowness of thinking from which consideration of the enduring significance of religion has been excluded. But 'when I look at the religious question as it really puts itself to concrete man', William writes, 'this command that we shall put a stopper on our heart, instincts and courage . . . seems to me the queerest idol ever manufactured in the philosophic cave' (477–8). Whatever the benefits of interpretation through 'pure insight and logic', these criteria 'are not the only things that really do produce our creeds' (464).

This continued presence of a religious dimension, although secularised, had been recognised by Henry James back in 1873, in reply to a letter from Charles Eliot Norton. Norton had written of Christianity's influence being 'a thing of tradition, rather than an actual force exercising control over the conduct & character of man'. As a creed it had exhausted any vibrancy it may once have had, he suggested, and the wait for 'the new morality which is to be the organizing power & animating spirit of the new society' might be a long one.[41] James's reply conceded the growing irrelevance of formal Christianity – 'civilization, good & bad alike, seems to be certainly leaving it pretty well out of account' – yet as an animating force, detached from denominational or institutional manifestations, he judged 'the religious passion' (notice the Peircean vagueness) to be of enduring importance: '[W]hen one thinks of the scanty fare, judged by our usual standards, on which it has always fed, & of the nevertheless powerful current continually setting towards all religious hypotheses, it is hard not to believe that *some* application of the supernatural idea, should not be an essential part of our life' (*Letters*, I, 363). Despite the cautious double negatives here, the characteristically indirect assertiveness, James's feeling for the impoverished state of the purely secular sensibility is clear. Reviewing a collection of poems by William Dean Howells in 1874, he transcribes in full one – 'Lost Beliefs' – which had, he noted, a 'charm' that was 'permanent':

> One after one they left us;
>   The sweet birds out of our breasts
> Went flying away in the morning:
>   Will they come again to their nests?
>
> Will they come again at nightfall,
>   With God's breath in their song?
> Noon is fierce with heats of summer
>   And summer days are long!
>
> O my life, with thy upward liftings,
>   Thy downward-striking roots,
> Ripening out of thy tender blossoms
>   But hard and bitter fruits!
>
> In thy boughs there is no shelter
>   For the birds to seek again.
> The desolate nest is broken
>   And torn with wind and rain!

James declared, somewhat generously, that Howells had produced 'a little masterpiece' of a poem with his description of spiritual malaise, of the loss of those 'sweet birds' who could find 'no shelter' amongst the now 'hard and bitter fruits' of the poet's life. The poem, he felt, could best be enjoyed during one of 'those quiet moods' that, although not in themselves melancholic, were yet 'tolerant of melancholy' (*EAE*, 484). Howells's writing hinted at 'some *vague* regret, felt or fancied' (my emphasis), some 'bitter-sweet sense of a past' which James was able to appreciate (*EAE*, 483).

Occasional sadness at the passing of a more formally religious culture was something James noticed again when reviewing Ernest Renan's memoirs, *Souvenirs d'Enfance et de Jeunesse* (1883). Here Renan, whose *Vie de Jésus* (1864) had so undermined conventional interpretations of biblical authority, described his religious training for the Catholic priesthood, an education which had left an indelible impression on his thinking, regardless of later disagreements and controversies: '"Le pli était pris – the bent was taken," as he [Renan] says,' James writes (*EWP*, 637). Later in the review James chooses to translate a passage from the preface to the memoirs which tells of the legend of Is, a town engulfed by the sea but whose tolling church bells it is still possible to hear on calm days. 'It seems to me often', the translation continues, 'that I have in the bottom of my heart a city of Is, which still rings bells that persist in gathering to sacred rites the faithful who no longer hear. At times I stop to lend an ear to these trembling vibrations, which appear to me to come from infinite depths, like the voices of another world' (*EWP*, 641). It is easy to understand the attraction of a passage like this to Renan's reviewer. The language is pure Jamesian – indeed one might argue that it *is* James's language through virtue of his translation. 'Sacred rites', 'trembling vibrations', 'infinite depths', all are phrases indicative of both the delicacies and extremes of sensibility, of the presence of the unexpected and the uncanny. The period of Renan's religious orthodoxy may be past, but it lingers as a mode of thought which cannot be entirely banished. For James, Renan offers an attractive possibility of the clerical frame of mind, 'the groundwork' as he calls it, 'embroidered' with less ascetic interests, with 'an artistic feeling', an 'urbanity' and 'the air of being permeated by civilization' (*EWP*, 637).

For the sake of comparison, we can turn to James's review eight years earlier of another clerical memoir, that of the American Unitarian minister Ezra Stiles Gannett. Gannett, he notes, 'was a born minister; he stepped straight from his school days into the pulpit, and looked at the world, ever afterwards, from the pulpit alone' (*EAE*, 279). Unlike Renan, 'what is called the "world" said little or nothing' to him; 'in his tastes, in his habits, in his temperament, he was a pure ascetic' (*EAE*, 280). The 'mechanical development of conscience' (*EAE*, 281) which Gannett's religion has promoted in New England is as inflexible and limited as James's words suggest. It is the embodiment of the Woollett sensibility of *The Ambassadors*, a moral climate which produces automatons such as Lambert Strether, instructed and expected to function specifically and solely as the long arm of Mrs Newsome and her rigid mission. Renan displays a cosmopolitanism that provokes James's interest in his continuing religious sensibility; it is the Frenchman's ability to combine successfully the secular with the sacred, to the detriment of neither, which raises him above the 'extreme dryness' of Gannett's narrowly conceived moralism (*EAE*, 280).

On a basic level, the recurring religious presence which James detected in Howells and Renan often takes the form in his own work of specific choices of vocabulary. In *The Ambassadors* for example, Lambert Strether's drama is consistently couched in terms of mystery, miracle and faith:

> 'I've been sacrificing so to strange gods that I feel I want to put on record, somehow, my fidelity – fundamentally unchanged after all – to our own. I feel as if my hands were embrued with the blood of monstrous alien altars – of another faith altogether.'[42]

> 'Yet was n't her whole point' – Strether weighed in – 'that he was to be, that he *could* be, made better, redeemed?'
> (II, 172)

> Still he could always speak for the woman he had so definitely promised to
> 'save'. This wasn't quite for her the air of salvation; but . . .   (II, 204)

One of the central questions of the novel could be said to resonate around
the implications offered by these particular word choices: who in fact saves
whom? Who is offered the chance of redemption as a result of the Parisian
encounters? The possibilities are played out by James's characters. Strether
tells Madame de Vionnet, the object of Chad's attentions, 'I'll save you if
I can' (I, 255); Strether's Puritanical, American acquaintance Waymarsh
regards him in a manner that 'fairly sounded out – "to save you, poor
old man, to save you; to save you in spite of yourself"' (II, 103); another
concerned American, Mamie Pocock, had hoped to influence Chad's
salvation, but she is 'too late for the miracle' (II, 172). Moreover, within
the flexible potential of spiritual metaphor, James's Europe discloses further possibilities as Miss Barrace paints Little Bilham in the image of a
failed missionary: '"You come over to convert the savages . . . and the
savages simply convert *you*"' (I, 205). The effect, I suggest, is one of
vestigial recognition; spiritual metaphor acts to enhance the possibilities
of communication by tapping into a history of experience already written into the language and, because ancestrally familiar, still current in
the structure of our feelings. Like Renan's tolling bell, the vibrations of
an originally religious diction continue to resonate and offer meaning,
such that the secular and the sacred co-exist and the distinction between
the two often becomes blurred. James Senior, as 'editor' of his fictionalised autobiographical narrative (which I discuss in chapter 1), noted just
this merging of the two realms when he commented on the difficulty
he had in distinguishing where his persona's 'secular consciousness left
off and his religious consciousness began'. 'All his discourse', he writes,
'betrayed . . . an unconscious, or at all events unaffected, habit of spiritu-
alizing secular things and secularizing sacred things.'[43]

Yet beyond the examples of specific religious imagery, James was also
exposed by his father to a particular (and endlessly theorised) dynamic of
spiritual regeneration, which, because of its essentially dramatic nature,
offered an attractive theme around which the novelist could elaborate
his variations. James Senior's religious master, Emanuel Swedenborg, had
developed an intricate system of biblical interpretation which was enjoying an upsurge in popularity in America during the spiritual revivalism of the early nineteenth century.[44] Swedenborg had appropriated the
archetype of the 'fortunate fall', recasting the creation story as the rescue
of man from his debilitating innocence through a liberating encounter
with experience, to conceive of true selfhood as created through a dramatic encounter with the unfamiliar, the Other. For both Swedenborg
and James Senior, 'otherness' included spiritual evil which only the

immature sought to avoid; for James this becomes secularised into an immoral but nevertheless attractive (usually European) playground for his (usually American) innocents. Encounters with the unfamiliar provide the opportunity for a rigorous testing of selfhoods hitherto considered fully formed. In the first chapter I discuss the several autobiographical writings of both Henry Jameses, and the diverse strategies which they employ to describe the development of their mature selves. Noting James Senior's rejection of the orthodoxy of an individualised and economically inquisitive self (a politicisation of the Emersonian figure in which Emerson himself was complicit), I show how Peirce's idea of the value of fallibility is embodied and celebrated in the autobiographical narratives of both father and son. Of particular interest are the ways in which both writers dispense with the shackles of verifiable fact in their quest to convey truth as an *essence* not dependent upon historical accuracy. For James, events during the Civil War are offered as formative, if aesthetically embellished; for James Senior the pivotal episode is his spiritual breakdown of 1844, his 'vastation', described on more than one occasion and with increasing archetypal emphasis. It is this dynamic of self-redefinition, the process by which maturity is attained, which is central to both men's work.

Chapter 2 explores the issue of inheritance as it becomes refracted through the distorting lens of Emersonian transcendentalism. Emerson looms large in this book as a central intellectual presence whose personality and ideas are variously read and interpreted by the James family. Examining more fully than have previous studies the nature of the relationship between James Senior and Emerson, I chart the changing nature of the elder James's acquaintance with the Concord seer over almost forty years. Writing to a friend in 1852, James Senior would characterise Emerson as one who displayed 'no faith in man, at least in progress. He does not imagine the possibility of "hurrying up the cakes" on a large scale.'[45] The reasons behind this judgement on Emerson's solitariness and quietism are various – in part indicative of a more practical temperament, in part a reflection of a less liberal religious background than Emerson's Unitarian-based individualism, in part too pointing at a professional rivalry in which James Senior would remain the junior player. I choose to highlight one area around which their philosophical differences crystallised, the nature and purpose of evil, as indicative of the wider disagreements at play between the two men. The elder James misinterprets Emerson on this subject; by reading the Concord writer too narrowly he chooses to emphasise disproportionately those elements where Emerson seems blissfully oblivious to evil's reality, at the expense of a more accurate and complex representation of the dualistic nature of this aspect of his philosophy. Henry James confirms this 'partial portrait' provided by his father, transforming it from its original theological critique into a form of cultural dissatisfaction with America. Despite a difference in emphasis, both men depict a figure exhibiting a moral blankness, living a secluded existence in a quasi-Edenic state. James Senior's criticism of Emerson's apparent ignorance of evil goes untested by his son, who wishes to fashion for himself a literary identity respectful of American tradition yet is desirous too of a more cosmopolitan, European focus. Emerson is a prominent figure in James's literary sensibility, to the extent that the site of paternal influence expands to incorporate him, for the intellectual and instinctual differences between James Senior and Emerson provide the novelist with an instructive and concentrated antagonism.

The European focus is the subject of chapter 3, where I discuss *The Portrait of a Lady*, examining how Isabel Archer is depicted as an Emersonian figure whose untested approach to life is challenged and shown to be inadequate when confronted with the manipulative reality of thoroughly Europeanised Americans. Surveying Emerson's shifting and uneasy relationship to the notion of the fall, I suggest that James reimagines his father's more assured doctrine of the beneficial fall to describe his heroine's exposure to history and experience. Isabel's initial preference for effacing the past corresponds to the transcendentalists' refutation of their European inheritance and celebration of a uniquely American future. This often pronounced ahistoricism is the cultural context which provoked James Senior's criticism of the aggrandisement of American innocence. In *The Portrait of a Lady* James employs the inverted arc of the fortunate fall in narrating Isabel's journey towards epistemological maturity, in so doing offering a critique of perceived Emersonian provinciality. Chapter 4 suggests that the paternal inheritance was less productive for James when he attempted to incorporate more directly into his writing the cultural milieu and subject matter recognisably James Senior's own. One of the factors which contributed towards the germ for James's *The Bostonians* was his father's recent death; in his stated desire to write a specifically American novel, to forego (if only temporarily) the literary successes of the European encounter, James is conscious of the need to, at least in part, pay tribute to his father's memory, a desire felt all the more strongly given William James's appropriation of the mantle of paternal promoter. Discussing the elder James's writing on two of the issues which Henry's novel addresses, gender roles and spiritualism, my reading of *The Bostonians* seeks to explain the ways in which certain aspects of James Senior's thinking were incorporated into the narrative, but not, as Alfred Habegger would have it, in any seamlessly ideological manner. Although the character of Basil Ransom articulates many of James Senior's more reactionary sentiments, these are embedded within the excesses of a romantic Carlylean rhetoric (of which the elder James was highly critical), ensuring that the novel refrains from confidently endorsing any position, reformist or conservative. *The Bostonians* finally illustrates the degree to which the presence of competing (and at times apologetic) discourses prevents its author, almost in spite of himself, from submitting to crude partisanship.

The final chapter returns my discussion of paternal influence back to the more profitable framework (for James, at least) of James Senior's estimation of the relative worths of America and Europe. The elder James held a more fluctuating and conciliatory opinion of Europe than that expressed by Emerson, whose nativistic embrace of the New World spurned the history-burdened Old. James Senior's response to Europe was to a large extent dependent upon his readership or audience. His articles for Horace Greeley's *New York Tribune* often articulated the standard Romantic line of American superiority to the European institutions of Church and State. Yet this view is seriously qualified elsewhere, particularly in lectures tailored to a more specific audience, where the significance of the Old World is more soberly recognised – to the extent that an encounter with it is viewed as potentially liberating. In *The Ambassadors*, Paris is presented as an environment profoundly disorientating to a mind steeped in a combination of the Puritan and genteel Emersonian traditions. Lambert Strether's embrace of this unfamiliar world and his unintentional succumbing to vulnerability and fallibility enables him to approach the kind of cosmopolitan sensibility which results in the manifestation neither of a Rooseveltian American nationalism nor of a blinkered embrace of the Old World.

This book argues for a reassessment of Henry James Senior and his relationship with the intellectual culture of nineteenth-century America. Typically viewed as an eccentric tirelessly advocating a theological system for a rapidly secularising society, he is considered here both in his own right as a figure engaged with many of the preoccupations of his time and as a complex influence on his novelist son. The fact that the nature of this influence has often been exaggerated to satisfy the preconceived agendas of critics means that to approach the subject without an overt ideological axe to grind may appear merely tentative and suggestive, a pale imitation of more strident readings. This I would maintain is no bad thing, for James's narratives are firmly resistant to the certainties of programmatic interpretation. The traces of cultural transmission reverberating across from one generation to the next are what this work seeks to detect, those elements of confluence which point at shared concerns or ingrained ways of thinking. James certainly felt them: writing to his nephew in 1912 about his progress with the autobiographical narratives that would become *A Small Boy and Others* (1913) and *Notes of a Son and Brother* (1914), he confessed to becoming 'at every step of my process, more intensely "Family" even than at the step before'.[46]

1

Autobiography and the writing of significance

In 'The Diary of a Man of Fifty', a short story first published in 1879, Henry James describes a man actively engaged in the process of reconstituting his past – a process not dissimilar to that which would characterise James's own autobiographical narratives of over thirty years later. In a succession of diary entries (in themselves a form of autobiography) the middle-aged hero of James's tale, revisiting Florence, is prompted to revive memories of an unhappy love affair conducted there years before. Initially the past seems quite familiar, a sequence of events recalled with unerring accuracy. 'Everything is so perfectly the same', he notes, 'that I seem to be living my youth over again.'[1] But the process of memory soon proves to be surprising, as things once thought forgotten return unexpectedly to active consciousness, prompting the narrator to ask, 'What in the world became of them? Whatever becomes of such things, in the long intervals of consciousness? Where do they hide themselves away? In what unvisited cupboards and crannies of our being do they preserve themselves?' (334). The sequence of unearthed memories proves endless, chaotic and a touch oppressive ('They have been crowding upon me ever so thickly' (339)), with each recollection suggestive of something further: 'Everything reminds me of something else, and yet of itself at the same time.' The diarist's recapturing of the image of his lost love becomes a physical as much as a mental act, one in which his senses strain to be released from the confines of the present: 'The place was perfectly empty – that is, it was filled with her. I closed my eyes and listened; I could almost hear the rustle of her dress on the gravel' (335).

This emergence of unexpected memories is encouraged by his encounters with the daughter of the woman he had once loved and with that daughter's suitor, a man who seems to the diarist to be so perfectly the embodiment of his earlier self that he is led to declare with amazement that 'the analogy is complete' (340). James's sentient central character feels himself to be re-experiencing his past through this surrogate self, for, commenting on the suitor's bliss, he remarks, 'I confess that in the perception of his happiness I have lived over again my own' (351). The idea of 'living over again', in the sense of not merely recalling the past as a museum piece, preserved and labelled, but encountering it anew in different ways and for different purposes, is central to the epistemological process at work in the Jamesian autobiography (that of father *and* son). Indeed at the beginning of *A Small Boy and Others* James declares his desire 'at the same time to live over the spent experience itself' (*A*, 3), such that apparently exhausted ('spent') history may be reanimated by the process of memory. As Wolfgang Iser has observed, in a discussion of Laurence Sterne's novel of autobiographical strategies *Tristram Shandy* but also in terms which can usefully be applied to James here, 'writing can never coincide with life, and facing up to this fact is a sign of the moral integrity of the historian'. Indeed, such integrity is 'violated whenever life and representation appear to coincide'. Autobiographies that seem to achieve such matching 'are nothing but illusory fulfilments of set purposes which substitute interpretations of life for life itself'.[2] By a deliberate aestheticising of the autobiographical project, both Henry Jameses attempt to articulate a sense of their own understanding of themselves and of the routes which have led to such understanding; both use the autobiographical form as a means of capturing the essences of certain experiences, essences which render creative significance to their lives in more fundamental ways than would adherence to mere chronological accuracy or factual fidelity.[3]

I

One of the earliest extended sequences of memory in *A Small Boy and Others* is James's recollection of the building of the Hudson River Railroad in New York in 1851, part of the New York Central Rail line that linked New York City with towns further north in the state and ran parallel with the Erie Canal. As a boy walking home from his tutor's house, the construction scene presented to his impressionable imagination 'a riot of explosion and a great shouting and waving of red flags', a potentially dangerous arena, a 'test' demanding a demonstration of bravery if it were to be passed successfully. James recollects that 'the point of honor among several of us, was of course nobly to defy the danger, and I feel again the emotion with which I both hoped and feared that the red flag, lurid signals descried from afar, would enable or compel us to renew the feat'. But instead of continuing to brave the 'fragments of rock' which would 'hurtle through the air and smite to the earth another and yet another of the persons engaged or exposed', James prefers to describe an alternative route ('one of the other perambulations of the period') (*A*, 15). His young self walks home via 'the country-place, as I supposed it to be, on the northeast corner of Eighteenth Street', a brownstone mansion whose grounds teemed with animal life, 'browsing and pecking and parading creatures'. The recollection of this scene prompts James to 'wonder at the liberty of range and opportunity of adventure allowed to my tender age', and he concludes, with the benefit of an autobiographer's hindsight, that his childhood freedom 'can only have had for its ground some timely conviction on the part of my elders that the only form of riot or revel ever known to me would be that of the visiting mind' (*A*, 16).

The workings of the 'visiting mind' ensure that the past is not so much retold as created anew by the imagination. Barriers of time and space are dissolved as, from the comfort of Lamb House, the elderly James sensually revisits and re-experiences the scenes of his childhood, simultaneously present at his younger self's wanderings: 'I at any rate watch the small boy dawdle and gape again, I smell the cold dusty paint and iron on rails of the Eighteenth Street corner rub his contemplative nose' (*A*, 16–17). The image of the boy studying the collection of animals becomes evidence for the autobiographer of his future. Just as the autobiographical project as a whole can be considered as James's final preface to the work of his writing life, so this childhood experience is conceived as the germ or donnée of a story that expands into the career of the novelist, enabling him to trace the seeds of himself as a mature imaginative artist back to their origin: 'He is a convenient little image or warning of all that was to be for him . . . For there was the very pattern and measure of all he was to demand: just to be somewhere – almost anywhere would do – and somehow receive impressions or an accession, feel a relation or a vibration' (*A*, 17). In this episode the young James is situated by his older self at a moment of intersection in urban development, at the point where the burgeoning industrialisation of New York is encroaching on the more pastoral world of the country house and its animals. Henry Ward Beecher, the popular New York clergyman and journalist, described the changing situation in a sketch of 1854, sympathising with those living in mansions such as that which the young James passes and who now find themselves at the mercy of the new technology. The owner of such a property all of a sudden discovers that

> his own grounds are wanted. Through that exquisite dell which skirts along the northern side of his estates, where he has wandered, book in hand, a thousand times, monarch of squirrels, bluejays and partridges, his only companions and subjects – are seen peering and spying those execrable men that turn the world upside down, civil engineers and most uncivil speculators. Alas! the plague has

broken out. His ground is wanted – is taken – is defiled – is daily smoked by the passage of the modern thunder-dragon, dragging its long tail of cars ... They have spoiled one of God's grandest pictures by slashing it with a railroad.[4]

Although, as Ross Posnock has pointed out, the 'denaturing' of the land-scape of New York by the railroad was 'inseparable from the construction of a new category of the natural',[5] ensuring that the small boy was lo-cated in a shifting and transitional geography, Henry James is nevertheless quite specific about his choice of route – past a fragile but still resistant pastoralism. It is a journey which is significant, for, as James weighs the evidence of his memory, he can recall no repetition of the walk home via the railroad, a walk which would involve him in a public display of masculine bravery, a burst of defining action in the face of America's newest animal, the 'modern thunder-dragon' of technological progress. The alternative has the advantage of possessing the more private delights of the country scene with its 'more vivid aspects, greater curiosities and wonderments' (*A*, 16).

Such a rejection of public action, turning instead to the 'far from showy practice of wondering and dawdling and gaping' (*A*, 17), was a decision, I suggest, encouraged by the peculiar circumstances of the James house-hold and the powerful presence (in both positive and negative senses) of its patriarch. James Senior's interrogation of the self inspired an irreverence towards conventional modes of authority and identity. An abjuration of society's constructions and its expectations of the individual pervades his writing: 'Society affords no succour to the divine life in man', he states. 'Any culture we can give to that life, is owing not to society, but to our fortunate independence of it.'[6] 'Society' for the elder James entailed the accumulation of both formal and informal social restrictions – it could be any social institution or any commonly recognised moral authority, since morality and society were, for him, two aspects of the same propo-sition. This suspicion of hegemonic structures promoted a commitment to willed vulnerability, an openness to unfamiliar experience which em-bodied a strategic resistance to the constricting ideologies of both genteel New England culture and the more aggressive, individualising aspects of rapid American urbanisation.

With the publication of *Democracy in America* (in two parts, 1835 and 1840), Alexis de Tocqueville emerged as one of the earliest commenta-tors on this latter phenomenon. Discussing the American inclination to construct society around the totem of the primacy and stability of the individualised self, he argued that the philosophical tradition of America was relatively unformed compared with that found in Europe. The prin-cipal 'philosophical method' employed by the New World citizen, de Tocqueville suggested, was one in which 'each American appeals only to the individual effort of his own understanding'. Furthermore, this was the manifestation of a philosophy that, although not identified and categorised, was nevertheless inevitable given the circumstances in which the nation found itself. Although 'Americans do not read the works of Descartes, because their social condition deters them from speculative studies', they nevertheless 'follow his maxims, because this same social condition naturally disposes their minds to adopt them'. The absence of European class distinctions, the growth of social mobility and the rapid accumulation of wealth had ensured that 'every one shuts himself up in his own breast, and affects from that point to judge the world'. De Tocqueville warned that the elevation of this essentialised self to a position of omniscience inevitably led to a belief in that self's infallibility. 'As [Americans] perceive that they succeed in resolving without assistance all the little difficulties which their practical life presents,' he wrote, 'they readily conclude that everything in the world may be explained, and that nothing in it transcends the limits of the understanding.'[7] The effect of American democratic life on the habit and practise of philosophy was thus to divorce the mind from the influence of tradition, the accumulated knowledge of the past, and to throw it back instead on the notion of individual authority as the supreme interpretive agency. For de Tocqueville, this signified a dangerous and impractical state of affairs in which the goal of social consensus – indeed the goal of social cohesion – would be forever unattainable:

> If every one undertook to form all his own opinions, and to seek for truth by isolated paths struck out by himself alone, it would follow that no considerable number of men would ever unite in any common belief. But obviously without such common belief no society can prosper, – say, rather, no society can exist; for without ideas held in common, there is no common action, and without common action there may still be men, but there is no social body.   (146)

The 'independence of individual minds' is all well and good to a degree, but 'unbounded it cannot be' (147). Although de Tocqueville was careful to distinguish individualism ('a mature and calm feeling, which disposes each member of the community to sever himself from the mass of his fellows' (193)) from solipsistic excess ('a passionate and exaggerated love of self, which leads a man to connect everything with himself, and to prefer himself to everything in the world' (192–3)), he nevertheless was pessimistic about the prospects of individualism. 'In the long run', he warned, 'it attacks and destroys all others, and is at length absorbed in downright selfishness' (193).

As Ian Watt notes, the very word *individualism* was coined by Henry Reeve, the first translator of de Tocqueville's text, to describe the unique American conditions, the French *individualisme* having no existing

English–language equivalent.[8] *Democracy in America* identifies both the establishment of an orthodoxy of individualism – one might paradoxically say its institutionalisation – and the nation's affirmation of the link between individual identity and epistemological stability. Against de Tocqueville's strictures, Emerson takes up (although does not acknowledge) Descartes' formulation of *cogito ergo sum* in his essay 'Self-Reliance' (1841) to describe a state of affairs in which he sees that stability now compromised: 'Man is timid and apologetic; he is no longer upright; he dares not say "I think," "I am," but quotes some saint or sage. He is ashamed before the blade of grass or the blowing rose' (*CWE*, 1, 67). Of course there is an unrecognised irony in that Emerson is paraphrasing another writer at the same time as he warns of the dangers of such indebtedness. Nevertheless, as I discuss in chapter 3, here is a characteristic description of one of the consequences of the fallen condition: a debilitating outbreak of self-consciousness (man is 'ashamed') which prevents an original relationship to the universe. No longer able to proclaim a secure individuality, to exercise and express self-authorship, man is compromised and reliant upon other authorities. Lacan's formulation of the 'mirage which renders modern man so sure of being himself even in his uncertainties about himself' has been shown to be just that – a mirage.[9] The posture of Emerson's man is dented; the upright figure, embodiment of the *I* pronoun, now slumped and uncertain.[10]

That the elder James's dismissal of the social ('our fortunate independence of it') seems to conform to a definitive Emersonian position is a judgement requiring qualification. The American celebration of a unitary and apparently infallible self, socially reinforced and mandated, was something he sought to question. Cartesian self-complacency was rejected for a conception of selfhood created through process, through a vibrant and often difficult dynamic *with* society which instils a sense of identity, but which in turn is found to be only provisional and ultimately unsatisfactory: 'the process of creation involves or necessitates a two-fold consciousness on the part of the creature; first a finite or imperfect consciousness, or a consciousness of selfhood distinct from God; and second, an infinite or perfect consciousness, a consciousness of a selfhood united with God'.[11] The formation of this second, true selfhood involves 'no ostentatious self-assertion, no dazzling parade of magical, irrational, or irresponsible power'; rather it depends upon 'an endless humiliation',[12] upon the realisation of 'a burdensome and abject servitude, from which there is no release but in the fetterless air of the spiritual world'.[13] James Senior's notion of an identity based on process, rather than one rooted in the security of a specific society, finds a telling parallel in Francis Grund's *The Americans, in Their Moral, Social, and Political Relations* (1837). Grund, an Austrian who had emigrated to America in 1827 and who was to live there for over ten years, offered an alternative conception to de Tocqueville's focus on the physical and political factors influencing the genesis of the American sensibility. For him, America was not defined by its actual geography but existed as an imaginative moral site which could never be destroyed since it was always in the process of being realised. America was present only as an idea, a potential location, and the world acted as the means by which that potentiality could actualise itself (albeit imperfectly):

> America is to [the American] but the physical means of establishing a moral power, the medium through which his mind operates – the local habitation of his political doctrines. *His country is in his understanding*; he carries it with him wherever he goes, whether he emigrates to the shores of the Pacific or the Gulf of Mexico; his home is wherever he finds a mind congenial with his own. (my emphasis)[14]

James Senior shared this conception of society based not on local conditions of nationality and race but rather one united in a moral project still to be achieved. Mankind's 'great final development into the unity of the race, is what remains for us to see; that development which shall make all the nations of the earth one society . . . when in a word his sympathies shall flow forth towards every brother of the race, according to the good that is in him'.[15]

The limitations of the socially sanctioned realm of activity or construction of identity might be opposed by the recognition of alternative potentials or unexpected combinations. Incongruity and contradiction were central to the James family ethos – James remarks that 'the presence of paradox was so bright' that the children 'breathed inconsistency and ate and drank contradictions' (*A*, 124). The intellectual ferment emanating from the family is evident in a letter written by William in which he describes 'people swarming about . . . killing themselves with thinking about things that have no connection with their merely external circumstances, studying themselves into fevers, going mad about religion, philosophy, love . . . breathing perpetual heated gas and excitement, turning night into day' (*WJ*, I, 225). The tone of dissatisfaction, of detachment from the fray, which William's words express is present again in a more significant form in *A Small Boy and Others*. Recalling their walks together in London and Paris, Henry discloses details of a conversation he had with his brother in 'after days':

> W.J. denounced it to me . . . as a poor and arid and lamentable time, in which, missing such larger chances and connections as we might have reached out to, we had done nothing, he and I, but walk about together, in a state of direct propriety . . . We might, I dare say, have felt higher impulses and carried out larger plans – though indeed present to me for this, on my brother's so

> expressing himself, is my then quick recognition of the deeper stirrings and braver needs he at least must have known, and my perfect if rueful sense of having myself had no such quarrel with our conditions: embalmed for me did they even to that shorter restrospect [*sic*] appear in a sort of fatalism of patience, spiritless in a manner, no doubt, yet with an inwardly active, productive and ingenious side.   (*A*, 170)

James depicts his brother here as the intellectual superior, defining himself as deferring to William's need for greater and more challenging stimulation, 'the larger chances and connections', compared to his own less substantial requirements. William is elevated in his apparent thirst for 'higher impulses' and 'larger plans'; the more easily pleased Henry had 'no such quarrel with our conditions'. James makes a concession in the direction of his brother – no doubt the circumstances were 'spiritless' – but for him they still retained an 'active, productive and ingenious' quality. Despite his own feelings of personal fulfilment, James seriously entertains an alternative, less reassuring judgement of his childhood existence, namely that 'we had done nothing'. That this possibility endangers the very ontological foundations of the small boy which James has attempted to establish for the reader is clearly recognised, and he proceeds to consider William's argument once again before finally rejecting it:

> What could one have asked more than to be steeped in a medium so dense that whole elements of it, forms of amusements, interest and wonder, soaked through to some appreciative faculty and made one fail at the most of nothing but one's lessons? My brother was right in so far as that my question – the one I have just reproduced – could have been asked only by a person incorrigible in throwing himself back upon substitutes for lost causes, substitutes that might temporarily have appeared queer and small; a person so haunted, even from an early age, with visions of life, that aridities, for him, were half a terror and half an impossibility, and that the said substitutes, the economies and ingenuities that protested, in their dumb vague way, against weakness of situation or of direct and applied faculty, were in themselves really a revel of spirit and thought.
>   (*A*, 171)

Resonances queer and small, dumb and vague, stand in opposition and in preference to the more obvious intellectual rewards of 'direct and applied faculty'. Henry finally cannot share his brother's suspicion of apparently pointless drifting; unlike William, he feels that such activity provides an energy and vitality, a potential source of creativity which, he insists, only 'temporarily' seems purposeless. Again the autobiographer has an eye on his younger self's future development.

The foregrounding in the narrative of the process of 'taking in' experience nevertheless remains problematic for James, and the passage describing William's doubts about the value of such a strategy as a mode of *living* (their 'perambulations', James thought, signified for his brother their 'poverty of life' (*A*, 172)) reflects Henry's own anxieties throughout the text about a narration that voraciously consumes so much diversity but that may not, finally, cohere in any meaningful form. James's uneasiness is made apparent by his constant anticipation of the reader's response to his narrative, a continual attempt to air possible objections in order to pre-empt them: 'I am divided between their [James's memories] still present freshness and my sense of perhaps making too much of these tiny particles of history', he worries at one point (*A*, 15). This doubt can only afford to be momentary though, for on its dismissal depends the continuation of the ambitious project on which he has embarked. Thus he moves to reassure himself and us of the significance of his text: 'no particle that counts for memory or is appreciable to the spirit can be too tiny, and that experience, in the name of which one speaks, is all compact of them and shining with them' (*A*, 16). This rapid transition from doubt to artistic justification is replayed throughout *A Small Boy and Others*: the disquieting possibility that James's 'assimilations small and fine' are merely 'refuse, directly interesting to the subject-victim only' is dispelled by the assertion that he feels himself to be 'morally affiliated, tied as by knotted fibres, to the elements involved' (*A*, 105) and thus aesthetically vindicated.

The 'vague processes' which William criticised, Henry 'came to glorify . . . and see . . . as part of an order really fortunate' (*A*, 199); the realms of action and speculation which William preferred to keep distinct are merged by his brother into a creative synthesis. Henry's 'pedestrian gaping' is his 'sole and single form of athletics' (*A*, 113). Ross Posnock has usefully described the uneasy tension existing within William's rhetorical strategies as indicative of a pragmatist's belief in 'overlap and continuity among individual streams of consciousness' combined with, and often overpowered by, a more repressive conviction that the self is 'an engine of rationalistic control, shaping its experience by ceaselessly selecting and eliminating'.[16] Pragmatism's vocabulary of fluidity, merging, development and uncertainty is contained within a philosophical framework that seeks to emphasise practicality and usefulness, to rein in the meandering extravagances of what William considered to be 'wayward theoretical curiosity and wonder' (Posnock's phrase; 40). Such language of restrained direction, implied in Henry's account of his brother's anxieties over the kind of apparently purposeless activity in which he, Henry, indulged, is revealed in a lecture William delivered before the Harvard Natural History Society. In 'Great Men, Great Thoughts and the Environment' (first published in the *Atlantic Monthly* in October 1880), he suggests that the human mind becomes 'efficient' only 'by narrowing its point of view', otherwise 'what little strength it has is dispersed, and it loses its way altogether'. It is 'a *necessity* laid upon us as human beings to *limit* our view' (my emphasis). In the interests of productivity, and to be able to perform most effectively the function of being human, the infinite perspective of the immature mind must be brought under control and into more specific focus. Later in the lecture William amplifies on this point in explicitly vocational terms:

> Societies of men are just like individuals, in that both at any given moment offer ambiguous potentialities of development. Whether a young man enters business or the ministry may depend on a decision which has to be made before a certain day. He takes the place offered in the counting-house, and is *committed*. Little by little, the habits, the knowledge, of the other career, which lay so near, cease to be reckoned even among possibilities. At first, he may sometimes doubt whether the self he murdered in that decisive hour might not have been the better of the two; but with the years such questions themselves expire, and the old alternative *ego*, once so vivid, fades into something less substantial than a dream.[17]

The vocational uncertainties offered by the possibilities of alternative careers, William suggests, are dispelled once the choice of a particular direction has been made. But not only is this procrastination ended, the lingering presence of those alternative potentials, those other jobs unpursued, gradually fades, until finally that other self, representative of a life unlived, becomes something insubstantial and forgotten. Joseph Thomas has demonstrated how William developed a theory of 'habit' which was employed as a buttress against the myriad of forces at work in late nineteenth-century culture – what William called the 'big, blooming, buzzing confusion' of reality. 'Habit for James', Thomas writes, 'is meant to perform a kind of midwifery, easing entry into a more secure, less "uncanny" world'.[18] So the philosopher's pragmatism is inflected with an awareness of limits, of protective structures which enable us to 'build the flux out'.[19] In an 1879 review of a work by the philosopher Charles Renouvier (an early and lasting influence), William notes that 'in every wide theoretical conclusion we must seem more or less arbitrarily to *choose* our side'. Choice, even arbitrary choice, is essential for any philosophy which seeks to make a 'practical difference' in everyday life.[20]

In the second lecture of his 1906 course on Pragmatism, William famously tells his anecdote of a camping trip during which a philosophical dispute arises over a hypothetical squirrel attached to and circling around a hypothetical tree trunk. The animal moves in tandem with an observer also circling the tree, such that it is always hidden. 'The resultant metaphysical problem now is this,' William writes. '*Does the man go round the squirrel or not?* He goes round the tree, sure enough, and the squirrel is on the tree; but does he go round the squirrel?' The solution to this conundrum lies in 'what you *practically mean* by "going round" the squirrel . . . Make the distinction, and there is no occasion for any further dispute.'[21] For William then, questions of truth are necessarily contingent and viewpoints are multiple. But ultimately such plurality and ambiguity needs resolution if the *practical* applicability of pragmatism is to have any currency. 'Make the distinction', William counsels, and once made the situation clarifies while still acknowledging the partial framework in which that clarification has been achieved. Whereas William seems to be advocating a gradual sharpening of focus and a necessary division of labour – Howard Feinstein describes his 'keen awareness of . . . the disastrous psychological consequences of the failure to recognize and affirm the boundaries between persons'[22] – Henry James is happy to rest in the act of observation. His is a paradoxically self-conscious and energetic feat of non-participation, one in which the demands of the enquiring mind can never be satisfied fully. James's 'vague processes' depend upon further, but never final, interpretation. Again, Charles Sanders Peirce proves helpful, for his notion of 'vagueness' is of a kind which, 'leaving its interpretation more or less indeterminate, . . . reserves for some other possible . . . experience the function of completing the determination'.[23] It is worth noting that the additional clarifying piece of information is only 'possible', for absolute elucidation can never be assured, although attempts at closure may be endlessly offered.

The notion that everything is potentially significant, that nothing lies outside the realm of experience, was promoted by the James family's idiosyncratic estimation of 'waste', of that usually deemed inconsequential. James Senior displayed a deliberate perversity in his concern for 'the whole side of the human scene usually held least interesting'. He found in what was conventionally considered waste 'much character and colour and charm, so many implications of the fine and worthy' which 'enlarged not a little our field and our categories of appreciation and perception' (*A*, 301–2). The frantic atmosphere of heated intellectual stimulation, to which William's letter quoted earlier alluded, is present in Henry's claim that the family 'breathed somehow an air in which waste, for us at least, couldn't and didn't live, so certain were aberrations and discussions, adventures, excursions and alarms of whatever sort, to wind up in a "transformation scene"' (*A*, 302). Nothing was considered irrelevant – irrelevance indeed was celebrated for its 'intensity and plausibility and variety' (*A*, 112). At the most base level, for example, the use of sewage in European agriculture had become for James Senior a powerful symbol of how the material makes possible the spiritual: 'Only think of this! Europe actually depends for her material salvation upon a divine redemption mercifully stored up for her in substances which her most pious churchmen and wisest statesmen have always disdained as an unmitigated nuisance!' That which we 'would gladly hurry into the abyss of oblivion', he marvelled, 'teems with incomparably greater renovation to human society than all the gold, silver, and precious stones ever dug from earth to madden human lust and enslave human weakness!'[24] Henry James echoed this interest in the excremental when considering his sense of the value of his first trip to Italy in 1869. 'Let it lie warm and nutritive at the base of my mind, manuring and enriching its roots', he instructed himself rhetorically (*Letters*, 1, 208).

James returned to the notion of 'waste' again three years prior to the publication of *A Small Boy and Others*, contributing to the collection of essays brought together under the title *In After Days: Thoughts on the Future Life*. (It also included writing from such contemporaries as Julia Ward Howe, Thomas Wentworth Higginson and William Dean Howells.) That James's philosophical piece was a departure from his preferred prose forms, that with it he was approaching literary territory more comfortably inhabited by his father and brother, is something of which he was well aware. Writing to Elizabeth Jordan, the editor of *Harper's Bazar* (the magazine that had originally commissioned the collection), he confessed to finding 'the little business distinctly difficult, so that I had – it being a sort of thing that is so little in my "chords", to work it out with even more deliberation than I had allowed time for'.[25] The finished composition, 'Is There a Life After Death?', reveals its author pondering with great care the difficulty of determining what can be considered extraneous – what in fact constitutes a wasted life – and alive to the danger of asserting too narrow a conception of value. Such an assertion, James believes, is indicative of an arrogance which may serve only to reveal the actual inadequacies of our understanding:

> The probability is, in fact, that what we dimly discern as waste the wisdom of the universe may know as a very different matter. We don't think of slugs and jellyfish as the waste, but rather as the amusement, the attestation of wealth and variety, of gardens and sea-beaches; so why should we, under stress, in respect to the human scene and its discussable sequel, think differently of dull people?[26]

The infinite variety of reactions which consciousness displays, its creative awareness, is evidence for James of 'us as establishing sublime relations', after which, he asks, 'how can we . . . hold complete disconnection likely?' (228). Consciousness then is 'consecrated' (elsewhere James writes of 'the consecration of knowledge' (*A*, 560)), a fact which allows him to entertain the possibility of infinite existence in the face of science's determination to prove secular man finite, a mere laboratory brain.

'Magnificent waste', as James describes it, is what is left over of 'one's visionary and speculative and emotional activity' once those elements which have had even the most 'traceably indirect bearing' on our actions have been subtracted (222). This glorious sense of excess, of potential not necessarily directed *at* anything, defines the possibility of an afterlife. Finally, James suggests, it is in the performance of 'beautiful things' in the context of a *communal* and not isolated experience that we are able to become emancipated from the shackles of the present: 'The truth is that to live, to this tune, intellectually, and in order to do beautiful things, with questions of being as such questions may for the man of imagination aboundingly come up, is to find one's view of one's share in it, and above all of its appeal to *be* shared, in an infinite variety, enormously enlarged' (224). 'Magnificent waste' then is something to be experienced with others, to the extent that as a result not only does one find one's own place in the 'infinite variety' on offer, one is also potentially changed, 'enlarged' by the process. As Beverly Haviland has recently noted, 'one's very self may be consumed and dispersed in an act of imagination that takes one far beyond the limits of the actual'.[27] This is a liberating conclusion, for it enables James to assert that 'even should one cease to be in love with life it would be difficult, on such terms, not to be in love with living' (222). If our experience of living points us in the direction of an on-going and expansive consciousness, why should we assume that it will cease at the moment of physical death? This question of consciousness's regenerative quality is expressed again in a famous letter James wrote to Henry Adams following publication of *Notes of a Son and Brother*. Adams had read James's volume with growing pessimism, writing in March 1914 to his friend Elizabeth Cameron that 'Poor Henry James thinks it all real, I believe, and actually still lives in that dreamy, stuffy Newport and Cambridge, with papa James and Charles Norton.'[28] James's reply to a now lost letter from Adams, one presumably in the same vein, is a concentrated statement of his artistic belief, reiterating a faith in the vitality and significance of consciousness as a defining characteristic of human existence:

> You see I still, in presence of life (or of what you deny to be such), have reactions – as many as possible – and the book I sent you is a proof of them. It's, I suppose, because I am that queer monster the artist, an obstinate finality, an inexhaustible sensibility. Hence the reactions – appearances, memories, many things go on playing upon it with consequences that I note and 'enjoy' (grim word!) noting.   (*Letters*, IV, 706)

Faced with the infinite variety of life in all its 'splendid waste' (as he chooses to describe it in the preface to *The Spoils of Poynton*), James, it seems, simply cannot help himself. The excess allows for the 'sublime economy of art' which 'rescues' and 'saves' (*EWP*, I, 139), such that, in his letter to Adams, James is 'still' besieged by impressions which 'go on' affecting his consciousness, as if without any prompting from him.

In that volume by James which Adams so failed to appreciate, the author describes himself as being 'actively inert in his own behalf' (*A*, 336), a phrase perfectly expressive of the combination of physical stasis and mental agility. He practises, we are told, a blankness which is 'inclusively blank . . . rather than poorly, and meanly, and emptily' blank (*A*, 234). In recollecting his younger self's visit to Sing-Sing prison in the company of his cousin Gus Barker, James muses on the nature of his feelings of envy towards his 'little red-headed kinsman' (*A*, 99), on the fact that 'I seem to have been constantly eager to exchange my lot for that of somebody else, on the assumed certainty of gaining in the bargain.' In admitting this James is eager not to misrepresent his emotion as jealousy, something which for him, significantly, 'bears . . . on what one sees one's companions able to *do*' (my italics). His envy takes the form of 'an acuity of perception of alternatives', an aesthetic curiosity at the possibility of inhabiting the consciousnesses of others (*A*, 101). What James so admired in Balzac, namely his skill at 'transmigration' (*EWP*, 115), his ability to 'get into the constituted consciousness, into all the clothes, gloves and whatever else, into the very skin and bones, of the habited, featured, colored, articulated forms of life that he desired to present' (*EWP*, 132), this quality is the imaginative facility which James remembers his young self wishing for, and the source of his envy.

As Ross Posnock noticed, qualities customarily held to compromise the integrity of the self are deliberately (even perversely) celebrated by James. Indeed in the writing of this autobiography the very assumption of an essential, organic self is what James is seeking to undermine. By effectively revising conventional attitudes to such notions as blankness, vagueness and envy, he attempts to locate himself at some distance from the reigning values of an increasingly aggressive and ambitiously accumulative society. 'By defamiliarizing . . . concepts . . . which usually signify negation, sterility, and poverty', Posnock observes, 'James releases their stored-up energy, which was hitherto repressed as terms of opprobrium in the culture.'[29] For the unconventional self of the dawdling observer, the redefinition of these conventionally pejorative and limiting values opens up enlarged possibilities of perception and experiential enquiry. Recalling in *The Middle Years* (1917), the posthumously published and uncompleted third part of his autobiographical project, his first protracted visit to London, James writes of his sheer enjoyment at being 'in the midst of . . . perversities, idiosyncrasies, incalculabilities, delightful all as densities at first insoluble, delightful even, indeed, as so much mere bewilderment and shock'. An openness to this kind of potentially disorienting atmosphere induced, we are told, sensations of excitement and danger, a heightening of consciousness in which James's provoked feelings would 'melt more or less immediately into some succulence for the mind'. A London breakfast 'disconnected' the writer from all that was familiar, 'all that I had left on the other side of the sea'. The deliberate, 'delightful' challenging of the expected, the obdurate desire to place oneself in the flow of the unfamiliar and potentially embarrassing, 'was above all what I had come out for, and every appearance that might help it was to be artfully and gratefully cultivated' (*A*, 558–9). Selfhood becomes highly contingent and enjoyably precarious, inseparable from the process of experiential inquiry and interpretation; as James notes in his preface to *The Princess Casamassima*, 'it seems probable that if we were never bewildered there would never be a story to tell about us'. Without bewilderment, he continues,

> we should partake of the superior nature of the all-knowing immortals whose annals are dreadfully dull so long as flurried humans are not, for the positive relief of bored Olympians, mixed up with them. Therefore it is that the wary reader for the most part warns the novelist against making his characters too *interpretative* of the muddle of fate, or in other words too divinely, too priggishly clever.   (*EWP*, 1090)

As I will show, 'novelist' here can just as easily be substituted with 'autobiographer', for the interpretative powers of that archetypal Jamesian creation, Henry James himself, are at significant moments clouded in a deliberate yet enticing cloud of obscurity.

II

James Senior's command to his children to 'Convert, convert, convert!' (*A*, 123), to take the bare facts of existence and create with them a life expressive of a deeper significance, succinctly summarises Henry James's autobiographical project. Both father and son were aware of the potentially liberating effect of illustration. For the future novelist, whose 'face was turned from the first to the idea of representation – that of the gain of charm, interest, mystery, dignity, distinction, gain of importance in fine, on the part of the represented thing' (*A*, 149–50), the possibility of the play of imagination on 'the very home of the literal' (*A*, 124) was irresistible; in the preface to *The Spoils of Poynton*, James declares that 'the fatal futility of Fact' could be overcome in the 'richer soil' of artistic creation (*EWP*, 1140). Henry's fascination with and eager consumption of the scenic arts is extensively revealed in his recollections of hours spent at the theatre and art galleries in both America and Europe. James Senior's passion for theatre and art was pursued as part of his celebration of the unorthodox and spontaneous aesthetic sensibility. Aesthetic activity was also linked with the sacrament, in which, as Wendy Graham has described it, 'the artist consecrates the work of his hands by casting off the shackles of convention in pursuit of an ideal that will bring him closer to a spiritual reunion with God'.[30] The creation of art is an inclusive and democratic process, 'man's characteristic activity', writes the elder James, one which 'excludes from its field neither the saint nor the sinner, neither serpent nor dove, but perfectly authenticates the aspiration of both'.[31] In an article in the *Harbinger* newspaper, house journal of the utopian Brook Farm Association, he writes despairingly of the clergyman who 'stifles alike the voice of natural desire, and the inspirations of spiritual attraction, in the sole obedience of duty or social obligation'. He laments a state of affairs in which a 'taste for the opera would be thought very inconsistent with [the clergyman's] calling, and a visit to the Theatre would be tantamount to professional suicide'. In a footnote to the same article James Senior relates an anecdote about his encounter with an orthodox clergyman in Paris 'a few years since' who felt liberated by the sensual delights offered by the city: 'He had an eye for spectacle, and very decided gastronomie [*sic*] tendencies, and the way he would cut about from cafe to restaurant, with the nicest relish of the distinctive merits of each . . . was really marvellous and beautiful in one whose individuality had been so long falsified.'[32] As *The Ambassadors* illustrates, with the ascetic life and its narrow focus left behind, Paris offers a more hospitable vista for one already in possession of 'an eye for spectacle'.

The preference for the freedom offered by an aesthetic conversion of fact over the restrictions of the literal is a strategy which both Henry James and his father employed in their respective autobiographical writings. The desire to convey an impression of significance, for which a mere chronicling of events would prove inadequate, is evident in James Senior's fragment of autobiography, written as a result of urging by his children and published posthumously by William in 1884. That James Senior chooses to adopt the narrative technique of a persona, Stephen Dewhurst, a fictitious friend who allegedly gave the elder James his letters requesting him to transform them into a book, immediately emphasises the extent to which the reader is unable to assume a transparent communication of the 'facts' of the past. Dewhurst enables James Senior to conceal biographical information in order to promote spiritual meaning.[33] In an earlier, unpublished autobiographical piece, 'Essay on Seminary Days', James Senior had disguised his story (or 'the little Iliad of my private bosom', as he described it) as a series of letters to his former Princeton Theological Seminary classmate Parke Godwin; but the representative significance of the autobiographical act was nevertheless made explicit. Godwin's earlier requests for James Senior's life story had apparently been denied. Now its teller finally felt ready to 'hold the *clinique* you then demanded, and give you my own mental or rather sentimental autopsy, in order that you, having before you in miniature form the science of the evil, as I at least understood it, may without difficulty apply it yourself to the large personality of civilized mankind'.[34] William James's words in a letter of 1885, comparing his father to Thomas Carlyle, are pertinent here. Whereas both men flouted 'reasoning', regarding it as 'only an unfortunate necessity of exposition', James Senior 'had nothing to correspond to Carlyle's insatiable learning of historic facts and memory'.[35] Fact, for William's father, could be put to one side in favour of philosophical exemplification. Indeed the first words of his posthumously published sketch proudly declare an aversion to identifiable chronology: 'I will not attempt to state the year in which I was born, because it is not a fact embraced in my own knowledge.' What is important for Dewhurst is the birth of his 'historic consciousness', the genesis of his own sense of identity. This can be dated, he writes, from his presence at the celebrations in March 1815 – James Senior was three months off his fourth birthday at this date – marking the signing of the Treaty of Ghent to conclude the 1812 war with Britain. His memory of the event is focused on a specific and insistent pair of opposing images: 'The only impression left by the illumination upon my imagination was the contrast of the awful dark of the sky with the feeble glitter of the streets; as if the animus of the display had been, not to eclipse the darkness, but to make it visible.' The conquering of the 'feeble glitter' by the 'awful dark' (with the conscious Miltonic allusion to 'darkness visible') points to the presence of a spiritual struggle which the author would wish us to believe was felt even at this early age, a struggle which we are meant to understand as an allegorisation of the human condition. These hints are made explicit when Dewhurst chooses to interpret his experience as being 'rather emblematic of the intellect', emblematic in the sense that 'its earliest sensible foundations should thus be laid in "a horror of great darkness"'.[36] The sketch is not intended simply as a memoir. It insists on being read as a religious parable expressing what James Senior believed to be the liberating truths of his own brand of Swedenborgianism. In Stephen Dewhurst, the elderly James Senior envisages an idealised *alter ego* reflected back into his youth, a spiritually whole self who, despite similarities in education and background, had reached a state of maturity at a much earlier stage in his life than had his creator. In the preface to the fragment, James Senior as 'editor' comments that 'It costs me nothing to admit that my friend, both intellectually and morally, was of a more robust make than me.' He is 'astonished' and 'disconcerted' by the 'cosmopolitan ease and affability . . . in all the range of his religious conscience'. Whereas James Senior had 'almost no suspicion of the spiritual or interior contents of Revelation', Dewhurst was 'insensible to the pretension of a distinctly moral righteousness'.[37]

James Senior's theology was inextricably connected to his personal history, to the extent that his autobiography was deliberately aestheticised to highlight spiritual meaning. In an article in the *Harbinger* from 1848 he writes that 'It is true the old theologians will tell you that they derive their views of the divine character and of human destiny from revelation, but it is none the less true that *every one's perception of revelation is exactly moulded upon his experience of life*' (my emphasis).[38] The 'vastation' episode at Windsor in 1844, James Senior's pivotal moment of psychic breakdown, provides him with further material to transform so that the empirical facts of the incident become almost irrelevant compared to its spiritual reality. The writing is of such a vividness that the story deserves to be quoted at some length:

> In the spring of 1844 I was living with my family in the neighborhood of Windsor, England, much absorbed in the study of the Scriptures. Two or three years before this period I had made an important discovery, as I fancied, namely: that the book of Genesis was not intended to throw a direct light upon our natural or race history, but was an altogether mystical or symbolic record of the laws of God's *spiritual* creation and providence . . . During my residence abroad . . . I hoped to be finally qualified to contribute a not insignificant mite to the sum of man's highest knowledge . . .
>
> One day, however, towards the close of May, having eaten a comfortable dinner, I remained sitting at the table after the family had dispersed, idly gazing at the embers in the grate, thinking of nothing, and feeling only the exhilaration incident to a good digestion, when suddenly – in a lightning-flash as it were – 'fear came upon me, and trembling, which made all my bones to shake.' To all appearance it was a perfectly insane and abject terror, without ostensible cause, and only to be accounted for, to my perplexed imagination, by some damnèd shape squatting invisible to me within the precincts of the room, and raying out from his fetid personality influences fatal to life. The thing had not lasted ten seconds before I felt myself a wreck, that is, reduced from a state of firm, vigorous, joyful manhood to one of almost helpless infancy. The only self-control I was capable of exerting was to keep my seat. I felt the greatest desire to run incontinently to the foot of the stairs and shout for help to my wife, – to run to the roadside even, and appeal to the public to protect me; but by an immense effort I controlled these frenzied impulses, and determined not to budge from my chair till I had recovered my lost self-possession.[39]

James Senior at the beginning of this passage is a successful man by his own standards. In apparent rude health, enjoying the beauty of the Windsor location (which 'furnished us a constant temptation to long walks and drives' (44)), he is confident too in his intellectual abilities – certain that his investigations into the biblical Genesis story will warrant him a place amongst those who have added to 'man's highest knowledge'. The unsettling confrontation which he experiences with this ill-defined form (it is '*some* damnèd *shape*') is transfigured into something archetypal of the experience of discarding selfhood, 'that which keeps our manhood so little and so depraved' (47). As a result his studious theological labours are abandoned as worthless and self-serving: 'I had never really wished the truth, but only to ventilate my own ability in discovering it. I was getting sick to death in fact with a sense of my downright intellectual poverty and dishonesty' (48–9).

Howard Feinstein has demonstrated the extent to which James Senior seems to be borrowing from other sources in his retelling of this event, most especially from Bunyan's *Pilgrim's Progress* but also from Swedenborg and the Bible.[40] The reference to 'fear and trembling' (Job 4:14), a biblical example of a mystical experience in which what is revealed is man's inability to understand God's ways, serves to introduce James Senior's own instance of punctured hubris and radical incomprehension. There is also an intriguing, although probably unknowing, echo of Søren Kierkegaard's 1843 meditation on the Abraham and Isaac story of the same name, like James Senior's account, a narrative of renunciation of conventional values for the sake of moral and spiritual innovation.[41] What is worth remembering is that this most extensive treatment of the Windsor experience was not published until 1879, three years before its author's death. By this time it had become imbued with an archetypal trajectory and serves not so much (even if at all) as a document of historical event than as a testimony of a well-rehearsed spiritual position. As Feinstein observes, 'The sequence of James's story is Bunyan in microcosm: reading the Bible, being cast into despair, hiding the matter from his family, and then telling them the awful truth that launches him on his solitary quest for the Heavenly City.'[42] For the purposes of his religious parable James Senior must locate the genesis of his spiritual journey at the point where he first encounters the writings of Swedenborg. Where numerous doctors and expensive water cures have failed, his eager perusal of *Divine Love and Wisdom* and *Divine Providence* initiates a healing process. The enigmatic Mrs Chichester (a figure identified by Henry James in *Notes of a Son and Brother* (*A*, 340)) introduces him to the idea of vastation as an explanation for what he has experienced. Her pupil is duly grateful: 'In expressing my thanks for her encouraging words, I remarked that I was not at all familiar with the Swedenborgian technics, and that I should be extremely happy if she would follow up her flattering judgement of my condition by turning into plain English the contents of the very handsome Latin word she had used.'[43] Within the rules of the narrative, a profession of ignorance is necessary if Swedenborg is to act as James Senior's saviour in his hour of need. This proves to be the case:

> I read from the first with palpitating interest. My heart divined, even before my intelligence was prepared to do justice to the books, the unequalled amount of truth to be found in them. Imagine a fever patient, sufficiently restored of his malady to be able to think of something beside himself, suddenly transported

where the free airs of heaven blow upon him, and the sound of running waters refreshes his jaded senses; and you have a feeble image of my delight in reading.[44]

But as Feinstein has noted, there is ample reason to suggest that this was by no means James Senior's first encounter with Swedenborg's ideas. Certainly he had already struck up an acquaintance with the London Swedenborgian James Garth Wilkinson before his Windsor experience. Wilkinson had written to him three months prior to it, in February 1844, affirming his belief in one of the central tenets of Swedenborg's philosophy, that of the doctrine of correspondence, whereby humankind is to be encouraged 'to cultivate a finer sense, and to receive it as a settled truth that there is ever something more in nature than the order first presented to the senses'. In the same letter Wilkinson had enthused about the establishment of the Swedenborg Association, and encouraged James Senior to anticipate, 'by the blessing of Divine Providence', his promotion to a 'station of use, either as an Author, or as an oral teacher'.[45] And one further piece of evidence can be marshalled to question James Senior's apparent ignorance of Swedenborg prior to Mrs Chichester's ministrations. In a letter of 1843 written to Joseph Henry, his former science teacher and now a professor of natural philosophy at Princeton University, James Senior outlines a philosophical conviction that can be said to anticipate that described in Wilkinson's later communication. 'Again and again,' he writes, 'I am forced by scriptural philosophy to the conviction that all the phenomena of physics are to [be] explained and grouped under laws exclusively spiritual – that they are in fact only the material expression of spiritual truth.'[46] Joseph Henry's reply would have done nothing to deter the direction of his former pupil's thinking, affirming his belief that 'all the phenomena of the external universe and perhaps all those of the spiritual [are] reduced to the operation of a simple law of the Divine Will . . . I believe that every phenomena is connected with every other' (388).

It is likely, then, that James Senior was at least already receptive to certain ideas and influences which would have led him to espouse more readily those of the Swedish thinker. Moreover in writing his own account James Senior was attempting to create a close link between *his* biography and that of Swedenborg. Wilkinson's life of Swedenborg had appeared in 1849, and it is surely not coincidental that James Senior's vastation is strongly identified with his friend's account of one of the series of experiences that Swedenborg claimed for his own crisis-filled years of 1743, 1744 and 1745. Like James Senior, Swedenborg is dining in his room, labouring on a philosophical study from which his revelations would relieve him: 'Towards the end of the meal I remarked that a kind of mist spread before my eyes, and I saw the floor of my room covered with hideous reptiles... I was astonished, having all my wits about me, and being perfectly conscious... From that day forth I gave up all worldly learning, and labored only in spiritual things.'[47] The coincidences are striking: the prior contentment brought about by food and study; the lack of a precise description of the manifestation; the resultant renunciation of work previously cherished and valued. It is a narrative which James Senior seems to appropriate for his own conversion to Swedenborgian ideas, yet, as I have suggested, in the memoir the existence of prior knowledge is suppressed. The vastation experience is, like the autobiographical fragment, a deliberate refracting of personal history, a means of communicating a more important reality. Henry James had offered his own slant on this formulation in one of his Italian travel essays, where he noted that in recapturing his experiences the importance rests in 'giving the particular thing as much as possible without at the same time giving it, as we say, away'. To achieve this requires 'a necessary indirectness, ... a little art'.[48] The artist must be allowed to respond to certain memories in a creative manner, which may mean taking the reality of something only as a starting point for the conversion process. The danger of 'giving away' is that of presenting something in a manner which precludes the detection of vibrations of further significance. In this way the capacity for autobiography to deliver accurate information from the past does not depend necessarily on fidelity to an objective chronology of brute facts. In some instances a distortion of the fact might allow for a more accurate depiction of the experiential aspect of a subject's life.

Adopting this strategy became particularly problematic for James in a way that he perhaps was not expecting when he decided against merely transcribing certain family letters, choosing instead to edit (and in some instances rewrite) them prior to their inclusion in *Notes of a Son and Brother*. Letters which James wrote to William's son, Henry III, indicate the extent to which William's family was concerned about James's intentions towards his brother's words. The family's desire that William should not be misrepresented is felt in James's assurance, even before embarking on the second volume, that 'the principle of selection of letters from the correspondence at large should be preferentially and supremely... the illustration of character, personality, life etc.' (*Letters*, IV, 796). A further letter, in November 1912, finds James unable to make any specific promises to his nephew about the use he determines to make of the family archive: 'Don't insist, but trust me as far as you can' (*Letters*, IV, 798). After completion of the book he wrote again to William's son, and in a dense but richly illuminating piece of writing set out his defence against criticisms of editorial licence. At the outset James admits that his style is not 'the ideal of documentary exactitude, verbatim, literatim et punctuatim – free of all living back imaginatively'. He cannot adhere to a 'high standard of rigid editing... with no relations for the letters but their relation to their utter text' (*Letters*, IV, 800). Instead what James describes is his sense of a kind of spiritual communion with his dead brother, one in which, in a curious transference of authorial control, the revised versions of the letters which appear in his book seem initiated by William himself, ghost-written with Henry merely acting as a loyal amanuensis:

> I found myself again in such close relation with your Father, such a revival of relation as I hadn't known since his death, and which was a passion of tenderness for doing the best thing by him that the material allowed, and which I seemed to feel him in the room and at my elbow asking me for as I worked and as he listened. It was as if he had said to me on seeing me lay my hands on the weak little relics of our common youth, 'Oh but you're not going to give me away, to hand me over, in my raggedness and my poor accidents, quite unhelpful, unfriended, you're going to do the very best for me you can, aren't you, and since you appear to be making such claims for me you're going to let me seem to justify them as much as I possibly may?' And it was as if I kept spiritually replying to this that he might indeed trust me to handle him with the last tact and devotion – that is do with him everything I seemed to feel him like.
>
> (*Letters*, IV, 802)

Note again the concern with 'giving away' that James projects on to his brother. William's ventriloquised anxiety about being revealed metaphorically unclothed – 'in my raggedness' – legitimises James's editorial elisions. Any notion of the sanctity and inviolability of William's words becomes irrelevant for James; any truth which he feels it to be his duty to evoke does not lie in the accurate transcribing of symbols, but rather in the process of refining and capturing the felt essence of those symbols. Truth is not something external and objective, but instead to be discovered through a creative interaction between subject and object – James has 'to the last point the instinct and the sense for fusions and interrelations, for framing and encircling... every part of my stuff in every other' (*Letters*, IV, 803).[49] Although fact is the necessary raw material of art, the duty of art in return is to heighten and embellish, transforming fact into a mode of representation in which aspects that retain a straightforward significance *outside* the world of the text are simultaneously held *within* the text in an alternative, parallel pattern of meaning. James's exploration of the capacities of fiction as an imaginative and narrative form reinventing the processes of history leads to the redefinition of history itself found in *The American Scene*. After apologising for one of the narrative digressions which, he feels, seem to abound in the record of his visit to America in 1904–5, James writes: 'I draw courage from the remembrance that history is never, in any rich sense, the immediate crudity of what "happens", but the much finer complexity of what we read into it and think of in connection with it.'[50] In the final section of this chapter I want to discuss how this strategy is problematically entwined for James with the question of vocation and the pressure to *do*. How does one escape from the 'immediate crudity' of a historical situation which demands a certain kind of behaviour, one in which the luxury of 'much finer complexity' may be thought to be a form of moral cowardice?

III

I have already shown how James Senior, in an article in the *Harbinger*, had castigated the clergyman for his lack of aesthetic spontaneity and his 'conviction to duty'. In the same article he also focused his ire on the growing phenomenon of the businessman, one, he categorised, who 'seeks chiefly the satisfaction of his natural desires, and devotes himself to the acquisition of wealth as their instrument': 'No one truly esteems the man himself, merely because he has become rich.'[51] Work for James Senior could only be countenanced if its performance expressed an independence of spirit and an originality of thought – hence his lauding of the artist figure. He praises 'the man of whatsoever function, from king to cobbler, who follows his function from taste and not from necessity or duty, who cultivates it not with a view merely to a livelihood or to fame, but purely because he loves it and finds it its own exceeding great reward'.[52] In 'Universality in Art', a lecture he included in an 1852 collection, work as obligation – as 'duty' – again comes in for criticism as he hymns the 'sovereign activity' of Art which 'embraces all those products of human genius, which do not confess the parentage either of necessity or duty'. This enveloping of the idea of work in a protective blanket of aesthetic significance (a theory whose practical application was no doubt aided by the cushion of considerable inherited wealth) is evident in the importance which he attaches to 'the man who . . . works from an ideal, works to produce or bring forth in tangible form some conception of use or beauty with which not his memory but his inmost soul is aglow'.[53]

The world 'in which people sat close and made money' (*A*, 30), as Henry James recalled defining business in his childhood, was one that remained alien to the James household. Throughout *A Small Boy and Others* especially, James comments on the family's ignorance of all matters pertaining to conventional careers and vocations:

> Our consciousness was positively disfurnished, as that of young Americans went, of the actualities of 'business' in a world of business . . . We touched it and it touched us neither directly nor otherwise, and I think our fond detachment, not to say our helpless ignorance and on occasion (since I can speak for one fine instance) our settled destiny of understanding, made us an unexampled

and probably, for the ironic 'smart' gods of the American heaven, a lamentable
case. (*A*, 35)

The ambiguity of feeling in this passage is delicately weighed: James feels
himself 'positively disfurnished', a phrase asserting either the strength of
feeling or the value attached to that feeling, or a position somewhere
between the two. 'Fond detachment' jostles for attention with 'helpless
ignorance'; and one wonders how much credence the reader is supposed
to give to the judgement of the American gods in their sophisticated and
'ironic' heaven. Certainly tension exists in James's attitude towards his
father's deliberate refusal to find value in conventional modes of work,
such that we find him repeating the familiar pattern of statement, followed
by doubt, followed by justification of the initial statement. He stresses
again the fact of the family's complete detachment from the world of
business:

> The word had been passed, all around, that we didn't, that we couldn't and
> shouldn't, understand these things, questions of arithmetic and of fond calcu-
> lation, questions of the counting-house and the market; and we appear to have
> held to our agreement as loyally and to have accepted our doom as serenely
> as if our faith had been mutually pledged. The rupture with my grandfather's
> tradition and attitude was complete.

The assertiveness of these final words is impressive, and one might think
that nothing more could be said on the subject. Yet the feeling that
somehow the family's position is improper, that something is 'the matter',
breaks through the apparent closure: 'What was the matter with us under
this spell, and what the moral might have been for our case, are issues of
small moment, after all, in face of the fact of our mainly brief duration.
It was given to but few of us to be taught by the event, to be made to
wonder with the last intensity what had been the matter.' These may be
'issues of small moment', but the fact that James is prepared to consider
them at all indicates the degree to which they remain important so many
years later. The apparent ease with which he dismisses the questions
he has raised only serves to confirm this impression: 'This it would be
interesting to worry out, might I take the time; for the story wouldn't
be told, I conceive, by any mere rueful glance at other avidities, the
preference for ease, the play of the passions, the appetite for pleasure'
(*A*, 109).

Not then for any base or selfish reason did the family shun the world of
work; the real explanation, as James defines it, is the fact that the opportunities provided by the business world were ultimately inadequate – 'there
were not enough of these, and they were not fine and fair enough, to
engage happily so much unapplied, so much loose and crude attention'
(*A*, 110). James can assuage any anxiety he may have about the validity

of his father's action by relying on the argument that the alternative to it simply did not exist. Instead, he tells us, the family was 'thrown so upon the inward life' (*A*, 35), where conventional notions of value and success (like those of waste referred to earlier) were ignored. Success as generally understood, for example, became 'a reward of effort for which I remember to have heard no good word, nor any sort of word, ever faintly breathed' (*A*, 123). Indeed although Stephen Dewhurst in James Senior's autobiographical narrative obtains a position in the Treasury Department in the nation's capital, 'which his ability and probity qualified him to fill with advantage to the country', the effect on his health and circumstances is marked. James Senior as 'editor' comments that 'his constitution had been signally robust, but he had lost his wife and his only son a year or two before, and I could easily see that he was now devoting himself with forced activity to the increased labors thrown upon him in common with all the government servants by our unexampled war [presumably the Civil War]'.[54] Dewhurst finally succumbs to 'a chronic malady resulting from a fever which he had contracted at the close of the war, and which had been at length fatally determined by the weight of his official labors and cares' (140). Conventional employment has been, quite literally, a deadening activity, and the identification of Dewhurst with James Senior is at its loosest here; as editor, the elder James notes that neither he nor Dewhurst 'contemplated a life of idleness', but he is strangely quiet about his own occupation. Behind the problem of 'forced activity' lay, James tells us, the fear of 'narrowing' (*A*, 269), of restricting the free play of one's consciousness by a commitment to a particular form of activity which then 'dispensed with any suggestion of an alternative' (*A*, 268). That Henry felt ambiguous about this seemingly liberating philosophy is understandable. After all, one could not remain unattached, floating in an idealised realm indefinitely; despite the luxury of significant family wealth, the need to find a vocation was felt strongly by both Henry and William (hence William's thoughts on the subject, quoted earlier). Yet the paternal warning of the dangers of making finite what should remain infinite encouraged the development of that familiar Jamesian stance of the incessantly curious observer. Although he ultimately could not share his father's radical embrace of inertia and non-participation, James was able to convert for his own creative purposes those same qualities, 'to work [them] for all [they] were worth' (*A*, 279).

James Senior of course was not unique in his condemnation of the motivating drives behind a rapidly expanding capitalist culture. In 'The American Scholar' address of 1837, Emerson pre-empted the fate of Stephen Dewhurst by declaring that the world of business was destructive to young men of idealistic promise, those 'inflated by the mountain winds, shined upon by all the stars of God'. Descending from such heights, they 'are hindered from action by the disgust which the principles on which business is managed inspire'; a capitalist culture results in men who 'turn drudges, or die of disgust, some of them suicides' (*CWE*, I, 114). Later, in his essay 'Success' (first published in 1870 but delivered as a lecture as early as 1852), Emerson remarked on what he diagnosed to be the American proclivity to perform, the need to be in a continual state of activity: 'Our American people cannot be taxed with slowness in performance or in praising their performance. The earth is shaken by our engineries' (*CWE*, VII, 283). He regarded this condition as the inevitable response of a young and acquisitive society, driven by a sense of purpose and urgency, in which industrial and vocational success had become a mark of social esteem and stature: 'We respect ourselves more if we have succeeded. Neither do we grudge to each of these benefactors the praise or the profit which accrues from his industry' (*CWE*, VII, 286). But the American preoccupation with success, a phenomenon which Emerson identifies as developing in conjunction with the process of American colonisation and expansion, is nevertheless not something to be embraced wholeheartedly. The maxim of 'Rien ne réussit mieux que le succès', he warns, leads to financial and moral tainting, 'as our bankruptcies and our reckless politics may show. We are great by exclusion, grasping, and egotism' (*CWE*, VII, 289). Emerson rejects this conventional understanding of *material* prosperity in favour of a kind which emphasises a self-reliance of the mind, an attitude which scorns public opinion and has no need for society's approbation: 'I fear the popular notion of success stands in direct opposition in all points to the real and wholesome success. One adores public opinion, the other private opinion; one fame, the other desert; one feasts, the other humility; one lucre, the other love; one monopoly, and the other hospitality of the mind' (*CWE*, VII, 308).

The irony of course is the degree to which the ideal of self-reliance, in an Emersonian sense connected with a profound wariness of the social body and the promotion of a 'hospitality of the mind', becomes transformed into something redolent of mercantile competition, representative of the very kind of striving after pecuniary gain which Emerson seemed to so dislike. Yet, and this is indicative of the difficulty faced by any reader of Emerson's work in search of seamless consistency, this co-opting of his notion of the independent self by Jacksonian ideologues was at times encouraged by the sage of Concord himself, despite the anxieties expressed in 'Success'.[55] His frequent references from the mid-1840s onwards to *laissez-faire* economics were prompted by a profound distrust of communitarianism, both in America and further afield in Europe. In 'Wealth' for example (included in the *Conduct of Life* (1860)), he could state that financial prosperity 'brings with it its own checks and balances. The basis of political economy is non-interference. The only safe rule is found in the self-adjusting meter of demand and supply . . . [T]he law of self-preservation is surer policy than any legislation can be' (*CWE*, VI, 105). This echoing of the language of Adam Smith and the free market did not go unnoticed by Emerson's interpreters, for in a piece in the *North American Review* in 1903 celebrating the centenary of Emerson's birth, W. Robertson Nicoll went so far as to remark that 'from his works a book might be compiled on the conduct of life, which hard-headed business men would distribute among their employees', a volume which would 'give mind, soul, heart and body to business'.[56] Yet, as Sacvan Bercovitch has suggested, Emerson's endorsement of Jacksonian rhetoric was undertaken with the desire 'to de-ideologize the entire issue';[57] *despite* the specific deleterious effects of individualist economics (represented by 'exaggerating schemers, maniacs who go about in marts'), Emerson could claim in 1851 that the overall effect would ultimately prove beneficial, regardless of 'the madness of a few' (*Journals*, XI, 392). He recognised (as had de Tocqueville) that the philosophy of self-reliance, until the early 1840s the province of the Party of the Future and one of the transcendent myths upon which America insisted on defining itself, had become institutionalised and made concrete, 'organic to a certain society, in a certain place, as a tendency toward perfect union inherent in its laws, customs, assumptions, and institutions'.[58]

Instead of fearing this appropriation, Emerson uneasily chose to regard it as a means to an end – its excesses were disliked but tolerated. Indeed Philip Schaff, a Swiss theologian teaching in Pennsylvania (and no supporter of Emersonianism generally), seemed to affirm Emerson's idealism in the face of capitalist endeavour, judging in 1855 that the 'acquisition of riches is to them [the Americans] only a help toward higher spiritual and moral ends; the gain derived from the inexhaustible physical resources of their glorious country only the material ground-work toward the future of civilization'.[59] However, Emerson's endorsement of Jacksonian America has been read less favourably. Strongly individualistic, his philosophy, Daniel Aaron remarks, 'spoke for equality of opportunity in economic and political affairs, and it lent support to the belief in *laissez-faire* and the necessity of the minimized state'. For Perry Miller, individualism rapidly expressed the economic orthodoxy such that its radicalism (as Emerson had conceived it) was softened: it 'came to seem not at all dangerous, but rather the proper code for a young businessman with get-up and go'.[60] So Emerson's ideal of manly self-empowerment was inevitably appropriated for the service of capitalist endeavour by the emerging middle class, an appropriation which ultimately he could do little to control or influence. From the seclusion of Concord he had looked on this new sector of society with a mixture of nervousness and admiration, comparing it, in all its virtues and vices, to one of his Representative

Men, the figure of Napoleon. This chapter of Emerson's book has long been regarded as one of his most significant explorations of the contemporary American political scene.[61] The French Emperor, he suggested, embodied the assumptions and aspirations of 'the middle class of modern society; of the throng who fill the markets, shops, counting-houses, manufactories, ships, of the modern world, aiming to be rich' (*CWE*, IV, 252). Napoleon's reign had ushered in an exciting period of 'expansion and demand': 'A market for all the powers and productions of man was opened; brilliant prizes glittered in the eyes of youth and talent' for a class which he describes as 'self-relying' (*CWE*, IV, 242, 224). That this was a change which resulted in a beneficial mirroring of the American situation is rendered explicit, for the 'old, iron-bound, feudal France' has become transformed into 'a young Ohio or New York' (*CWE*, IV, 242). Yet Emerson's unease with his celebration of middle-class values is finally apparent in the lecture's closing paragraphs. 'The brilliant picture has its reverse', he warns, and the final judgement has the effect of muting the excited fascination which has permeated all that has come before: 'In short, when you have penetrated through all the circles of power and splendor, you were not dealing with a gentleman, at last; but with an imposter and a rogue; and he fully deserves the epithet of *Jupiter Scapin*, or a sort of Scamp Jupiter'. Napoleon's 'sensual and selfish' character reflects a wider society 'of property, of fences, or exclusiveness' which will ultimately 'leave us sick' (*CWE*, IV, 253, 256, 258).

Patrician disdain here competed, at times uneasily, with Emerson's admiration of Napoleon's personal force – and by extension with Emerson's wonder at an aspiring, industrious America. In a study charting the development of American working habits, Daniel T. Rodgers details the importance which the mid-nineteenth century attached to the idea of work as an antidote to the pernicious effects of leisure and idleness: 'the elevation of work over leisure involved not an isolated choice but an ethos that permeated life and manners'. This doctrine of work as 'duty' gave a moral impetus to the debate, for, as Rodgers comments, '[W]ork made men useful in a world of economic scarcity; it staved off doubts and temptations that preyed on idleness; it opened the way to deserved wealth and status, it allowed one to put the impress of mind and skill on the material world.'[62] Work was not only linked to an idea of moral welfare however; it was also an important factor in the construction of ideas of masculinity. Speaking to the congregation of a church in Providence, Rhode Island, Augustus Woodbury made explicit the gendered assumptions of the work ethic. The carpenter, Woodbury claimed, 'would find that he was doing something more than driving nails, and hewing timbers, and wearily shoving the plane; that he was giving form to ideas; that he was growing into a love of the beautiful and the true, and that every day's labor was aiding in the noiseless but certain work of building up the structure of a manly and noble character'.[63] In an increasingly mechanised work-place traditional ideas of manliness such as artisan independence, dedicated hard work and pride in one's labour were challenged in an emerging marketplace which stressed competition, the necessity of risk and the imperative of calculation. Work became energised by the fear of business failure and an aggressive aspiration for dominance.

The gulf between the different roles expected of men and women in this new economy, a separation which had previously seemed less gaping when the sites of economic productivity had often been situated in the household itself, emphasised the ethos of the self-made man under the imperative of maximising individual gain in a competitive market. Measured against a cultural orthodoxy of this kind of assertive masculinity, it is not surprising that James at times felt the disparity between society's requirements and those upheld by his father. Alfred Habegger comments, quite accurately, that James Senior 'was independently wealthy and thus, unlike all American men, without a job or career; he lived on the fringe of man's world'.[64] However, Habegger goes on to contend that a 'power vacuum' was left in the younger Henry's life by his 'visionary, erratic, and ineffective' father, precisely because James Senior 'lacked a professional or public role in a country that defined men by the way they earned a living away from home' (258–9, 272). As a result of this dispersal of potential male influence, the future novelist 'became an observer because he could become nothing else in a world where boys and men were supposed to be bellicose and mean, to get in there, hustle and fight' (58). Habegger's portrait of the young Henry is of a boy apparently crushed and humiliated by the 'crude complacency of power' (*A*, 129) displayed by the other, more successfully initiated boys who had been able to solve the basic problem of 'how to find a possible male role' (268). James failed to achieve a masculine identity, Habegger maintains, because of this 'aborted masculine initiation'; furthermore, and of most significance, this failure is 'a type of deformity, and . . . this deformity impaired his writing' (255).

Habegger's thesis is that James's formative years instilled in him a sense of profound alienation from society because of his inability to partic-ipate in the customary and culturally inscribed rites of masculine de-velopment. In effect he argues that James's sensibility was denied the requisite raw material for him to be successful as a novelist creatively engaged with his environment. Consequently James's importance to lit-erature lies in the fact that he 'made the novel available for the interests and strategies of modernism mainly because he knew so little' (255). This argument flounders around its dubious assertion that a rejection of a particular form of cultural orthodoxy (however dominant it may be) is somehow both artistically and biographically impairing. There is no question that writers *are* subject to their specific social reality, with the result that, because their writing is circumscribed by historical conditions, the discourse they produce may *re*produce the social conventions already in place. George Santayana's analysis of the genteel tradition, with its 'slightly becalmed' mind 'float[ing] gently in the back water' might be said to characterise this sense of passive receptivity to and imitation of the cultural status quo.[65] But conformity of this kind co-exists with the potential for disruption: writers can also reject existing power structures or create alternative ones, and by so doing offer resistance to hegemonic standards.[66] Such a rejection for James, despite the acknowledged difficulties of his father's romantic and impractical conception of the value of work, is, I contend, aesthetically liberating. One small incident in *A Small Boy and Others* serves to illustrate this point. James recalls how William offered him a sharp rebuke when he once expressed the desire to play with his brother and his friends. '"*I* play with boys who curse and swear!"' (*A*, 147), William asserts, declining his brother's request to be included. James, in recounting this episode, admits that he 'simply wasn't qualified' to participate in this childhood version of the adult male world. As a result he took refuge 'easily enough in the memory of my own pursuits, absorbing enough at the time to have excluded other views . . . I was so often engaged at that period, it strikes me, in literary – or, to be more precise in dramatic, accompanied by pictorial composition – that I must have again and again delightfully lost myself' (*A*, 148). Annexation from the realms of conventional, if childish, masculine activity engenders the early stirrings of Henry's artistic desire. Far from feeling excluded from the traditional (and expected) rites of boyhood, his alternative is overpowering, intoxicating, a release from the pressures focused on the non-conforming self. In turning to the alternatives afforded by a mind disposed to literature, James tellingly writes that 'I . . . delightfully lost myself.' Selfhood is reconfigured, made challengingly fallible.

James exhibited patterns of behaviour and response which, although only retrospectively visible to the autobiographer, would eventually lead him to literary creativity – patterns which would not immediately locate him in the male universe of action, with its codified initiations, skills and occupations. The outbreak of the Civil War in 1861 provided James with the severest test of his ability to maintain an uncompromised stance of deliberate vagueness – his ability in short to remain outside the reaches of society's demands on the masculine self. The war inevitably provoked and authorised a demonstration of decisive manhood, of public and patriotic action as an easily available means of defining a selfhood acceptable to society – a selfhood which James described as the 'conventional maximum'. On Memorial Day 1885, his friend, Oliver Wendell Holmes, Jr, himself three-times wounded in the conflict, would recall and perpetuate

an ideal of noble and active bravery of a kind to which James had little inclination or for which he demonstrated any particular aptitude. In
opposition to the 'wallowing ease' of the false patriot who, 'under the
name of cosmopolitanism', sought out 'a place where the most enjoyment may be had at the least cost', Holmes celebrated the code of 'high
and dangerous action' which affirmed the legitimacy of a soldier who
would 'throw away his life in obedience to a blindly accepted duty'. War
was a shared 'communicable experience' for Holmes, but only through
remembrance and rewriting could it become so for Henry James.[67] His
decision to enrol at the Harvard Law School in the autumn of 1862 can
be seen as a concession to the 'conventional maximum' – it is 'the flag
I publicly brandished', he admits. Yet there lingers the recognition of
the inadequacy of his action when compared to the national upheaval
in which many of the other young men of his age (such as Holmes)
were participating. His flag shrinks, as if out of shame and impotence,
to become an 'emblazoned morsel', 'a light extravagant bandanna rolled
into the tight ball that fits it for hiding in the pocket' (*A*, 411), where
'light' and 'extravagant' suggest both the insubstantiality and the inappro-
priateness of his response. Attending Harvard is a provisional strategy, an
option which leaves James's potential as far as possible undefined and uncircumscribed. The paternal inheritance of experiential freedom and fear
of personal narrowing, of the creative uses of indeterminacy, is reflected
in James's disclosure that his decision had 'the positive saving virtue of
vagueness'. But 'to be properly and perfectly vague', he admits, 'one had
to be vague *about* something' (*A*, 412).

James's representation of his experience of the Civil War is indeed
shrouded in such a tantalising and suggestive nebulousness, and its importance for him remains profound. As an aspiring artist in a time of
conflict, striving to maintain an attitude of detachment from any aggressive and expected display of manliness, James had, he writes, 'under
stress, to content myself with knowing [the war] in a more indirect and
muffled fashion than might easily have been'. Yet despite its indirectness,
the experience stays significant for the elderly autobiographer 'as a more
constituted and sustained act of living, in proportion to my powers and
opportunities, than any other homogenous stretch of experience that my
memory now recovers' (*A*, 382–3). The recollection of the war's outbreak in 'the soft spring of '61' (*A*, 414) is directly linked by James with
the suffering of his 'obscure hurt', that much-discussed mysterious injury
incurred while fighting a fire in Newport. For the author, the incident
is important yet, he admits, of an imprecision which makes the nature of
its importance hard to describe. James's late style, with its pauses, indirections and attempts at clarification, finds its ideal subject in an event that
refuses to come into focus. It is recalled as 'a passage of personal history

the most entirely personal, but between which, as a private catastrophe or difficulty, bristling with embarrassments, and the great public convulsion that announced itself in bigger terms each day, I felt from the very first an association of the closest, yet withal, I feel, almost of the least clearly expressible' (*A*, 414). Leon Edel's biography revealed that, in terms of historical accuracy, the yoking together of these two events, the personal injury and the public war, in such a direct manner is misleading. Edel's painstaking reconstruction finds evidence that the fire to which James alludes occurred six months after the outbreak of the war, not simultaneously as the autobiographer seeks to imply. He also identifies the precise nature of James's suffering as a back injury, in part, it seems, as an attempt to rescue James from those critics who have understood the affliction to be something more disabling – castration.[68] Yet his reading of these autobiographical distortions and evasions provokes him into accusing James of a deliberate and cowardly attempt to mislead his readership over the extent of his involvement in the war. James, Edel writes, 'seems to have felt that by vagueness and circumlocution he might becloud the whole question of his non-participation' (1, 147). Such a negative assessment ignores the extent to which James positively insists upon obscurity and emphasises his own lack of conventional engagement – it is a period of his life 'the least clearly expressible'. The various attempts made to clarify and explain James's narrative are indicative of the task increasingly demanded of biography; any new life of a well-documented figure finds its *raison d'être* in the revelation of a hitherto unknown 'key' to that life. In the case of James, banishing the clouds of obfuscation for the sake of biographical judgement merely imposes a selection of specific historical events and medical conjecture on to a text which refuses to be accommodating. Edel's theory of a back injury is simultaneously equally as valid and as irrelevant as any other interpretation.

The notion of the non-participation of his eldest sons in the war was not something about which James Senior, at least initially, had any qualms. Writing to an unknown correspondent at the beginning of the conflict, he explains his unwillingness to see William and Henry enlist:

> The way I excuse my paternal interference to them is, to tell them, first, that no existing government, nor indeed any now possible government, is worth an honest human life and a clean one like theirs; especially if that government is likewise in danger of bringing back slavery again under our banner: than which consummation I would rather see chaos itself come again.[69]

Here then is the father's characteristic disavowal of sectarianism, the fear of moral pollution which a definite commitment to the vocation of government-sponsored war would engender. The concern about a possible retreat from Lincoln's moral condemnation of slavery is revealed again in the Newport annual Independence Day address, which James Senior delivered in 1861. The speech, entitled 'The Social Significance of our Institutions', is an eloquent piece of rhetoric, infused with a consciousness of the historical circumstances of the moment. Slavery is a 'prison'

> grown so rank and pervasive . . . that each successive administration of the country proves more recreant to humanity than its precursor, until at last we find shameless God-forsaken men, holding high place in the government, become so rabid with its virus as to mistake its slimy purulent ooze for the ruddy tide of life, and commend its foul and fetid miasm to us as the fragrant breath of assured health.[70]

The conflict is important to the elder James as evidence of the ushering in of 'the transition from youth to manhood, from appearance to reality', with the effect, he says, that 'we are not fighting for our own country only, for our own altars and firesides as men have fought hitherto, but for the altars and firesides of universal man' (117). The world of *realpolitik*, in which maintaining the union at the expense of an outright moral condemnation of slavery was felt to be the most appropriate response, gets short shrift: 'The Republic is much, but it is not all. It is much as a means, but nothing as an end. It is much as a means to human advancement, but nothing as its consummation' (120). Indeed at the speech's conclusion, instead of reaching a climax of patriotic fervour and a proffering of best wishes to the North's leaders (as one might perhaps expect on 4 July), he intones a sober warning:

> For my part, if I thought that our rulers were going to betray in this agonizing hour the deathless interest confided to them, – if I thought that Mr Lincoln and Mr Seward were going at least to palter with the sublime instincts of peace and righteousness that elevated them to power and give them all their personal prestige, by making the least conceivable further concession to the obscene demon of Slavery, – then I could joyfully see Mr Lincoln and Mr Seward scourged from the sacred eminence they defile, could joyfully see our boasted political house itself laid low in the dust forever.   (120)

James Senior's decided unease about the execution of the war, his need to understand it as primarily a moral conflict indicative of a growing sense of universal unity, coupled with his anxiety that such fine thinking might be sacrificed for the sake of short-term political expediency, could not have gone unnoticed by young Henry. James's strong awareness of the inadequacy of his response to the pressure of making a public gesture is combined with a sense of his unfitness for such an action. His solution to this problem in his autobiography is to reconstitute the past in such a way that his younger self's non-conformist sensibility does not hinder him from becoming, in his own eyes and in his own way, an active participant in the war. The 'obscure hurt' is the means by which James achieves this transformation, for he writes of feeling 'a huge comprehensive ache' when 'one could scarce have told whether it came most from one's own poor organism, still so young and so meant for better things, but which had suffered particular wrong, or from the enclosing social body, a body rent with a thousand wounds and that thus treated one to the honour of a sort of tragic fellowship' (*A*, 415).

The mysterious injury which James sustains is transfigured into something positively liberating, resonating with a seemingly infinite 'interest' (a telling, and highly valued, Jamesian word):

> The interest of [the injury], I very presently knew, would certainly be of the greatest, would even in conditions kept as simple as I might make them become little less than absorbing... Circumstances, by a wonderful chance, overwhelmingly favoured it – as an interest, an inexhaustible, I mean... Interest, the interest of life and of death, of our national existence, of the fate of those, the vastly numerous, whom it closely concerned, the interest of the extending War, in fine, the hurrying troops, the transfigured scene, formed a cover for every sort of intensity, made tension in fact contagious – so that almost any tension would do, would serve for one's share. (*A*, 415–16)

We find James remembering his injury as a source of life-enhancing connection, nurtured within an 'enveloping tonic atmosphere' which inspired its 'growth'. The waste of national war has proven to be fertile ground, as differences between public and private suffering are blurred, and the distinction between action and observation is dissolved in this sense of universal belonging, of 'tragic fellowship'. The incident becomes recast as a 'vast visitation' – a descriptive distending of James Senior's own pivotal moment of significance, his 'vastation'. Removed from the public realm of battle, James at the moment of his injury finds himself 'jammed into the acute angle between two high fences' (*A*, 415), a perfect analogy for his imagined combination of (acute) detachment and identification, and for the resolution of the seemingly incompatible polarities of national exertion and private speculation.

In April and May 1898, as the United States went to war with Spain over that country's colonisation of Cuba (the conflict would extend further afield to the Philippines as America herself responded to the temptations of imperial power), James was in London and preoccupied with reviewing for the *Literature* magazine a number of newly published American works focusing on the Civil War. Reading these books in the knowledge that his country was again in conflict, James's judgement of them is almost uniformly negative. (The exception is a volume of Whitman's letters to his mother between 1862 and 1864 in which 'the good Walt' describes his hospital work with the injured and dying, with, James comments, 'a note of native feeling, pity and horror and helplessness'.) But accompanying these unfavourable estimations are hints at the continuing resonance of the war for James, regardless of the unin-spired representations of it currently before him. George Cary Eggleston's *Southern Soldier Stories*, a collection which James suggested might be 'another case of the dreadful "boys' story"' (*EAE*, 672) with its deter-mination to 'make the grimmest things rosy' (*EAE*, 673), nevertheless gave him cause to ponder his own fitness to judge such a work. It was, he noted, the 'kind of volume, I feel, as to which a critic who is a man of peace finds himself hesitate and perhaps even slightly stammer – aware as he is that he may appear, if at all restrictive, to cheapen a considerable quantity of the heroic matter'. As a non-combatant, a 'man of peace', James is sensitive to the disparity between his own experience and that described (however inadequately) in Eggleston's book. As he admits, 'the man of military memories can always retort [to the reviewer] that he would like to see *him* do so well'. James's solution to these hesitancies is a blunt and not totally convincing one, but a solution nevertheless with which we are swept along as he starts to focus on the work itself. As a critic, he remarks, his role is only to concern himself with the task of judging the merits of the book before him. The only 'doing' that matters, and against which his own competency can be compared, is that which has produced Eggleston's stories. 'A critic [as opposed to a soldier] has, of course, only to do with Mr Eggleston's book' – a job for which James feels himself to be fully qualified. The 'of course' here is a little too easy; I have shown how, a few years later in *Notes of a Son and Brother*, James would reimagine the experience of the war as something in which he had a stake – he is able to claim a share in what he calls the 'high privilege' of the conflict (*EAE*, 672). Retreat behind the protective immunity of lit-erary criticism is no longer adequate in 1914, when facts are refashioned to enable retrospective participation. That James saw the potential for this imaginative recasting is evident in a review he wrote in April 1898 of W. A. Dunning's *Essays on the Civil War and Reconstruction*. The dry material contained in this volume (James confides that the discussions of the historical, constitutional and legal issues pertaining to the con-flict had failed in conjuring up for him 'a picture') nevertheless offered a 'roundabout and sentimental interest' of an important kind. James is able to inscribe into Dunning's work a more personal rewriting: 'I have found it irresistible to *read into them*, page by page, some nearer vision of the immense social revolution of which they trace the complicated legal steps' (*EAE*, 665; my emphasis). The 'drama' of the war 'more and more rounds and composes itself' as the actual event recedes in history, so that, for a sensibility possessing a keen and sympathetic imagination, James is able to report that the 'huge complexities' fall 'into place and perspective' (*EAE*, 666). Dunning's book has provoked the possibility of this 'nearer vision'; without direct influence or interest, it has nevertheless authorised the possibility of a more personal and comprehended history, one which would be told in James's autobiographical volume.

To accuse James of self-interest in his retelling of these experiences is to misunderstand his intentions.[71] The 'truth' of his life is ultimately not to be gauged against the available facts of it; as subjected to the process of artistic conception, historical episodes are redefined in relation to an expressive whole. In writing of his Civil War experiences James is confronting once again those questions of vocation and masculinity which he faced as a young man, aware of the difficulty of justifying an artist's sensibility in an America torn by violent action and partisan loyalties. In reconstituting this period he manages to maintain his young self's artistic potentiality and at the same time feel that he is not hiding from the conflict. Indeed it is because of this potentiality, because of his openness to a creative fusion and interrelatedness, that James is able to connect in an enduringly significant manner with the war. Paul John Eakin's considered reading of the 'obscure hurt' episode argues that, although James's injury was an 'enabling event', it nevertheless had the deleterious effect of being 'the cause of his inveterate and increasingly problematic passivity'.[72] But passivity, however problematic, is not quite the effect which James's obfuscations instil. James asks the reader to see that the individual artistic triumph of recollected consciousness is to be accorded a success too in the wider world – the means by which James finds a way of combating the problem of vocation, the opportunity it allows him to construct an actively engaged yet resolutely uncircumscribed identity.

The James autobiographies live up to the imperative to convert the bare materials of life into a form redolent of enduring significance. For the elder James, as I have shown, the details of his early life and his watershed experience at Windsor reverberate with a sense of their symbolic function. What James Senior undergoes in microcosm is the redemptive process which he feels is necessary for the whole of society to experience in order for it to achieve a state of true humanity. The particulars of his biography are consequently of less importance than their sense of conveying a representative and, for him, fundamental dynamic of lost selfhood and regenerative being. The conversion of history into parable, life into paradigm, the finite into the infinite, is the rhetorical strategy that enables him to achieve this. James's autobiographies similarly depend upon a rejection of the demands of documentary exactitude for an aesthetic of accumulated sensations, a commitment to openness and to the infinitely revisable self. The autobiographical narrative then is reforged, such that there are crucial differences between the textual representation of the self and the autobiographer's actual experience. Extra-textual fact is not held to be sacrosanct; there is no empirical truth contained within these narratives which ineluctably and necessarily corresponds to the writer's life. The focus can be said to have shifted from a concern with documenting that life to reimagining the self as it lived it, or, as James Olney has defined the process, 'the "I" that coming awake to its own being shapes and determines the nature of the autobiography and in so doing half discovers, half creates itself'.[73] Autobiography may reveal the writer's character, but that character is not inextricably wedded to the historical figure who performed certain actions in the past. The autobiographical narratives of both father and son play with this notion of the freed self, allowing James Senior to present the events of his life as exemplary and educational, offering Henry James the possibility to reshape his anxieties about masculine activity into an accommodation which he can offer as both aesthetically untainting and socially acceptable.

2

Reading the 'man without a handle': Emerson and the construction of a partial portrait

Henry James's disposition of withheld involvement was frequently felt by his critics to be at odds with the development of a proudly committed, nativist American literary culture. An anonymous writer in the *New York Herald* in 1904 lamented the fact that American fiction had remained unchanged since the Gilded Age of the 1890s; only 'from the dilettante point of view' could James's *The Golden Bowl* and William Dean Howells's *The Son of Royal Langbrith* be classed as 'the finest' writing of that year. Many current tendencies, including Theodore Roosevelt's election to the presidency, suggested that Americans endorsed the 'strenuous life' which its literature chose to ignore: 'our novelists remain untouched by the forces . . . seething around them'. In preference to the 'trivial details' and 'dainty ineffectualities' of writers like James and Howells, the reviewer proposed Kipling, Hardy, Conan Doyle and Rider Haggard as more virile antidotes. Although British, these were authors felt to be more expressive of 'the mental struggles of the age' than any American equivalent.[1] An earlier critic of James, the Unitarian historian George Willis Cooke, identified the differences in contemporary writing with similarly gendered nuances, although *his* nomination for literary greatness was quite different. In 'Emerson's View of Nationality', one of the lectures given at the Concord School of Philosophy in 1883 (William James also lectured there that year), Cooke rhapsodised on the Emersonian themes of American exceptionalism: 'The true America is in the soul that is free, intelligent, and aspiring. The country of man is the genuine America. It does not lie here or there, but towards the way of hope and promise, where men rise up to liberty and justice, where they live in the light of the ideal.'[2] America 'centres in itself the freshest impulses of an age full of activity and dancing' (332). Opposed to such energies, he suggests, stands Henry James. Unable to appreciate the native talents

61

of Nathaniel Hawthorne, James is in error in strikingly similar terms to those expressed in the *Herald* of 1904: he 'forgets that the highest of all literary motives come [*sic*] from sympathy with man in the daily struggles of his own inward nature, and that literature has other purposes than artistic form and beauty' (321). The 'mental struggles of the age' become the 'daily struggles of... inward nature' from which James has removed himself. Cooke's recommendation was 'the rugged verse of Whitman', representative of the transcendentalist philosophy because of its 'intense appreciation of the struggling and urgent life of America'; by contrast, and pre-empting Roosevelt's critique, James's writing was effeminate 'polished prose', offering a weak 'pseudo-Americanism which imitates what is shallow and pretentious in European society' (322–3).

In this chapter I want to examine James's relationship with American (and particularly Emersonian) transcendentalism, exploring Cooke's polemical dichotomy (and the vocabulary used to express it) to suggest that James's understanding of this protean philosophy is refracted through his father, whose own estimation of Emerson is more critical (although less sophisticated) than has previously been recognised. F. O. Matthiessen noted that collectively the Jameses' writings on Emerson 'compose by themselves a chapter of American intellectual history'.[3] Certainly Emerson was a familiar figure within the family circle: James tells how soon after being born William was proudly displayed as if for the approval of his father's new friend, Emerson apparently happy 'to admire and give his blessing' (*A*, 7); James Senior and Emerson, through their shared interests, soon commenced a relationship which, I will argue, was to become increasingly difficult to sustain; and James accompanied Emerson on part of the latter's final European trip in 1872, writing two major reviews incorporating an estimation of the Concord writer the following decade.

Many of the prominent elements of the relationship between Emerson and James Senior have already been sketched by other critics in addition to Matthiessen: Hansell Baugh sympathises with James Senior's final disillusion in his brief essay 'Emerson and the Elder Henry James'; Ralph Barton Perry, in his mammoth work *The Thought and Character of William James*, transcribes much of the James Senior–Emerson correspondence, but he is hampered in his ability to offer a considered interpretation of the relationship by the demands of his book's insistent chronology; and William T. Stafford, in 'Emerson and the James Family', skirts over much the same ground as Perry but with even more haste.[4] Here I look in detail at that portion of Matthiessen's New England intellectual history represented by the encounter between Emerson and the Jameses. Through an examination of the available James Senior–Emerson material and an understanding of the tradition out of which both men emerged, it is possible to see how their relationship became characterised by inequality and incompatibility, leading James Senior to misread or exaggerate certain areas of Emerson's text in order to sustain an identifiable and independent philosophical position. Representative of this kind of partial interpretation is James Senior's discussion of Emerson's understanding of evil: in this chapter's final section I outline both men's conception of the term in an attempt to assess the degree to which this particular aspect of the Concord writer's thought and character is understood only inaccurately and polemically by the elder James. Henry James perseveres with this repressed reading of Emerson, a reading that is uncomfortable with its subject's shifting perspectives and embrace of contradiction. The picture that emerges is of an Emerson whose radicalism is contained and neutralised; he is rewritten as an example of the kind of homogenous and provincial America from which James was self-consciously trying to distance himself. Both Jameses impose a framework of simplification on to both Emerson's fluctuating prose and his cultural presence. For different reasons, these readers of Emerson are unable to follow his own advice, in an essay on Montaigne, about interpretive plurality: 'Why fancy that you have all the truth in your keeping? There is much to say on all sides' (*CWE*, IV, 157).

Over a period spanning the years 1842 to 1874 James Senior and Emerson were regular correspondents. There were, however, frequent periods of epistolary silence between the two men – and not only during those times when one or the other of them was in Europe. There is no evidence to suggest, for example, that the two men communicated at all between James Senior's return from England in late 1844 and a letter (no longer extant) written by Emerson to him in March 1847.[5] The underlying reasons for this break (and others like it, although none for so long) soon become evident as one reads the letters with a growing feeling for what has been suppressed as much as for what is present in the text. James Senior's words present the reader with a relationship characterised by initial idealisation and enthusiasm, soon prone to intermittent doubt, and eventually the cause of much frustration in the face of confirmed disillusionment.

The reaction of both men to a (at the time) notorious episode in the history of polite New York society encapsulates some of the differences that I want to go on to explore. In 1874 Henry Ward Beecher was embroiled in a highly public divorce suit, accused of adultery with Libby Tilton, the wife of one of his associates. James Senior knew Beecher from his own New York days (they had been members of a discussion group of prominent intellectuals),[6] and he felt compelled to offer his thoughts on the matter for general consumption. Emerson was to be his means to a wider readership. Writing to him at the end of October he outlined the project in some detail:

> I propose (with your consent, of course) to publish a pamphlet or small book, one of these winter days that are coming, bearing the following, or an equivalent, title, namely:
>
> What is Morality?
> Base or Superstructure?
> Being a Letter to Ralph Waldo Emerson suggested by recent events.
> By Henry James.
>
> The 'recent events' of course are the Brooklyn scandal, but I shall have nothing whatever to say of this matter but an allusion or two to it in the opening of the pamphlet, serving as an introduction to my theme. And there is nothing whatever that concerns you personally in the pamphlet but a few words of that same introduction, which read as follows:
>
> 'My dear Emerson:
> 'The last time I was at your house you spoke with manly sadness of Mr Beecher, whose fall in men's esteem then seemed imminent, and you deplored with generous warmth the discredit which his lapse might reflect upon the things of religion. <u>To think</u>, you said, <u>of one so brave and generous as he in every righteous cause, compelled at last to shun the face of day! I have known no tragedy like it! And then the licence it will give the scoffer!</u> How every ribald tongue in the land will claim instant and boundless holiday! And he himself, poor man, where <u>in broad Christendom can he go for refuge, without his fame going before to emphasize his shame! It seems to me the heart and hope of mankind have encountered no worse shock in our day!</u> Every word you attended in short, whether of rebuke or compassion, was instinct with a tender human kindness, and no note of pride mingled in the strain.'
>
> This is absolutely all that concerns you personally in the book; and it is besides all I have to say of direct reference to the scandal. I leave it – having served in this way to introduce my pamphlet – entirely behind me, and go on to what seems to me a very interesting inquiry into things which breed no scandal, and minister only peace to human society. I think you will read the work with great interest when it is printed.[7]

It appears from this summary that Emerson's role in all this was to provide reaction to the unfortunate specifics of the Beecher–Tilton case, in the form of the transcribed conversation (actual or embellished) that he had had with the author. James Senior would then have the opportunity to move the discussion away from Emerson's narrowly unpleasant focus to a more philosophical and benign realm in which issues of morality might be redefined so as to remove the kind of attention from 'every ribald tongue in the land' from which Beecher was suffering. Emerson's unusually prompt and adamant reply (written three days later) displays his lack of sympathy with the whole enterprise:

> No, once & for ever No, to your marvellous [i.e. extravagantly improbable] proposal of putting me or even my name into that mud: I told you that I avoided the reading after the first days broaching of the odious paragraphs & columns of the scandal & have kept until this a dear hope that the whole wretched story may yet prove to be a filthy plot. I never talk of it at home, much less abroad & wonder that I expressed any more to you than to shudder at the chance of one lump of the mud proving to be his. I beseech you not to name me with it . . . I beseech you let us all *three* keep our sanity & not touch this new shaken delirium.   (*LE*, x, 144)

Emerson, characteristically, was unwilling to lend his name to a discussion of such *public* and considerably messy matters. The journalistic temperament of James Senior, one in which ideological fads or, as in this case, the minutiae of social affairs required instant response and interpretation, was not shared by the Concord philosopher, for whom the whole Beecher episode reeked of the vicissitudes of the everyday – 'odious', 'wretched' and 'filthy' being his choice of adjectives. (In her journal of nineteenth-century New England life, the feminist writer Caroline Dall transcribes a description of Emerson by Bronson Alcott, one which is acute in its understanding of its subject's preferences: 'I know no man who more delights to write a lecture and deliver it to a fine company, no man who dislikes more to speak to a multitude or be reported in the newspapers.'[8]) For Emerson, publicity of this kind involved a direct encounter with a populace whose opinions he could not predict and upon whose sympathies he could not rely. Lecturing was appealing because it depended upon an informed and interested constituency; readers of Emerson's books made an even heavier intellectual (and financial) investment in him. Sustaining public controversy through the publication of a ghost-written letter effectively meant Emerson relinquishing control of the mode of reception of his words. He was being asked to place them in a context which was, for him, absolutely and alarmingly public. Not for the first time then did he decline to support his friend in his literary endeavours. James Senior's usually successful attempts to keep control of his dissatisfaction at Emerson's frequent lack of co-operation ensures that those occasions when frustration does seep through are all the more striking. In writing to close family, or to other correspondents towards the end of his relationship with Emerson, James Senior is less careful; and the chapter in *Spiritual Creation* devoted to the Concord writer, published posthumously by William James in 1884 as part of *The Literary Remains*, is a strong attack on the character of a generally esteemed, and recently deceased, public figure. What then were the reasons for this eventual intellectual and emotional dismissal of someone who had initially instilled in him so much hope? To what extent did these reasons constitute a sustainable critique of Emerson's philosophy? In attempting to address these questions I want first to outline the more prominent aspects of James Senior's intellectual history up until his first encounter with Emerson in New York in 1842.

I

James Senior's education at Princeton Theological Seminary commenced in 1835, at the tail-end of the so-called 'Second Great Awakening' that had swept over New England. The orthodox Puritan stress on man's absolute depravity and untrustworthiness, its insistence that the fate of men and nations lay solely in the arbitrary and mysterious will of God, was challenged by a proliferation of new sects and revelations that insisted that God was indeed benevolent, governing by reason and not mere capricious whim. The notion that His laws aimed to secure the stability and well-being of humankind seemed more in line with both the American experience of enlightened progress and the feeling that the nation held a unique responsibility to uphold the value of democratic institutions in the face of European decadence and its supposedly stultifying ecclesiasticism. The church historian William McLoughlin has characterised the nature of such religious sea changes in the following terms:

> [I]n times of cultural stress, when institutionalized religion is unable to sustain, even among the faithful, a sense of regular communion with God in formal church rites, the distance between Creator and created becomes intolerably great . . . Then the pendulum swings to the pole of divine immanence . . . God's absence from the churches is compensated for by his spiritual presence in nature; regular churchly practices begin to appear as a barrier rather than as a bridge to God.[9]

Towards the petering out of the first Great Awakening of religious revivalism (1734–50), Jonathan Edwards had written *A Treatise Concerning Religious Affections* (1746) in which he addressed some of the more disturbing aspects of this kind of polarised spirituality. During this period emotions were thought to constitute the source of religious experience; in the reaction that followed, all emotion had become suspect, indicative of a seductive yet facile religiosity. In his *Treatise* Edwards rejected the extremes of exclusive rationality and exclusive emotion, regarding both as posing a threat to religious conversion. Edwards's own stance was one of a highly refined and rationalistic philosophy of emotional religion, a carefully delineated position between the Enlightened man of the Newtonian universe and the Romantic celebrations of emotion soon to be articulated by Blake, Coleridge and Nietzsche. However, this theological synthesis of rationalism and pious emotion which both James Senior and Emerson inherited, and which Edwards had succeeded in balancing, had always threatened to fall apart in mutually opposing halves. Insisting on both a measured logic and a total warmth of emotion, the old Edwardsian Puritanism inevitably gave rise to disparate religious reactions.

Both James Senior and Emerson attempted to draw on both halves of the Puritan schism. Emerson, despite his obvious rejection of the constrictions which he felt organised religion placed on spontaneous thinking, was unable to sympathise with the pure emotional fervour of awakenings and revivals – the mysteries of the pietistic side of Puritanism remained attractive. A journal entry of 1841 points to his positive admiration for the spirit of the old Puritan faith:

> Great, grim, earnest men, I belong by natural affinity to other thoughts and schools than yours, but my affection hovers respectfully about your retiring footprints, your unpainted churches, strict platforms, and sad offices; the non-gray deacon and the wearisome prayer rich with the diction of ages. Well, the new is only the seed of the old. (*Journals*, VI, 53)

James Senior shared this sense of religious indebtedness to a Puritan culture in the process of being dismantled by a less rigid set of doctrines and practices. Writing in 1855 he noted that 'we are all of us more or less involved in some branch of the reigning ecclesiasticism, . . . either partakers of its spirit, or at all events indebted to its appreciable traditions'.[10] His early religious sense was characterised by an orthodox ardour and an intense focus on individual responsibility. In a letter of 1835 to his half-brother William, a Presbyterian minister, he set out a goal of regimental duty. 'I want drilling and disciplining,' he commands, 'I want advice and support in study – I want council in doubt, and a companion at all times – and such I know you will afford & be . . . I have zealously devoted myself by prayer and watching to clearing up the dark corners of my mind and heart, and opening them broadly for the full light of the Scriptures to penetrate and purify.'[11] Seventeen years later James Senior would recall his youthful devotions in similar terms: he had 'abounded in prayer, day and night', being 'studiously, even superstitiously pure in thought and act'. He had 'observed every precept of mystical and ordinary piety'.[12] Princeton Theological Seminary itself reflected the wider sense of religious diversification taking place, with the less orthodox wing of Presbyterianism breaking away in 1836 to found the Union Theological Seminary in New York City. James Senior remained at Princeton, at this stage distanced from the new thinking which was elsewhere questioning the validity of Calvinist assumptions, although, as described in retrospect at least, apparently chaffing against aspects of the ecclesiastical legalism of the establishment. In an unpublished autobiographical fragment he wrote that '[t]he aim of everyone we saw was to defeat frank spontaneous intercourse, and compel the human heart with its living extacies [*sic*] of joy & grief into the measure of a psalm-tune, into the movement of a hand-organ'.[13]

The Calvinist legacy that James Senior never managed to disinherit accounts in great part for his attraction to Robert Sandeman, an eighteenth-century Scottish theologian who, having renounced Presbyterianism, established an independent religious sect based solely upon the practices of the Apostolic Christian church. James Senior had interrupted his studies at Princeton in February 1837 for a trip to England and Ireland, and it is likely that while staying in England he had discovered Sandeman's book, *Letters on Theron and Aspasio* (first published in 1757).[14] Returning to America later the same year, he abandoned his studies at Princeton, and in 1838 published an edition of Sandeman's work, offering a two-page unsigned preface. *Theron and Aspasio* proclaims a shift from institutionalised Presbyterianism to a purified strain of Calvinism that dispenses with professional clergy and organised denominations. Sandeman believed that Protestant Christendom had lapsed from the clean simplicity of the early church, and his conception of its renewal was founded on a literal and direct reading of the New Testament. Scriptural interpretation offered by the mediating authority of the clergy was scorned for its encouragement of both superstition and the ritual of salvation by good works:

> We Protestants have laid aside the crucifix; we reserve no fragments of the wood of the cross. But what have we got instead of these? We have got a perverted gospel. We have got some insipid sentiment about the cross of Christ ... By this perverted gospel, many teachers tantalize the souls of men, leading those whose conscience is most easily touched, through a course of the most gloomy kind of anxieties.[15]

That James Senior should have been attracted to such an austere theological position is perhaps curious given his later immersion in Swedenborg and an interpretative strategy of human redemption heavily dependent on reading biblical allegory and symbolism. But at this stage his Presbyterian upbringing, coupled with the general atmosphere of dissatisfaction with existing ecclesiastical structures, led him to a form of Calvinism more radical in its purity than even Princeton, after the schism of 1836, could offer. The egalitarian and antinomian impulses of Sandeman's theology, with its insistent emphasis on what Giles Gunn has called 'the democratic solidarity of primitive Christianity',[16] were highly appealing to James Senior's early spiritual sensibility. Moreover Sandeman's strict interpretation of the central Calvinist tenet of justification by faith alone influences the paradox which lies at the heart of James Senior's understanding of the spiritual. The paradox simply stated was that only that which was secular and untainted by the self-serving nature of ecclesiasticism could hope to lay claim to being considered as truly spiritual. In turning away from a religion that was socially sanctioned to one focused and enacted within the theatre of the individual consciousness, James Senior suggested an exploration of spirituality unconnected to any denominational or doctrinal concern.

It is at this stage in his intellectual history that he encountered Emerson. His renunciation of orthodox Presbyterianism had led him to a congregation severe in its logic and rationality – Sandemanism had confirmed his Calvinist inheritance of sinfulness. Emerson would provide the impetus for him to enter a wider, non-sectarian intellectual world and to reconsider his adherence to a dry literalism and an insistence on close biblical reading. However the influence of Calvinism remained. Indeed James Senior's paradoxical notion of the tragic inevitability yet beneficial necessity of committing evil would prove to be an irreconcilable obstruction to his relationship with Emerson, for whom such a theory smacked too much of an unhealthy and lingering attachment to the debilitating notion of human depravity. As a result, James Senior's eventual critical position on his one-time friend is strongly expressed. It is a reading which proved highly influential for Henry James, whose estimation of the Concord writer, whilst certainly more charitable than that offered by his father, displays strong echoes of what James Senior had earlier articulated. In March 1842, however, the elder James was full of expectation.

II

James Senior was in the audience on 3 March 1842 at the New York Society Library for the first of a series of six lectures to be delivered by Emerson. His letter to the speaker, written immediately after listening to 'On the Times', is infused with a sense of excitement and anticipation; in Emerson he feels that he has discovered a potential spiritual guide, one whose level of maturity qualifies him in the role of teacher and translator:

> I listened to your address this evening, and as my bosom glowed with many a true word that fell from your lips I felt erelong fully assured that before me I beheld a man who in very truth was seeking the realities of things. I said to myself, I will try when I go home how far this man follows reality – how far he loves truth and goodness. For I will write to him that I, too, in my small degree am coveting to understand the truth which surrounds me and embraces me, am seeking worthily to apprehend, or to be more worthily apprehended of, the love which underlies and vivifies all the seeming barrenness of our most unloving world. (*WJ*, 1, 39–40)

He goes on to assure Emerson that even once his (James Senior's) 'own voice is known, I may now and then call him back to interpret some of the hieroglyphics which here and there line our way, and which my own skill in tongues may be unequal to' (*WJ*, 1, 40). The degree to which the writer has moved away from his austerely held belief in the literal authority of the Bible is revealed in the use of the word 'hieroglyphics', a multilayered symbolic language requiring skilled interpretation to reveal its true significance. The first sentence of Emerson's lecture boldly proclaims the Swedenborgian idea of a hieroglyphical correspondence between the natural and spiritual worlds: 'The Times, as we say – or the present aspects of our social state, the Laws, Divinity, Natural Science, Agriculture, Art, Trade, Letters, have their root in an invisible spiritual reality' (*CWE*, 1, 259). Swedenborg's first attempt to articulate this idea in a relatively thorough manner was in an unfinished essay (of 1741 or 1742), *A Hieroglyphic Key to Natural and Spiritual Arcana by way of Representations and Correspondences (Clavis hieroglyphica)*, printed in London in 1784.[17] He was acutely conscious that the principle of correspondence can swiftly become a problem of language when the symbols being used do not lead the reader beyond the immediate referent to the additional, superior (non-temporal) meaning. Swedenborg's interest in the Egyptian symbolic system lay in its expression not only of natural phenomena but at the same time an *interpretable* spiritual reality. The successful reading of hieroglyphics, the shifting from one realm to the other, aided in the revival of a primitive comprehension, a submerged wisdom lying dormant within man, only awaiting the suitable catalyst for its activation.

At the time of Emerson's lecture the key to deciphering hieroglyphics had only relatively recently been uncovered by Jean Champollion (in 1822). But for Sampson Reed, an important early American Swedenborgian, Champollion's explanations failed to do justice to the complexity of the symbols and thus the wisdom required to interpret them. In an article in the October 1830 issue of the Swedenborgian journal the *New Jerusalem Magazine*, he maintained that aspects of the hieroglyphics 'still remain obscure, and probably will be so until an examination is made of them *in a different spirit and manner, and on a different ground, from the present*' (my emphasis).[18] Inferred in Reed's doubt was the belief that the hieroglyphics must conceal some form of mysterious communication, some arcane Egyptian lore that the symbols Champollion had managed to translate simply did not convey. For Reed, elements of indecipherability remained, such that the unreadability of the markings was for him an indication of their genuineness and spiritual potential – only the initiated would be able to understand their meaning, and Reed doubted that this would be possible under present circumstances. The ability to read this language had been lost, he argued, for its primal purity had become progressively obscured and smothered by the arbitrary language of convention, by, as Emerson would later lament in his essay 'History', 'surface differences' which have prevented the attainment of a 'clearer vision' (*CWE*, II, 12). For James Senior, the reference in his letter to such symbols which only a privileged élite could comprehend (an élite which, his words reveal, he soon envisioned joining) highlights a growing interest in Emerson's uniquely American interpretation of Swedenborg's dualistic conception.[19] The transparency of language associated with the exegetical strategies of Sandemanism was being complicated and undermined by the discursive layerings of James Senior's new acquaintance.

'On the Times' is a dense collection of many of the key ideas of Emerson's developing thought. By using a rhetorical structure based on pairs of conflicting terms (Conservatism/Reform; the party of the Past/the party of the Future; actors/students), he focuses attention on the best way of developing a 'Moral Sentiment' (*CWE*, I, 289). Characterising the conservative viewpoint as 'a necessity not yet commanded, a negative imposed on the will of man by his condition, a deficiency in his force' (*CWE*, I, 260), Emerson goes on to analyse the alternative impetus to reform, whose origin 'is in that mysterious fountain of the moral sentiment in man, which, amidst the natural, ever contains the supernatural for men' (*CWE*, I, 272). His conclusion is a characteristic response: those elements that hope to improve the condition of man by organised structures (temperance societies, the anti-masonry movement, and the campaign against slavery are all cited) can only succeed in polluting the purity of the individual's ability to interpret the spiritual in the natural. By combining forces through collective action, Emerson argues, man is not empowered but dilutes and sullies his effectiveness at reading nature's hieroglyphics. However sincere the intentions, they cannot be realised:

> The impulse is good, and the theory; the practice is less beautiful. The Reformers affirm the inward life, but they do not trust it, but use outward and vulgar means. They do not rely on precisely that strength which wins me to their cause; not on love, not on a principle, but on men, on multitudes, on circumstances, on money, on party. (*CWE*, I, 276)

Emerson's joy in the impulse that has provoked man to organise reform movements is qualified by his disappointment that that same impulse has not been channelled into a concentration on the development of the individual mind: 'I urge the more earnestly the paramount duties of self-reliance. I cannot find language of sufficient energy to convey my sense of the sacredness of private integrity' (*CWE*, I, 279). His full approbation rests with the student who, despite society's resistance, attempts to pursue a life of 'solitude and meditation', one of (wonderful oxymoron this) 'ascetic extravagances' (*CWE*, 1, 283). The phenomenal world merely offers the opportunity to confirm knowledge already (and indeed always) present: 'To a true scholar,' Emerson asserts, 'the attraction of the aspects of nature, the departments of life, and the passages of his experience, is simply the information they yield him of this supreme nature which links within all' (*CWE*, 1, 289).

I have dwelt on this lecture because it introduced to its audience characteristic, although by no means consistently held, elements of Emerson's philosophy: a belief in the individual's ability to perceive the reality beneath surfaces; the fact that social groupings water down this ability; and the rejection of theories and practices of social improvement which encourage such groupings. As I go on to discuss, James Senior's later interest in the communistic theories of Charles Fourier and his development (via Swedenborg) of a theological system rooted in the necessity of rejecting any notion of the interpretative primacy of the self, indicates the degree to which this early inclination towards transcendental thought was reformulated. Even in an early letter, undated but thought by Perry to have been written in 1842, tension is already beginning to show. Here James Senior's ingrained Calvinist habit of delight in theological argument and persuasion seems to have come into conflict with Emerson's preference for unconfrontational affirmation. James Senior divides his correspondent into two contrasting figures, 'the Invisible Emerson, the Emerson that talks and bewitches one out of his serious thought when one talks to him, by the beautiful serenity of his behaviour' and 'the profounder Emerson who alone can do one any good' (*WJ*, 1, 41). The use of the word *serenity* here is, for James Senior, a heavily weighted term, signifying an innocent placidity and stasis that contrasts with his own desire to grasp at an understanding of the soul's construction. The same word is taken up again in two reviews by Henry James. Writing of James Eliot Cabot's 1887 memoir of Emerson he remarks: 'It must have been a kind of luxury to be – that is to feel – so homogenous, and it helps to account for [Emerson's] serenity, his power of acceptance' (*EAE*, 252). And in a review of a collection of the correspondence between Emerson and Thomas Carlyle published four years earlier, James sums up the relationship between the two men thus: '[Carlyle's] irritation communed happily for fifty years with Emerson's serenity; and the fact is very honorable to both' (*EAE*, 244). As I go on to suggest, James's conception of Emerson is not concerned with his theological limitations; unlike his father, the novelist makes no demands on him of that kind, his reflections having a more sophisticated sense of relaxed irony, of the superiority of his own society's evolution. But several of his father's judgements on Emerson's character are aired once more, as *theological* innocence is replaced by James with a retrospective judgement of a general American *cultural* artlessness.

But in this early and undated letter describing Emerson's split identities, James Senior's attitude towards his subject is far from serene. He is preoccupied with a desire to accumulate knowledge, regarding such an activity as definitive of his humanity. His mind is incessantly curious and unsatisfied, described in a manner reminiscent of his son's response to Henry Adams's gloomy analysis quoted in the previous chapter: 'Now my conviction at present is that my intelligence is the necessary digestive apparatus for my life ... Is it not so in truth with you? Is not your life continually fed by knowledge, and could you have nay life but brute life without it?' (*WJ*, I, 42). With his Presbyterian background and flirtation with Sandemanism, James Senior was well acquainted with polemical theological debate and the need for rational proof of Christianity's truth. His request that Emerson 'put up from his depths some heart-secret-law which shall find itself reproduced in mine and so further me, or at least *stay* me' (*WJ*, I, 43) is an oft-repeated one in his correspondence. So great is James Senior's need for approval and praise that any comment from Emerson regarding his work is prized, regardless of the tenor of the opinion which it expresses. For example, having read *Moralism and Christianity* (1850) Emerson makes the following remarks:

> Your writing is not as good a statement as your speech. At least, I think not. I do not pretend yet to have mastered the book. I read many fine things in it, and admirable special statements.
>
>   But I am awed & distanced a little by this argumentative style: every technical For & <u>suppose</u> & <u>Therefore</u> alarms & extrudes me. [A]nd moreover I find or fancy ... that you have not shed your last coat of presbyterianism, but that a certain catachetical [*sic*] & legendary Jove glares at me sometimes, in your page, which astonishes me in so sincere & successful a realist ... I see very well that the book is full of nobleness, & bright with health & reason, and as I become better acquainted with it, perhaps it will defend & acquit itself.
>
>   (*LE*, VIII, 238–9)

Emerson articulates two essential differences here between his own writing and that of James Senior. The first of these concerns his unease with his correspondent's use of language. Logical progression and the rhetoric of scientific evidence characterise much of the elder James's writing style, and arguments are repeated and summarised at regular intervals, for the benefit, one occasionally feels, of the writer as much as the reader. Emerson was uncomfortable with a reliance on this kind of systematic use of language as proof, especially with what he saw as James Senior's rigid logical structure. In Emerson's tripartite conception of language words signify natural facts, certain natural facts are symbols of certain spiritual facts, and nature as a whole is the symbol of spirit. A result of this formulation is an epistemological process in which words representing physical phenomena are adapted into symbols representative of further non-physical phenomena. Like Swedenborg, Emerson understood that language is thus always figurative, being a structure of tropes and images which, in their secondary use, may no longer remind us of their origin. Consequently language remains an imprecise tool. Words, as finite entities, 'cannot cover the dimensions of what is in truth. They break, chop, and impoverish it' ('Nature', *CWE*, I, 45). A language heavily reliant on logic and system errs in assuming an ability to capture truth's unboundable essence. Indeed a dogged probing of this kind only destroys spontaneity – 'if a man fasten his attention on a single aspect of truth and apply himself to that alone for a long time, the truth becomes distorted and not itself but falsehood' ('Intellect', *CWE*, II, 339). In his own use of language then, Emerson's compromise was to assert the poet's ability to penetrate into the subverbal regions of men where words would prompt a realisation of truths *already intuitively known*. Aware that a corrupted language could act as a barrier between man and his understanding of spiritual truth, Emerson used rhetoric against itself, where any recognition of truth felt by his audience would be attributable not to the authority and power of his words but would rather confirm man's inherent possession of that truth in the unconscious mind.

James Senior was less concerned with the status and efficacy of language. Any potential limitations it may exhibit were of less importance to him than the recognition that language remained the only means by which he could articulate his ideas. Enthusiasm for the systems of Swedenborg and Fourier ensured that his writings were more prone to sermonising exegesis than Emerson's more poetic and flexible raptures. Giles Gunn notes that 'systematic theology written in the moralistic tone of the familiar essay is not quite what he produced', but nevertheless 'it was what much of his writing sounded like'.[20] Indeed this inability to lose the voice of the pulpit is alluded to in Emerson's second criticism of James Senior's book, namely its author's propensity to cloak his words in the 'last coat of Presbyterianism'. Emerson remained unconvinced that James Senior had fully renounced the Calvinist conception of a distant and legalistic deity. James Senior's own doubts over Emerson's philosophy were also centred on just this issue, for in an earlier (1843) letter to Emerson he had allowed a few lines of criticism to slip into his generally appreciative comments:

> You don't look upon Calvinism as a fact at all, wherein you are to my mind philosophically infirm, and impaired as to your universality. I can see in Carlyle's writing the advantage his familiarity with this fact gives him over you with a general audience. What is highest in Carlyle is built upon that lowest. At least so I read. I believe Jonathan Edwards *redivivus* in true blue would, after an honest

study of the philosophy that has grown up since his day, make the best possible reconciler and critic of philosophy – far better than Schelling *redivivus*.

(*WJ*, 1, 47)

At this stage in his intellectual history James Senior could still appreciate Thomas Carlyle in terms of an antidote to what increasingly he felt to be Emerson's dangerously innocent optimism. To envisage Calvinism as a fact was to recognise the reality of human wickedness as part of life's experience; the notion of human fallibility appealed to him far more than a transcendental theology of human perfectionism achieved through refined perception. By positing two figures of such philosophical extremes, Edwards and Friedrich Schelling representing Calvinism and Romanticism respectively, James Senior makes a remarkably direct statement expressing his emotional and ideological distance from Emerson.

Yet in responding to Emerson's criticisms of *Moralism and Christianity* he reverts to the role of grateful disciple, finding those moments of honest engagement such as the one above difficult to sustain. It is as if, in trying to persevere with the relationship, James Senior must content himself with expecting little or nothing in the way of argument and debate from such an immovably placid figure. 'I prize every word of your criticism of my book so highly,' he insists. 'It is a real delight that I should have said anything that doesn't appear trite to you. But it is downright rapture that I have been able to make you shake your head, and ponder whether after all things be so or no' (*WJ*, 1, 67). Emerson's response to another of James Senior's works, the unexpectedly popular *The Nature of Evil* (1855), must have been similar in tone to that of the earlier book (the MS of the letter itself is incomplete), for it drew forth the following characteristic reply from its author: 'What you say about my book is only another instalment of your unequalled generosity, and I am not taken in. I have only to hear the book named by you, to feel at once how desperately faulty its form is. But I am past regrets on this score. I will do better in future.' Despite his doubts however, he is proud to announce the commercial success of the work, 'the whole edition – 1000 copies – is exhausted', allowing himself to wonder how 'a book of that dullness as to subject' could have sold out in just four months. He adds that he hopes that his fortunes may be about to turn and that his name may rank alongside others whose success and influence has already been assured: 'I may yet perhaps be mentioned with Emerson, Dickens, Thackeray, Carlyle and other popular authors' (*WJ*, 1, 81).

James Senior's constant call for Emerson's time and intellectual stimulation ('I really must see you without hindrance for one hour or many, as my need may require, and come into intelligible relation with your understanding and sympathy' (*WJ*, 1, 61)) seems to have been ignored as the two men settled into a relationship characterised by, respectively, overt admiration punctured by flashes of criticism and serene oblivious-ness occasionally roused to ambivalent judgement. One of the best of James Senior's outbursts represents his most sustained attempt in letters to Emerson at articulating an opinion of him which avoids mere uncritical regard:

> For really I find every want supplied here but that to which you minister, a want which grows, out of my American manhood, and which demands in one's cronies an openness of soul answering to one's own. This is certainly you, a soul full of doors and windows, a well-ventilated soul, open to every breeze that blows, and without any dark closets receptive of ancestral, political and ecclesiastical trumpery. I could sometimes wish indeed to find those gracious doors and windows a little more retentive of what comes in, or a little more humanly jealous of what goes too speedily out; I could wish, indeed, that those stately chambers should afford the hospitality of a frequent and spacious *bed*, in which the weary guest might lie down and sleep till the next breakfast time; but perhaps this is only my sensuality, and sure I am meanwhile that you are a matchless summer house, green with clambering vines, and girt with cool piazzas fit to entertain the democratic host as it marches from the old worn-out past to the beckoning and blossoming future.   (*WJ*, I, 83)

Emerson's soul here is envisioned as light and airy, free of any sinister inherited skeletons, 'ancestral, political and ecclesiastical'. But for James Senior this is damning with faint praise, for in fact Emerson's mind is *too* open, a mere conduit or corridor with little to detain the visiting and expectant mind. He is unable to find repose in Emerson, for there is little there to encourage him to stay. What is on offer instead is a slumber-ing, perhaps even soporific, summer house that James Senior is only able to accept once he manages to depersonalise its visitor from himself to 'the democratic host'. For such a vague entity Emerson becomes once more a suitable dwelling place at which the party of the future may be welcomed. Such use of the extended conceit of the house anticipates Henry James's 'house of fiction' metaphor in the preface to *The Portrait of a Lady* (1908). The father's description points at an important difference between Emerson and James, a difference which the novelist's own use of the image highlights. Emerson's house, at least to the personalised figure of James Senior, seems inhospitable: it is too tranquil in its composure and too secure in its construction to be aware of the presence of something or someone from outside of itself. James's image, by contrast, offers a con-sciousness placed within his house and restricted in its view of the outside, that view dependent upon the aperture at which it stands. The house does not offer that same relaxed impression as does Emerson's. The windows are 'of dissimilar shape and size', 'mere holes in a dead wall, disconnected, perched aloft'. Whereas Emerson's house seems blankly wide-open, the house of fiction declines such an expansive panorama – its apertures 'are not hinged doors opening straight upon life' (*EWP*, 1075). In James's fictional house there can be no sense of placid satisfaction because there can never be a single perspective which is able to achieve such an all-encompassing view. That sense of completeness which Emerson's mind offered to the frustrated James Senior, a mind so secure in its power that it no longer notices the disruption and potential stimulus represented by the invading other, is alien to James's artistic sensibility.

By the late 1860s the relationship between James Senior and Emerson had cooled to such an extent that the elder James could write this to William in 1868: 'Emerson's unreality to me grows evermore. You have got to deal with him as with a child, making all manner of allowances for his ignorance of everything above the senses, and putting such a restraint upon your intellect as tires you to death . . . I love the man very much, he is such a born natural; but his books are to me wholly destitute of spiritual flavour, being at most carbonic acid gas and *water*' (*WJ*, 1, 96–7). Whilst communication between the two men was civil and respectful (although not as regular as it had been), James Senior's increasing private criticism seems to have accounted for one of the very few instances during Emerson's lifetime when their differences were aired for public consumption. On 26 October 1868 James Senior was in an audience listening to Emerson deliver a lecture on his impressions of New England culture, 'Historical Notes of American Life and Letters'. In an expansive, anecdotal talk, which included sympathetic portraits of Thoreau and Bronson Alcott, Emerson expressed his criticisms of the Brook Farm community's conversion from a broadly transcendental ethos to one structured on Fourieristic principles. Although Fourier 'could not but suggest vast possibilities of reform to the coldest and least sanguine', Emerson could not finally take the Frenchman's 'mathematical mind' seriously. His projects for social amelioration were 'the most entertaining of French romances' in which 'poverty shall be abolished; deformity, stupidity and crime shall be no more. Genius, grace, art shall abound, and it is not to be doubted but that . . . all men will speak in blank verse' (*CWE*, x, 347, 348, 351). As he felt about all attempts at systematisation, Fourier's grand and elaborate scheme displayed for Emerson an inflexibility and harshness which reduced the precious individual to the status of mere object: 'Our feeling was that Fourier had skipped no fact but one, namely Life. He treats man as a plastic thing, something that may be put up or down, ripened or retarded, moulded, polished, made into solid or fluid or gas, at the will of the leader' (*CWE*, x, 352). James Senior's interest in Charles Fourier had flourished in the late 1840s, when between November 1847 and February 1849 he was writing regularly for the Brook Farm paper, the *Harbinger*. But by 1856 his enthusiasm had waned for the notion of individual human redemption being accompanied by a conscious and deliberate regeneration of society through specific, empirically measured economic and social practices. He insisted instead that a reliance on purely natural laws of organisation could not succeed. Society was not to be reformed out of its present incarnation; rather his conception of society was so new that it could only be envisioned as a future ideal:

> Fourier, St Simon, and the rest, no doubt deserve well for their attempts to embody this spirit, but we must not judge of the spirit itself from their conception of it ... I for my part am led to think, that the Socialists proper exhibit a very faulty conception of society. They all suppose it to be a product of purely *natural* laws. Thus their whole thought becomes absorbed in the invention of suitable gearing for society, while the crying want of the world is to be convinced of the bare *possibility* of society itself.[21]

By the time of Emerson's lecture in October 1868 the peak of James Senior's involvement with ideas of a socialist utopia had been reached some twenty years earlier. Yet James Senior's fundamental differences of temperament with Emerson established over many years ensured that a certain feeling of protectiveness towards his earlier, now discarded self arose. He declared his irritation in a letter to Caroline Tappan: 'I went ... as your proxy to hear Emerson on Brook Farm, and as such proxy, as well as on my own behalf, do not hesitate to pronounce him dreadfully seedy ... There was a slim account of the Brook farmers & an unprincipled (because ignorant) denunciation of Fourier; but the substance of the lecture was intellectual slip-slop of the poorest kind, & its form simply disgraceful.'[22] A month after the lecture, the *Boston Commonwealth* carried an article by 'Warrington' (William S. Robinson, a Concord native and distant relative of Emerson) declaring that James Senior was 'mad' about the criticism of Fourier. Eleven days later the *Springfield Daily Republican* reported James Senior's response, in which he confirmed that he was 'much shocked and chagrined at the monstrous misrepresentation Mr E. gave of F.'s books, when he represented them as inculcating self-indulgence upon men, in place of self-control'.[23] James Senior informed Emerson of the details of the incident in a letter of 7 December, again without retracting his original complaint (*WJ*, 1, 98); Emerson's response to this letter is unknown, but the criticisms which the elder James had allowed to occasionally surface in his letters to Emerson (and to which he had given full vent in that letter to William) had slipped into the public domain and beyond his immediate control.[24] Not until after Emerson's death did James Senior consider the idea of allowing the wider world to read what seems to be the accumulation and release of many years suppressed frustration. Ironically his own death prevented him from witnessing the reaction to his words. William assumed the mantle of guardian of his father's literary estate, publishing James Senior's harsh opinion of Emerson in 1884 and then choosing to follow it up with the publication in 1904 (one year after the centenary of Emerson's birth) of an earlier, much less critical lecture. It is to these two estimations of Emerson that I now turn.

III

On 16 February 1872 James Senior delivered a lecture on Emerson at the home of James T. Fields to a coterie of New England writers and thinkers. Three days earlier he had written to Emerson informing him of his impending talk, requesting an audience of Emerson's friends and family for a second reading of his piece. He did not want the subject of his lecture to be present at this event:

> I should like very much to read the piece, not to you, for you have too dainty a taste in literature for my wares, but to Mrs Emerson, say, and Ellen, and Elizabeth Hoar, or Miss Elizabeth Ripley, if they will grant me a hearing...I hope Mrs Emerson won't fancy that I am vain of my essay, that I propose reading it to her – not at all. I simply feel that I owe it to her to say nothing of you, which her heart does n't also say, in some sort. (*WJ*, I, 101–2)

Far from being worried about what Emerson might think of his efforts, James Senior had decided to flatter him, comparing his own literary skills unfavourably to that of his subject and wanting Emerson's wife present to confirm for him the reality of his early enthusiastic ardour. He fancies that Lidian will be able to recognise the qualities that he finds in her husband, and by doing so will somehow authenticate them. Emerson complied, and the lecture was delivered in his absence on the twentieth. We are left to conjecture on the response the address might have received, as its author returns to the past of his earliest letters to Emerson in a desire to re-establish that sense of youthful devotion. After his initiation into the intrusive practices of the American press, here James Senior is attempting to rehabilitate himself, to express in the strongest personal terms his discipleship of Emerson. Indeed it is on the personal aspects of Emerson that he chooses to focus, claiming (disingenuously, if the evidence of his letters is anything to go by) a lack of interest in Emerson's published philosophical and theological views:

> I think it has never once occurred to me in my long intercourse with Mr Emerson to prize his literary friendship, or covet any advantage which might accrue from it to myself. No, what alone I have sought in Mr Emerson is not the conscious scholar, but always the unconscious prophet, whose genius, and not by any means his intellect, announces, with unprecedented emphasis, spontaneity as the supreme law of life.[25]

The now older and more confident writer no longer feels that he has to attempt to extract from Emerson a theory of life, an underlying law of existence. Rather what he wants to recall and present to a wider audience is the emotion that was expressed in his first letter to Emerson thirty years earlier. 'He at once captured my imagination,' James Senior enthuses, 'and I have ever since been his loving bondman . . . I have often found myself, in fact, thinking: if this man were only a woman, I should be sure to fall in love with him' (740). This feminisation of Emerson becomes a characteristic means for James Senior of assessing him; feminine qualities here come to represent a form of purity and an energising spiritual force. Thus the way in which Emerson acts as an influence is described in terms of female infiltration and cleansing, 'as if the spotless feminine heart of the race had suddenly shot its ruby tide into your veins, and made you feel as never before the dignity of clean living' (741). And again, James Senior remarks that in Emerson 'the masculine or moral force, force of will, presents itself in his natural personality so refined, so sublimated into feminine or aesthetic force, force of spontaneity, that men instinctively do him homage, as a manifest token of divine power in our nature' (745). What is striking about this lecture is the way in which, both by emphasising Emerson's gendered purity and innocence and by recalling an admiration located at a much earlier time, James Senior manages to undermine the laudatory intent of his text. Many of those areas which he highlights here are taken up again in the later estimation where they are pointedly regarded as criticisms. Here, in his desire to write an appreciation he is unable to forget his intellectual objections: by foregrounding them to such an extent it is as if he is trying to fool his audience and himself into believing that they have been resolved. The nostalgic tenor of the whole lecture is characterised by the remark that 'it is impossible to read [Emerson] when you are young and as yet undismayed by the experience of life, without instantly speculating how you shall begin forthwith to live' (741). The appeal of the Concord writer then is to the unformed, because Emerson himself has managed to achieve a perpetual state of prelapsarian innocence. James Senior does not get drawn into overtly judging his subject here (as he would do in the later work), but his prose struggles to maintain that external veneer of esteem against the impulse to criticise. To quote one example where this tension is palpable: '[Emerson] has not the least vital apprehension of that fierce warfare of good and evil which has desolated so many profounder bosoms, which has maddened so many stouter brains' (743). Here an awareness of this conflict is felt to be essential to life, 'vital', yet Emerson, by apparently being unaware of it, has not been destroyed in the way that others, more intelligent than him, have been. Neither desolated nor maddened he continues to live in perfect serenity. Remaining untouched by fundamental warring impulses he has survived to represent the 'bud of a redeemed life of God in our nature' (744). On the surface of things it is the fact of Emerson's survival, and thus his continuing influence, which is important. Yet by characterising Emerson as a 'bud', he is maintaining that element of subtle confusion: he is both a precursor to a full-flowering of spiritual unity (elsewhere Emerson is called 'an American John the Baptist' (742)) and yet also unformed and protected in his inchoate state. As if in antagonism against his intent, James Senior manages to send disrupting ripples over the smoothness of his celebratory text.

Thomas Carlyle regularly proved a convenient opponent for James Senior – convenient both in the sense that he was a suitably polemical figure against which he could argue, and convenient on a more practical level in the fact that he lived in London and thus, unlike Emerson, beyond the consideration of James Senior's scruples. In this lecture Carlyle could freely be employed as a negative force compared to which Emerson's saintly qualities would stand out in even stronger relief. In effect Carlyle is used as a prop to help bolster this project of appreciation, with James Senior hoping perhaps to cloak his own dissension in the judgements of the dour Scot. The project of public endorsement is all too gratefully assisted by a pattern of Manichean simplicity. Compared to Emerson's almost preternatural goodness, Carlyle 'does not hesitate to regard the good and evil, the true and the false, the strong and the feeble that he discerns in men's persons, as finalities, clothing the universe of the divine administration in impenetrable gloom' (743). Although Emerson may remain unconscious of the divine drama of good and evil, Carlyle's crime is the worse because he accepts the polarities as absolute and static sartorial properties. For the purposes of his lecture then, James Senior accords Emerson the superior position: obliviousness to evil is preferable to a resigned acceptance of its immutable existence. Ignorance is bliss, one might say, and Carlyle is wheeled out to underscore the message.

Perry claims that Emerson's letter to James Senior arranging the date for the delivery of the latter's lecture marks the end of their correspondence. This is not the case, for four further letters to James Senior between 1872 and 1874 have been documented by the editor of Emerson's correspondence.[26] However it is clear that by the mid-1870s the stream of communication between the two men had all but dried up. The reasons for this become evident when reading James Senior's comments on Emerson in his posthumously published book *Spiritual Creation*. The Emerson chapter acts as a companion piece to the 1872 lecture, but here any pretence at control of those subversive tensions which he had previously struggled to contain is finally renounced. It represents the culmination of a growing dissatisfaction with, and an admission of the failure of, their relationship. Ambiguity is present from the outset: 'My recently deceased friend, Mr Emerson, for example, was all his days an arch traitor to our existing civilized regimen, inasmuch as he unconsciously managed to set aside its fundamental principle in doing without conscience, which was the entire secret of his very exceptional interest to men's speculation.'[27] It is difficult to settle easily on the tone of these words, and thus on the authorial intention behind them. Emerson may be an '*arch*-traitor' (no mere traitor he), but given James Senior's lack of sympathy towards conventional social structures one might wonder whether an opposition to the 'existing civilised regimen' is such a bad thing. Yet James Senior seems to arrive at a judgement that Emerson's appeal can be explained in its totality; his 'entire secret', and the one and only thing which provoked people's interest in him, was his lack of 'conscience'. Whereas James Senior had attempted in 1872 to react positively to Emerson's obliviousness to the 'vital' conflict of good and evil, ten years later this same condition was dismissed as being 'really all that he distinctively did to my observation' (293). Emerson's self-composure finally proves exasperating, and any slight lapse from the standard of perfection is greeted with mock outrage. Witnessing Emerson sipping wine and puffing at a cigar provokes this observation: 'I felt very much as if some renowned Boston belle had suddenly collapsed and undertaken to sell newspapers at a street corner. "Why Emerson, is this *you* doing such things?" I exclaimed. "What profanation! Do throw the unclean things behind your back!" But no; he was actually proud of his accomplishments!' (294).

I suggested that in the earlier lecture James Senior was attempting to confront his differences with Emerson by a deliberately public declaration of loyalty, by drawing attention to those very areas of Emerson's personality (and by extension his philosophy) with which privately he had most quarrel, as a way of convincing himself that the quarrel was in fact groundless. That public affirmation of allegiance contrasts starkly with this later work. Here Emerson's moral blankness, far from indicating an angelic superiority, is indicative of a fundamental lack of self-awareness, a perpetual state of infancy. Emerson was 'seriously incapable of a subjective judgment upon himself; he did not know the inward difference between good and evil, so far as he himself was concerned. No doubt he perfectly comprehended the outward or moral difference between these things; but I insist upon it that he never so much as dreamed of any inward or spiritual difference between them' (295). The fact of Emerson's inability to conceive of himself as morally fallible, as possibly existing in an inferior moral position to another person, is, according to James Senior, evidence of spiritual immaturity. He is convinced that Emerson never felt the temptation to sin, and therefore never reached the potential for salvation: 'I am satisfied that he never in his life had felt a temptation *to bear false-witness* against his neighbor, *to steal, to commit adultery,* or *to murder;* how then should he have ever experienced what is technically called a conviction of sin? – that is, a conviction of himself as *evil* before God, and all other men as *good*' (295–6). The lasting effects of James Senior's Calvinist inheritance, the roots of which I outlined earlier, are at play here, for the strong conviction of sin and of moral fallibility seem to have been impressed on the writer at an early age, if we are to accept an anecdote told in his autobiographical sketch published in the same volume as *Spiritual Creation.* A 'magical drawer', always left unlocked and containing a seemingly endless supply of money belonging to his father, is pilfered by the narrator of the sketch to pay a debt he has owing at a local sweet shop. The significance of this petty indiscretion is far-reaching:

> Thus my country's proverbial taste for confectionery furnished my particular introduction to 'the tree of knowledge of good and evil'. This tragical tree, which man is forbidden to eat of under pain of finding his pleasant paradisiacal existence shadowed by death, symbolizes his dawning spiritual life, which always to his own perception begins in literal or subjective darkness and evil. For what after all is the spiritual life in sum? It is the heartfelt discovery by man that God his creator is alone good, and that he himself, the creature, is by necessary contrast evil.   (166–7)

The urge to steal is a watershed experience for the narrator: it 'was absolutely my first experience of spiritual daybreak, my first glimpse of its distinctively moral or death-giving principle . . . Our experience of the spiritual world dates in truth only from our first unaffected shiver at guilt' (167–8). The religious significance attached to this story transforms it from mere anecdote to spiritual parable. The presence of sin is felt as a tangible force: 'For I myself have known all these temptations – in forms of course more or less modified – by the time I was fourteen or fifteen years old; so that by the time I got to be twenty-five or thirty (which was the date of my first acquaintance with Emerson) I was saturated with a sense of spiritual evil' (296). The accumulation of immoralities is regarded here almost as a source of pride, an indication of future spiritual maturity, and the implicit comparison with Emerson, who he first encounters when at sin saturation point, is neatly made.

James Senior again uses gendered terms to describe his subject, whose superiority is inherited 'like a woman's beauty or charm of manners; that no other account was to be given of it in truth than that Emerson himself was an unsexed woman' (297). However this is not quite the same feeling of feminised purity and spirituality which had earlier been implied: now Emerson's qualities are likened to physical and social attributes, and the fact that he is 'unsexed' as a woman implies an ineffectuality and lack of form. Such a dichotomised conception of human nature articulated

a version of selfhood endorsing characteristics that male opinion form-
ers assigned to themselves. It was a gendered rhetoric of judgement and
control which was self-re-enforcing. As Susan L. Roberson has shown,
Emerson himself was aware of the dangers of spiritual emasculation. In an
increasingly competitive world, he was anxious about his ability to gain
recognition for a declaration of intellectual and religious independence
which stood opposed to an unmanning conformity.[28] Writing in his
journal in 1823, the young Emerson states: 'I am hastening to put on the
manly robe' (*JMN*, II, 112). Moreover in a sermon first preached to the
Second Unitarian Church, Boston in 1829, he suggests that Christian
gentleness (the theme of his address) is completely consistent with
more manly expressions of heroic action: 'I do not believe that the
graces of the Christian character are ever incompatible with its most
robust strength and highest majesty. I believe its strength is infirm, and
its majesty incomplete, without them.' In an earlier sermon (of 1828),
the future direction of Emersonian man is anticipated: this ideal figure
is one 'who does not reckon on authorities . . . but appeals to his own
eye, and to his own conscience'.[29] Yet for Henry Adams, for example, it is clear that Emerson's construction of masculinity was uncon-
vincing – levels of manliness, it seems, could always be surpassed and
rendered impotent: Emerson's religious rebellion was merely ' *naïf* ', an
example of the feminising effects of Unitarianism, whose denominational brand saw disappear 'the most powerful emotion of man, next
to the sexual'.[30] An earlier variation on this came in 1840 from a visiting Australian Presbyterian clergyman, who, in describing his impressions of American religion, declared that 'Unitarianism is the disease to
which Christianity is subject in what may be called its frigid zone'. James
Senior's was a similar lament: 'religion in the old virile sense has disap-
peared, and been replaced by a feeble Unitarian sentimentality'.[31] Although not aimed directly at Emerson himself, behind this comment lay
the example of the elder James's struggles to force his friend to disclose
even the barest nugget of his thinking, to make tangible what he felt sure
would be worth the hearing. In *Spiritual Creation* James Senior dramatises
an instance of this frustration:

> I used to lock myself up with him [Emerson] in his bedroom, swearing that
> before the door was opened I would arrive at the secret of his immense supe-
> riority to the common herd of literary men! I might just as well have locked
> myself up with a handful of diamonds, so far as any capacity of self-cognizance
> existed in him . . . It turned out that an average old dame in a horse-car would
> have satisfied my intellectual rapacity just as well as Emerson.   (296–7)

His interest in specific ideas and religious questions was apparently not accommodated by Emerson's more relaxed, even detached, style: 'Emerson,

in fact, derided this doctrine, smiling benignly whenever it was mentioned. I could make neither head nor tale of him according to men's
ordinary standards – the only thing that I was sure of being that he, like
Christ, was somehow divinely begotten.' Emerson's desexualised nature
is thus echoed in James Senior's conception of the Concord sage's parentage – he is 'virgin-born' (298) and inherits that selfsame embryonic state:
'He was like a vestal virgin, indeed, always in ministry upon the altar;
but the vestal virgin had doubtless a prosaic side also, which related her
to commonplace people. Now Emerson was so far *unlike* the virgin: he
had no prosaic side relating him to ordinary people' (300).

Such cocooning spirituality, it is argued here, caused Emerson to pay
little attention to the wider concerns of his world. Although James Senior
was a severe critic of both conventional religious and social movements,
his strictures were always founded on a desire to engage with the support-
ers of such groupings, whether Swedenborgians, socialists, or orthodox
Unitarians. He accuses Emerson of renouncing that which he knows little about, so that instead of arriving at a considered position based on the
rigours of argument and debate, Emerson's wilful self-reliance blithely
asserts its own solipsistic reality:

> He had apparently lived all his life in a world where it [the Church] was
> only subterraneously known; and, try as you would, you could never persuade
> him that any the least power attached to it. The same profound incredulity
> characterized him in regard to the State; and it was only in his enfeebled later
> years that he ever lent himself to the idea of society as its destined divine form.
>
> (299)

For James Senior the establishment of a divinely ordered society, composed of regenerate man devoid of all his sectarian and divisive impulses,
was the utopian goal. He felt that Emerson's privileging of refreshed individual perception as the means by which spiritual recovery might be
achieved was a far too isolating and subjective process: Emerson 'had
no conscience, in fact, and lived by perception, which is an altogether
lower or less spiritual faculty' (299). A dependence on a change in vision, James Senior argues, does not match the fundamental importance
of 'conscience', that internal process by which man comes to regard his
socially constructed selfhood as evil, rejecting it in favour of one divinely
inspired and best able to realise itself in others. James Senior can find no
trace of an inner dynamic at work. Emerson 'had apparently no private
personality; and if any visitor thought he discerned traces of such a thing,
you may take for granted that the visitor himself was a man of large imaginative resources' (300). In Emerson 'everything seemed innocent by the
transparent absence of selfhood, ... in us everything seemed foul and false
by its preternatural activity' (301). Although the destruction of selfhood

is the ultimate goal of the spiritually enlightened, Emerson starts from a position in which that selfhood has not been initially established and thus the conscious choice to renounce it has not been taken. Innocence is the key to his life, 'the only holiness which [he] recognized' (302).

Writing an introductory note to the 1904 publication of his father's kinder judgement of Emerson, William James captured that essential difference between the two men. Borrowing Francis Newman's terminology, James Senior, he writes, 'was a theologian of the "twice-born" type, an out-and-out Lutheran, who believed that the moral law existed solely to fill us with loathing for the idea of our own merits, and to make us turn to God's grace as our only opportunity'. Emerson, by contrast, was 'a "once-born" man; he lived in moral distinctions, and recognized no need of a redemptive process'.[32] This discrimination becomes clearer when we recognise James Senior's intense interest in the Genesis creation story. In 1879 he recalled his intellectual preoccupation at the time of his vastation experience some thirty-five years earlier: 'I had made an important discovery, as I fancied, namely: that the book of Genesis was not intended to throw a direct light upon our natural or race history, but was an altogether mystical or symbolic record of the laws of God's *spiritual* creation and providence.'[33] One of his first public lectures, 'The Two Adams' delivered in 1843, was developed out of this revelation. The lecture is no longer extant, yet the title indicates the key to an understanding of its author's conception of Emerson. In chapter 1 of Genesis God creates man both male and female (Gen. 1:27); in chapter 2 man is formed out of dust and only afterwards is woman created out of Adam's rib (Gen. 2:7, 22). The apparent discrepancy is solved by James Senior through an allegorical reading in which both versions of the story are valid and indicative of distinct stages in human development. The New York *Evening Post*, summarising one of the earlier lectures in the 1843 series, announced that James Senior would speak of 'the man of the *first* chapter of Genesis, and the man of the *second* chapter; or the CREATED man and the MADE man'.[34] Without the evidence of the actual lecture, one can only conjecture how its author might have developed this idea, yet it is clear enough that James Senior had started to formulate a theory of creation based on man's initial physical formation followed by a second, spiritual making. In this reading, Emerson only exists in this first, amorally infantile self; without an internal knowledge of good and evil he cannot be constructed anew through the process of redemption. Thus he lives in a perpetual 'once-born' state.

This pervasive atmosphere of transcendental simplicity was conjured up once more five years later in Henry James's 1887 review of Cabot's memoir of Emerson. We can be fairly certain that James had read his father's more critical account of their shared subject. After William had completed editing those of James Senior's writings which he wished to include in *The Literary Remains*, he sent a copy of it to James, then in London, for his perusal. Henry's response to his brother indicates that parts of the book were indeed read, and although the letter contains a defensive assessment of his overall understanding of his father's philosophy, one can surmise that the chapter on Emerson would have proved more interesting to the novelist than other more abstractly theological sections. Cabot had commenced researching what would become his two-volume memoir of Emerson whilst James Senior was still alive. As an intimate, the elder James was asked if he had any objections to his letters to Emerson being quoted. His reply was direct and probably not what Cabot was expecting:

> I cannot flatter myself that any letter I ever wrote to Emerson is worth reading . . . Emerson always kept one at such arms length, tasting him and sipping him and trying him, to make sure that he was worthy of his somewhat prim and bloodless friendship, that it was fatiguing to write him letters . . . It is painful to recollect now the silly hope that I had, along the early days of our acquaintance, that if I went on listening, something would be sure to drop from him that would show me an infallible way out of this perplexed world. For nothing ever came but epigrams; sometimes clever, sometimes not.

This is by now a familiar refrain, a variation on the one that James Senior was in the process of composing to include in *Spiritual Creation*. Cabot however felt that this brief character sketch did not do justice to the true nature of its writer's relationship with Emerson: 'This, I am sure, is quite unjust to Mr James's real feeling about Mr Emerson, – it was written in illness and depression, just before his death.'[35] Yet as I have shown, the wider evidence suggests that James Senior's words were not merely written in the petulance of sickness and old age, but were rather the accumulation and culmination of years of frustration. James would have read his father's response to Cabot when he came to review the book for the December 1887 issue of *Macmillan's Magazine*. There he repeats the highly ambivalent attitude which the elder James had held towards his subject. James Senior had admitted the effect that the personality of Emerson had had on his young imagination before proceeding to undercut that impression with an attack on Emerson's innocence and simplicity. James similarly grants Emerson his peculiar genius but qualifies this evaluation with a recognition of the secluded and sedate nature of his life – 'he had led for nearly eighty years a life in which the sequence of events had little of the rapidity, or the complexity, that a spectator loves'. The implication is that Emerson's genius was only relative to his provincial surroundings. James Senior's emphasis on Emerson's moral blankness and spiritual virginity is echoed again in James's comment that 'we lay down the book with a singular expression of paleness – an impression that comes partly from the tone of the biographer and partly from the moral complexion of the subject, but mainly from the vacancy of the page itself' (*EAE*, 250). Moral placidity once more characterises the Concord writer; his 'pure spirit' is unruffled by life's complexities, it is 'so fair, so uniform and impersonal' that it represents 'a surface whose proper quality was of the smoothest and on which nothing was reflected with violence' (*EAE*, 251–2).

Whereas James Senior had focused almost exclusively on the dangers of Emerson's theological simplicity, making no reference to the social milieu in which both Emerson and he operated, James, by distancing himself from that antebellum atmosphere, viewed Emerson's insubstantiality in largely cultural terms. He had rehearsed this argument back in 1875 when reviewing a volume of William Ellery Channing's correspondence. Although a 'moral genius', James detected evidence of Channing's 'rather frigid form of. . . thought' (again, evidence of the characteristic labelling of the Unitarian sensibility) which he ascribed to his subject's 'narrow' horizon and the lack of 'what is called nowadays general culture' (*EAE*, 215). Such moral naïvety, which James Senior attributed in Emerson to nothing beyond an absence of the internal consciousness of good and evil, James viewed as indicative of a general provincial thinness: 'We seem to see the circumstances of [Emerson's] origin, immediate and remote, in a kind of high, vertical moral light, the brightness of a society at once very simple and very responsible' (*EAE*, 252). This sentence succinctly captures the sense of an idealistic moral vertigo from which James Senior felt that he had suffered in his contact with Emerson. The elevated position proved too isolating for him, the thin moral air of Emerson's vantage point not circulating freely enough among the shadowy but yet, for James Senior, more tangible elements of the human condition. James's reaction to this atmosphere of two-dimensional brightness is not in the same register as his father's. Distanced by time, the relationship less personal and James's concerns less theological, the estimation of Emerson is best characterised by a tone of polite yet incisive condescension, one in which Emerson's innocence is held up for admiration at the same time as it is recognised that contemporary cultural complexity means that such an attitude towards life now can only seem hopelessly dated. When James writes of an 'absence of personal passion which makes [Emerson's] private correspondence read like a series of beautiful circulars or expanded cards *pour prendre congé*' (*EAE*, 252) we are reminded of his father's complaint to Cabot of Emerson's style likened to carefully articulated epigrams of varying success, a writing form reliant upon a high degree of control and cool artistry. But the benefit of chronological distance allows James to remain comically detached from the religious upheavals which so characterised his father's circle, to the extent that he finds the shock produced by Emerson's break with the Unitarian church a cause for amusement – 'we admire a state of society in which scandal and schism took on no darker hue' (*EAE*, 253). The reviewer again chooses to place the emphasis on the lack of intellectual nourishment rather than on the peculiar condition of Emerson's soul. This prelapsarian and yet arid society, 'not fertile in its variations', is compared unfavourably to Europe, which offers 'a more complicated world'; but Emerson's preference for the New World means that there, in 'the undecorated walls of his youth ... he could dwell with that ripe unconsciousness of evil which is one of the most beautiful signs by which we know him' (*EAE*, 254). James is thus returning to a preoccupation of his father's, accepting James Senior's evaluation of Emerson's ignorance of evil but characteristically regarding this fact less as a matter of fatal spiritual immaturity than as something of a curiosity value. This impression is strengthened when James describes those of Emerson's writings detailing the immoralities of his milieu as 'quaint', a word expressive of both authorial interest and condescension. To emphasise the received notion of Emerson's blind benignity, James adds that 'almost the worst [Emerson] can say is that these vices are negative and that his fellow-townsmen are not heroic'. Such unawareness means that Emerson's Boston was 'like a ministry without an opposition' in which he 'has only a kind of hearsay, uninformed acquaintance with [its] disorders' (*EAE*, 254).

Concurring with his father, James acknowledges the power of Emerson in his public role as lecturer – his words in that context 'come home', for 'instead of treating the few as the many, after the usual fashion of gentlemen on platforms, he treated the many as the few ... [N]ever was the fine wine of philosophy carried to remoter or queerer corners' (*EAE*, 256, 257). This public persona however is all of Emerson that one can grasp – 'he had only one style, one manner, and he had it for everything – even for himself, in his notes, in his journals'. Such uniformity of aspect is perpetuated by depictions of the New England community in which its members seem to have been 'embalmed – in a collective way'. For James there is little interest in this kind of tableau representation. Even Margaret Fuller, that most vibrant of women ('imaginative, talkative, intelligent and finally Italianised'), has been reduced to 'one of the dim' (*EAE*, 260). A desire for moral complexity and narrative interest mean that, for James, his curiosity lies more with Emerson's aunt Mary. His curiosity in her had already been aroused, according to Emerson's daughter Ellen, by his presence in 1872 at a lecture by Emerson entitled 'Amita' (latin for 'aunt'), an affectionate but somewhat superficial memoir. Ellen noted that James 'took an interest in the character of Aunt Mary', an interest which he felt was lacking when reviewing Cabot's book fifteen years later.[36] What was required, James suggested, was the improvement which might be offered by the use of a novelist's skills: 'We miss a more liberal handling, are tempted to add touches of our own, and end by convincing ourselves that Miss Mary Moody Emerson, grim intellectual virgin and daughter of a hundred ministers, with her local traditions and her combined love of empire and of speculation, would have been an inspiration for a novelist' (*EAE*, 259). I described in the previous chapter how the notion of fictional enhancement of the factual to depict a more fundamentally truthful portrait is something prevalent to both James and his father. Certainly this preference for moral (and also, in the novelist's case, narrative) movement and complexity ensures that, for both men, Emerson's already constructed self (as they conceived it to be) could satisfy neither their spiritual nor literary requirements.

Whether consciously or otherwise, James repeats one of the exact complaints which his father had levelled at Emerson. The fact that Emerson seemed to have 'no personal, just as he had almost no physical wants' (*EAE*, 260) recalls James Senior's ineffectual plea to his correspondent that 'I know that you have the same wants as I have, deep down in your bosom hidden from my sight, and it is by these that I want somehow to know you' (undated 1842, *WJ*, 1, 42). James laments the omission of a chapter in Cabot's book which would attempt to uncover exactly what Emerson thought of his contemporaries – 'his inner reserves and scepticisms, his secret ennuis and ironies' (*EAE*, 264). This again is the preoccupation of the novelist, for the reviewer recognises the difficulty in revealing such aspects when the book's subject chooses to 'practise a kind of universal passive hospitality' – echoing James Senior's conception of Emerson's house as one of indiscriminate indifference discussed earlier. Emerson had 'polished his aloofness till it reflected the image of his solicitor' (*EAE*, 260).

In 1883, four years prior to the publication of this review, James had written an evaluation in the June edition of the *Century Magazine* of Charles Eliot Norton's two-volume edition of the correspondence of Emerson and Carlyle. There is no evidence that James had encountered his father's manuscript chapter on Emerson written the previous year, but again the similarities between his review and James Senior's work suggest that the latter's opinions were well known and indeed currency in the James family at this time. As in his father's 1872 lecture, James regards Emerson and Carlyle here as operating at opposing extremes of sensibility, but unlike James Senior he has no philosophical agenda which requires him to arbitrate between them: their radical difference makes such a choice impossible, so much so that the great novelist admits to being unable to conjure up a plausible fictitious scene depicting Carlyle's arrival on a visit to New England. It would have been a 'dramatic' situation,

James writes, but 'the catastrophe never came off': 'It is impossible to imagine what the historian of the French Revolution, of the iron-fisted Cromwell, and the Voltairean Frederick, would have made of that sensitive spot, or what Concord would have made of Carlyle' (*EAE*, 239). James's estimation of Emerson here brings to mind his father's own later study, with its bemused focus on Emerson's implacable optimism, which 'makes us wonder at times where he discovered the errors that it would seem well to set right... He had a high and noble conception of good, without having... a definite conception of evil.' Carlyle, by contrast, is described in terms also familiar to readers of James Senior's work, being 'a pessimist of pessimists' and having 'a vivid conception of evil without a corresponding conception of good' (*EAE*, 243).

Quite how this relationship remained successful is difficult to imagine, given the nature of the personalities involved. Although James could not conceive of even a credible fictional meeting between Emerson and Carlyle, a letter to James Senior from his friend James Wilkinson describes the actual scene of an apparently tense encounter in London in 1848:

> it seems that the two old friends and correspondents found out when they met, that they had neither an idea nor a sympathy in common. Their parting is said to have been painful in the extreme. I wonder if they did not know the state of their relations long before... Moreover at times [Carlyle's] very mind is repulsive, even horrific; and his whole intellectual force lies in the greatness of his despair; while Emerson is a son of hope even where hope is unreasonable, and occasionally becomes sublime from the forcible pencil of light which he sheds athwart a gloom. (*WJ*, 1, 54)

James however hints at a possible method of compromise when he notes that Emerson's 'much more luminous a nature' means that he only 'expresses... the disapprobation of silence' (*EAE*, 235). Thus Emerson's placidity, which James Senior found so infuriating, allowed him to pursue a relationship in which fundamental differences could be overlooked.

From the writings of both Jameses, then, we have a picture of Emerson as a figure whose personality seems to embody a set of disabling principles, either theological or cultural. Despite a difference in focus, both men emphasise someone exhibiting moral blankness, sheltered in a quasi-Edenic state – for James Senior, Emerson is a 'man without a handle' (*WJ*, 1, 51). Yet James Senior's assumption of Emerson's innocence of evil is handled with a polemical force which misrepresents the precarious reality of Emerson's position. By focusing on this issue in the final section of this chapter, I suggest that even if James Senior did not wilfully misread Emerson he did at least fail to recognise the fact that within the idealistic duality of his thought the existence of evil remains a major preoccupation. Although we may grant that the fundamental premises on which

Emerson and James Senior's philosophies are based are indeed different, the picture proposed of the Concord writer as somehow living beyond the knowledge of good and evil (a picture which Henry James seems to accept and comically reinforce) represents a reading which exerts a flattening and distorting perspective.

IV

In the late 1840s, reformist circles in New York were attracted to the mesmeric revelations of an uneducated shoemaker from Poughkeepsie, Andrew Jackson Davis. According to his autobiography, Davis was put into his hypnotic state by the touch of a 'magnetic operator' and so enabled to uncover the ultimate laws of nature: 'The grave-visaged operator ties a handkerchief about the youth's uneducated head – closing the world yet more out, and leaving him to his own psychical changes and transformations . . . His benumbed hands do quiver with a new sensation, and the muscles of his face do vibrate and tremble with the inflowing power.'[37] Davis's many revelations, witnessed by amongst others George Bush (a leading Swedenborgian and Professor of Hebrew at New York State University) and Edgar Allan Poe,[38] were transcribed and published in 1847. The weighty volume detailed an evolutionary history of the universe, fiercely attacked denominational Christianity, and outlined an alternative system of human government based on the ideas of Fourier. Like James Senior, Davis made selective use of Swedenborg to interpret his visions, rejecting wholesale devotion and noting instead that the important thing 'is to point out the good and practical parts of each [philosopher], that they may be preserved for future application; and if these are duly distinguished and preserved, all the unreal and excrescent parts of each revelation and philosophy will at once be disregarded, because of their non-importance'.[39] The elder James's more explicit connection with Davis however takes the form of his reaction to a pamphlet written in 1847 by Bush (in collaboration with another orthodox Swedenborgian, Benjamin Barrett) which set out to discredit Davis's revelations (although carefully maintaining that Davis himself was not a fraud). The two men argued that because they had detected certain doctrinal errors in Davis's interpretation of Swedenborg, the visions themselves must have arisen as a result of the influence of corrupting evil spirits. Consequently the whole enterprise should be disowned:

> Our conclusion therefore is that Davis has been grievously deluded by the arts and machinations of deceitful spirits and that *occasion* for all this has been given by the lack of a true faith, the product of a moral state rightly affected towards all divine things. He has thus been prevented from associating with a sphere of

pure truth and been made the subject of the most enormously false impressions in regard to the whole circle of religious doctrines.[40]

James Senior entered the discussion on the side of Davis, writing a review of the Bush–Barrett attack for the *Harbinger* newspaper in which he rejected the notion that the existence of evil spirits was reason enough to refute the validity of Davis's claims. Characteristically opposing the aura of infallibility which orthodox followers had allowed to settle around Swedenborg's writings, he asserted the idea that the concept of evil remained inextricably entwined with that of goodness, that to deny the presence of one was to also deny the possibility of the other. 'The attempt to crush Davis's book, by asserting its purely hellish genesis,' he wrote, 'in reality conveys a reproach to the Divine.'[41]

This, one of the more bizarre episodes in antebellum New York's intellectual life, serves to introduce an examination of James Senior's understanding of the origins and importance of evil. Davis's critics had preferred to shun any manifestation which they could attribute to its influence; James Senior regarded this as a dangerous moral myopia, as perverse as the childlike ignorance he saw displayed by Emerson. In *The Nature of Evil Considered in a Letter to the Rev. Edward Beecher, D.D., Author of 'The Conflict of the Ages'* (1855) he expanded on this view. His work is ostensibly, as its full title indicates, a communication to Beecher, the less flamboyant brother of Henry Ward and editor of the *Congregationalist* newspaper. Beecher had attempted, in his own book of 1853, to reconcile the antagonism between Calvinist assumptions of human depravity and the more liberal wing of Protestantism, which rejected the idea of a vengeful God:

> Good men are at this day as really and as thoroughly divided against good men as they ever were. At one time, the New School Theology (so called), proceeding from New England, seems to be carrying all before it in the Presbyterian church. Then there is a division, and a combination, not only without, but also within New England, to react upon it, and to restore the Old School theology to its original power. So it has been, in other ages and climes.[42]

Beecher's solution to this doctrinal tension was to assert that human souls had existed prior to their birth and were already sinful. By allowing man to be born on earth, God was in fact showing true benevolence in providing the circumstances and opportunity for his repentance. 'By supposing the pre-existent sin and fall of man, the most radical views of human depravity can be harmonized with the highest views of the justice and honor of God' (242). The world became a 'moral hospital' in which are collected 'the diseased of past ages, the fallen of all preceding generations of creatures' (232). Thus sin had taken place in a time prior to human existence and the emphasis now, Beecher argued, must lie in effecting forgiveness and spiritual regeneration.

James Senior could not conceive of sin as an event occurring in the past – indeed in a time *prior* to the past when sinning was inevitable and man impotent. (In a later review he would refer dismissingly to 'Dr Beecher's outlandish pre-adamite worlds'.[43]) Evil remained an ever-present reality, and his book, at times infuriatingly prolix and repetitive, is an attempt to articulate this belief. The one great evil in the universe, he declared, was 'the principle of selfhood, the principle of independence in man'.[44] Because man is totally dependent upon God, the instant he imagines for himself an autonomous reality and as a result feels proud or superior, he commits spiritual evil, denying God and the possibility of an ultimate union with Him: 'The sentiment of independent selfhood: the conviction of being the source of one's own good and evil: such is the sole ground of every evil known to the spiritual universe' (143). This principle is complicated by the addition of another element: the development of that independent selfhood, so morally destructive, is in fact *necessary* if man is to achieve spiritual maturity. That selfsame sense of independence is granted by God, and thus our selfhood is provisional until we realise our unhappiness and voluntarily choose to renounce it, conjoining with God as a result:

> Thus the life or freedom which distinguishes man from the brute, is not a natural possession of man, but a Divine endowment, and it is imparted to him not for its own sake or to enable him merely to transcend brute existence, but to serve as the basis or platform of a higher Divine communication which shall lift him into the eternal fellowship of God.   (98)

It is this aspect of freedom of choice, so absent in Beecher's theory where evil is effectively a *fait accompli*, that James Senior considers so important. The paradoxical nature of his message – the one thing making spiritual life possible, the sense of selfhood, also happens to be the location for that which prevents such a life – can only be surmounted by an expression of choice where, as a final act of independence, that independence is renounced. The logical workings of this equation are dizzying, and the resolution of the paradox not entirely satisfactory (the idea that man has to repent for a delusion of selfhood, a selfhood without which he cannot move towards God, is an uneasy proposition). But in broad terms we can see how James Senior envisaged the concept of evil as an indispensable part of moral and spiritual development, and how an apparent ignorance of it (in Emerson's case) or an apparent avoidance of the issues it raises (in the case of Bush and Barrett) were signs of immaturity. There is a certain degree of authorial arrogance in *The Nature of Evil*, something which a contemporary reviewer remarked upon, describing how the author places

'Dr Beecher before his chair, as a well-meaning little boy, who deserves
to have his somewhat gross errors explained to him'.[45] Yet James Senior's
assured sense of the correctness of his theory lies at the heart of his
criticisms of Emerson, for although not as dismissive of him as he is of
Beecher, his repudiation is based on an assumption that his (Emerson's)
provisional selfhood had never been formed, that his spiritual evolution
had halted prior to this fundamental phase and thus an awareness of
evil was an impossibility. In a contemporary review of William James's
edition of his father's literary remains, John Albee commented that 'it
is worthwhile to read what [James Senior] says about Emerson, as he
speaks from long and intimate acquaintance. His criticism of Emerson, as
an intellectual and spiritual being, is altogether unique, slightly perverse,
or in the spirit of contradiction, and shows in an objective manner Mr
James's idiosyncrasies on the spiritual side.'[46] It is precisely this assessment
of the perverse nature of James Senior's response to Emerson which I want
to pursue, by questioning the tempting and, because tempting, widely
held assumption of Emerson's moral innocence.

In Caroline Dall's at times wryly amusing record of the conversations
on Greek mythology which took place in Boston in 1841 under the
guidance of Margaret Fuller, there is an account of the discussion which
ensued following a retelling of the story of Cupid and Psyche. Psyche,
tempted by her sisters to kill Cupid, the husband she has been instructed
never to look upon, accidentally scalds him with oil from her lamp.
Enraged, he abandons her, and she must fulfil certain tasks as penance for
her act of disobedience. Dall's transcription of the ensuing conversation
focuses on the matter of Psyche's temptation, which, Fuller instructs her
listeners, would surely 'have come through her own soul' if it had not
originated with her sisters: 'There seemed to be a need of sin, to work out
salvation for human beings.'[47] Emerson's comment, which immediately
follows this, serves both as a statement of disagreement with Fuller and as
representative of the optative bias of his thinking which so troubled James
Senior. 'It was man's privilege', Emerson exclaims, 'to resist the evil, to
strive triumphantly; to recognise it – never! Good was always present to
the soul, – was all the true soul took note of. It was a duty not to look!'
(113). A strategy of willed obliviousness, of not looking, was evidence
for James Senior of a fatal spiritual short-sightedness.

The Divinity School Address of 1838 saw Emerson explicitly set out
his understanding of evil, conceiving it as a negation, as merely the absence of good: 'Good is positive. Evil is merely privative, not absolute: it
is like cold, which is the privation of heat. All evil is so much death and
nonentity. Benevolence is absolute and real' (*CWE*, I, 124). By choosing
to define his concept in terms of what it is not, rather than what it is,
Emerson's approach is radically different from that of James Senior, for

whom evil was not a negative aspect of goodness but rather a vital, positive force. Emerson's linking of the two states in a relationship of seeming inequality, whereby evil is viewed as the mere absent shadow of its opposite, might cause us to wonder if the evaluation of Emerson propagated by the two Jameses is correct after all. Emerson strenuously insists upon his position, as in his chapter on 'Swedenborg' in *Representative Men*, where he remarks that 'the less we have to do with our sins, the better. No man can afford to waste his moments in compunctions . . . Evil, according to old philosophers, is good in the making' (*CWE*, IV, 138). But to state what is perhaps an obvious point, his decision to define the nature of evil in these terms does not deny evil's existence: to regard it as a privation of something else does not make the Jameses' assumption that Emerson remained unaffected by it an accurate one. The problem lies, I would suggest, in the fact that James Senior failed to recognise (or chose to dismiss) the essentially dualistic nature of Emerson's philosophy; namely that Emerson was able to survey life from an absolute as well as from a relative viewpoint, always privileging the former in the sense that the relative, the human, could be subsumed in an all-encompassing absoluteness. Thus evil could be contained by a greater goodness. The differentiation of experience into human (and thus imperfect) and ultimate (and thus divine) realms plays no part in James Senior's scheme of things, where the one was an important precursor of the other; in Emerson the two realms exist simultaneously.

Philosophically, then, evil is considered in the realm of a mystical whole. But in the realm of actual and imperfect human experience, Emerson strictly upholds the division of 'good' and 'evil' ('Everything has two sides, a good and an evil. Every advantage has its tax. I learn to be content'; 'We live in succession, in division, in parts, in particles' ('The Over-Soul'; 'Compensation', *CWE*, II, 269; 120)), so that once evil becomes a problem constituent of everyday morality its presence is strongly felt:

> Saints are sad, because they behold sin (even when they speculate) from the point of view of the conscience, and not of the intellect; a confusion of thought. Sin, seen from the thought, is a diminution or *less*; seen from the conscience or will, it is pravity or *bad*. The intellect names its shade, absence of light, and no essence. The conscience must feel it as essence, essential evil. This it is not . . .   ('Experience', *CWE*, III, 79)

Here is that duality of viewpoint succinctly expressed – moral and intellectual; human and absolute. Evil viewed from the intellectual and absolute perspective '*is* a diminution', whereas Emerson is careful to say that, seen from the moral and human perspective, man '*must* feel it as essence, essential evil'. The one is offered as an irrefutable fact, the other as a psychological necessity from the burden of which we are relieved once our vision is readjusted. In this manner Emerson is able to insist that human experience combines good and evil, and also that below that level, in the essential existence underlying the phenomenal, evil is the absence of essence, being, or God, and in that context can work neither good nor harm: 'Under all this running sea of circumstance, whose waters ebb and flow with perfect balance, lies the aboriginal abyss of real Being. Essence, or God, is not a relation or a part, but the whole. Being is the vast affirmative, excluding negation, self-balanced, and swallowing up all relations, parts and times within itself' ('Compensation', *CWE*, ii, 120–1). James Senior's response to Emerson suggests that his grasp of these twin strands of Emerson's thought was an imperfect one. The Concord writer's undoubted preference for the absolute perspective clouds James Senior's appreciation of those less prominent but still recognisable aspects which insist upon the moral problems caused by sin. In 'Experience' for example Emerson warns that 'everything runs to excess; every good quality is noxious if unmixed, and, to carry the danger to the edge of ruin, nature causes each man's peculiarity to superabound' (*CWE*, iii, 65–6). To recognise the difficulty of attaining virtue implies a corresponding recognition of the force of evil.

Yet although Emerson at times can willingly engage with the physical reality of evil and pain when regarded from the vantage point of the human, when this angle is given up, his attitude, far from becoming gently optimistic, displays an at times alienating severity and coldness. Suffering and pain, he asserts, are merely delusive sensations:

> Pain is superficial, and therefore fear is. The torments of martyrdoms are probably most keenly felt by the by-standers . . . Our affections and wishes for the external welfare of the hero tumultuously rush to expression in tears and outcries: but we, like him, subside into indifferency and defiance when we perceive how short is the longest arm of malice, how serene is the sufferer.
>
> ('Courage', *CWE*, vii, 265)

This belief in the ultimate victory of serenity over conflict is possible to maintain as long as Emerson makes his final evaluation of man's situation from God's point of view, or the whole, rather than from man's, or the part. F. I. Carpenter contended that the prime theme of Emerson's work is the ' "disparity" between man the suffering, confused, and selfish actor in the human tragedy, which is also "the divine comedy", and man the ideal made in the image of God'.[48] By asserting a God-like perspective (that of an omnipresent first-person narrator, one might say), Emerson can remain detached from the human tragedies unfolding around him, relying on a lightly comic vision which can accept Carpenter's disparity in the knowledge that ultimately beneficial natural laws are in motion. By contrast, James Senior's notion of the 'fortunate fall', whereby personal and very real acquaintance with evil leads to an eventual union with God, relies upon an essentially tragic conception of life in which the hazardous gaining of experience (selfhood) to realise one's sinfulness is the essential (and very Puritan inherited) element. The absolute realm, already existing for Emerson, is not tapped into merely through the refinement of an individual's angle of vision, but rather can only be achieved through the creation of a society in which humankind has collectively renounced its individual identities for one divinely inspired and universal.

The differences between the underpinnings of Emerson and James Senior's philosophies are real enough. Their letters suggest strong disparities of sensibility, and one sympathises with James Senior in his inability to crack the shell of Emerson's passive hospitality. Yet that aspect of Emerson's thought and character which most preoccupies the elder James, the question of an awareness of evil, is polemicised. Henry James's adoption of his father's line continues this unbalanced assessment. Many years ago, Arthur Christy offered a more measured attitude, arguing that Emerson's optimism, 'instead of being blindness or indifference [to evil], is a most persistent type of therapeutics'.[49] The perspective of the absolute is not a method of ignoring the difficult facts of life, but rather a method for coping with them by giving them their proper valuation. In implying a self-identity of theological and cultural superiority, both Henry Jameses presume a form of naïvety in Emerson that comfortably negates the tense complexity of his philosophy.

3

'Under certain circumstances': Jamesian reflections on the fall

Society, The Redeemed Form of Man (1879) was the last of James Senior's volumes to appear in print during his lifetime. Like many of his preceding efforts, the book is a series of letters addressed to an unnamed correspondent who, the author feels, is in need of spiritual guidance. The work is extensive yet unfocused, ranging across the whole spectrum of James Senior's intellectual and religious concerns, and includes the autobiographical mythologising of his vastation experience back in 1844. In the same year that *Society* was published, Henry James was preoccupied with the composition of his first major work, *The Portrait of a Lady*. The germ of the novel came to him as early as 1876: writing to William Dean Howells in October of that year he had mentioned that his new book 'was to be an *Americana* – the adventures in Europe of a female Newman', a reference to the hero of an earlier novel, *The American*, which Howells had started publishing in instalments in the *Atlantic* magazine four months previously (*Letters*, II, 72). The gestation period for this new book was a lengthy one: two years later James was writing to his brother William that 'the "great novel" you ask about is only begun' (*Letters*, II, 179); during 1879 he seems to have hit a creative impasse, confessing to Howells that the novel that he was 'waiting to write, and which, begun sometime since' was still only 'an aching fragment' (*Letters*, II, 244); and writing to his father from Florence in 1880 he admits to 'taking a holiday pure and simple – before settling down to the daily evolution of my "big" novel' (*Letters*, II, 277). James Senior's own newly published volume had already been sent to his son in London the previous year, and James's reaction to it in a letter to his mother is characteristically ambiguous: 'really to read it I must lay it aside till the summer. I have dipped into it and found a great fascination' (*Letters*, II, 230). Filial loyalty and admiration is combined with an unwillingness to plough through the intricacies of his father's philosophical system; James prefers to put off the event until a later, more leisurely time. He does admit to perusing its pages however, registering those aspects of it which interest him. Many of the ideas must have been familiar, if not in the sometimes prolix manner in which they are often expressed in print, then in the less quantifiable but still significant sense of the accumulation of their general spirit and feeling – as Kenneth Graham has accurately remarked, 'James was formed not by formal education but by family.'[1] In *Notes of a Son and Brother* James writes that 'In the beauty of the whole thing, again, I lose myself... in the fact that we were all partaking, to our most intimate benefit, of an influence of direction and enlargement... [T]erms of living appreciation, of spiritual perception, of "human fellowship"... were the very substance of the food supplied in the parental nest' (*A*, 336).

I do not wish to propose that through reading James Senior's book his son found an invaluable philosophical source for his own project, but *Society* does retread one important aspect of the elder James's thought that is reflected in *The Portrait of a Lady*. In articulating a reaction against the Emersonian tendency to idealise an Edenic existence, one in which the fall into experience is to be regretted and a recapturing of the prelapsarian state something desirous, James Senior's version of the Genesis story insists upon both the inevitability and the necessity of the fall, the importance of encountering the dangers of experience as a means of achieving full spiritual maturity. In Isabel Archer, James creates a character imbued with Emersonian idealism, one whose theoretical approach to life is insufficient when faced with the machinations of the inhabitants of the Old World. James's debt to his literary fathers Emerson and Hawthorne has been acknowledged by a long tradition of criticism,[2] but the influence of his biological father, who posited an antidote to what he regarded as the regressive fantasies of the American Romantic tradition, has been largely overlooked. In this chapter I want to suggest that in *The Portrait of a Lady* James explores (unconsciously or otherwise) his father's theological doctrine of the beneficial fall, recasting it into something suited to James's more secular yet still intensely moral preoccupations. At times employing Miltonic language, James describes Isabel's expulsion from the secluded protection of Albany and Gardencourt into the manipulative, history-saturated Europe of Florence and Rome. Her fall into history and experience corresponds to James Senior's insistence on the necessity of a similar descent. Isabel's initial preference for effacing the past, her desire to renounce the nearly blank page of her external history (James writes that 'she had a desire to leave the past behind her and, as she said to herself, begin afresh'[3]) locates her alongside a brand of transcendentalism that sought to refute America's European ancestry in favour of the blank page of a distinctly New World present. It is this phenomenon which I examine first: namely the cultural context that provoked James Senior's critique that such insistent ahistoricism could only result in spiritual stunting.

I

In his slight poem 'An Appeal to Time', G. N. Barbour neatly encapsulates in one stanza the ideology of regression which, although more elaborately and attractively expressed by Emerson, forms a central part of the Concord writer's philosophy:

> O Time! give back my childhood days,
> Those halcyon days of truth,
> And I'll give up my manhood ways,
> And be once more a youth.[4]

This nostalgic desire to renunciate adulthood and its 'ways' for an earlier, purer time stands in stark contrast to the Calvinist doctrine of original sin, a central component of New England theology since the continent's Protestant colonisation. In 1757 Jonathan Edwards had composed a treatise on the subject, *The Great Christian Doctrine of Original Sin*, in which he sought to establish beyond any doubt the *a priori* sinfulness of humankind, 'the true tendency of the natural or innate disposition of man's heart, which appears to be its tendency when we consider things as they are in themselves'.[5] Edwards was unsparing in his assessment of humanity's moral malaise; unlike Barbour, for the great Puritan divine even children were no sooner born than they demonstrated their fallen state, being 'by nature children of wrath' (215). The possibility of childhood innocence was refuted, for Edwards argued that 'in relation to the *positive* acts and hurtful effects of vice' the case was not proven that the young 'have not corrupt nature within them' (423).

As a doctrine predicated upon the assumption of an inherited taint caused by the fall in Eden, original sin came to symbolise for its apostates that enslavement to the Old World and its traditions which the new nation of America had the unique opportunity to reject. Abandonment of the past thus also coincided with an assertion of national innocence, of cultural youthfulness. In 1843 William Cullen Bryant predicted an American–European contest for 'power [which] holds and governs the world', one in which 'the mind of England, old and knit by years and wisdom into strength' was nevertheless well-matched by its fresh adversary, an America 'roused to new duties in its youth, and in the van with opinions born of the hour'.[6] Bryant, the long-serving editor of the organ of Jacksonian politics, the New York *Evening Post*, was frequently explicit in his advocacy of American self-sufficiency. The publication of

James Fenimore Cooper's novel *Home as Found* (1838), for example, had provided him with the opportunity to remind his readers of their nation's proud independence. In his book Cooper had lamented America's provincialism, one in which (echoing the words of de Tocqueville quoted in chapter 1) 'every man, as a matter of course, refers to his own particular experience, and praises or condemns agreeably to notions contracted in the circle of his own habits, however narrow, provincial, or erroneous they may happen to be'.[7] Bryant, in an editorial, opposed the novelist's admiration for the 'polished nations' of Europe, maintaining that America was far from being a country of individuals acting in isolation from one another, without any sense of social contract:

> Without staying to examine whether all Mr Cooper's animadversions on American manners are perfectly just, we seize the occasion to protest against this excessive sensibility to the opinion of other nations. It is no matter what they think of us. We constitute a community large enough to form a great moral tribunal for the trial of any question which may arise among ourselves. There is no occasion for this perpetual appeal to the opinions of Europe. We are competent to apply the rules of right and wrong boldly and firmly, without asking in what light the superior judgment of the Old World may regard our decisions.[8]

The New World, devoid of historical ancestry according to this particular time line, brought an immediacy and freshness which could more than counter the accumulated and immobilising weight of the tradition of the Old. Bryant's language of American exceptionalism stressed moral maturity and an independence of thought verging on proud isolationism.

William Ellery Channing, one of the founding fathers of American Unitarianism and an early influence on Emerson, had sought to undermine the tradition of European Calvinism in an essay review published in 1820. 'The Moral Argument Against Calvinism' was an attempt to rehabilitate fallen man, to rescue him from the fear engendered by orthodox and unsympathetic Protestantism. Channing stated what he saw to be the absurdities of the Calvinist position in the bluntest terms. The doctrine 'owes its perpetuity to the influence of fear in palsying the moral nature. Men's minds and consciences are subdued by terror, so that they dare not confess, even to themselves, the shrinking which they feel from the unworthy views which this system gives of God.'[9] Instead of depending upon an outdated theological tradition for guidance in religious matters, Channing asserted (in terms which Emerson would later come to echo) that 'it is an important truth, which we apprehend has not been sufficiently developed, that the ultimate reliance of a human being is and must be on his own mind' (340). The historical force of Calvinism, he hoped, was 'giving place to better views . . . Society is going forward in intelligence and charity, and of course is leaving the theology of the sixteenth century behind it' (343). Emerson's own sense of the dead weight of a more recent past litters his writing. In an early (1822) letter to a Harvard classmate on the eve of the fourth of July celebrations he confesses his preference to 'expend' his 'patriotism in banqueting upon Mother Nature'. Determined to remain detached from the national lauding of the country's revolutionary heroes, his reaction is explicit: 'Tomorrow is the birthday of our pride: our self complacent orators stand on tiptoe when the day is named.' Retiring to 'certain cherry trees of the country', Emerson chooses to repudiate one of the unavoidable effects of nation-hood, its delight in shared memory and historical celebration (*LE*, I, 121).

George Forgie has suggested that a sense of belatedness affected the members of Emerson's generation. 'The fact of being born too late to experience the Revolution,' he writes, 'but in time to be raised by the generation that had fought it, informed the way that many members of this later generation identified and thought about themselves.'[10] For some, the effect of this chronological limbo manifested itself as a lingering attachment to the golden post-Revolutionary age of the 1820s, a period in which memory of the nation's founding was still fresh and its li-onised participants still living. As one article on Henry Clay, John Quincy Adams's Secretary of State, nostalgically expressed it, 'the heroes . . . were still walking among the people . . . Multitudes of memories and traditions of the great deeds done back then, were still current. The whole heart of the nation was warm, the whole mind of the nation was lifted up.'[11] For others, the so-called 'Young Americans', the legacy of the fathers was accommodated in an aggressively expansionist and nationalistic project which defined them as distinctive from but not in opposition to the previous generation.[12] Emerson and transcendentalism were located on the path between these two positions, unwilling to pay slavish respect to the past and, at least initially, wary of a capitalist ideology that privi-leged the material life at the expense of the spiritual. (Although, as I have shown, Emerson would be drawn towards the Young American camp and free-market economics as the stance of individual unfettered new-ness became increasingly difficult to maintain.) Emerson's rejection of the early nineteenth-century's process of immortalising the leading figures of American history is evident in an 1841 journal entry in which he asks, 'What business have Washington or Jefferson in this age? You must be a very dull or a very false man if you have not a better or more advanced policy to offer than they had' (*JMN*, VIII, 58). In 'Nature' (1836) the desire to discard history in celebration of the naturalness of childhood is given deliberate expression. The fact that 'our age is retrospective', its vision clouded by the aggregated mass of its past, prevents 'an original relation to the universe'. Desiring a 'spirit of infancy even into the era of manhood', Emerson claims that surrounded by nature a man is able to 'cast off his years . . . and at what period soever of life, is always a child. In the woods, is perpetual youth' (*CWE*, I, 3, 9).

An editorial in the monthly mouthpiece of American nationalism, the *United States Magazine and Democratic Review*, neatly summarises the tendency I have outlined here: 'Probably no other civilized nation has at any period of its history so completely thrown off its allegiance to the past . . . The whole essay of our national life and legislation, has been a prolonged protest against the dominion of antiquity in every form whatsoever.'[13] Although rejecting the Puritan inheritance of original sin, this deliberate ahistoricism was perfectly consistent with that other Puritan myth of America as the land of apocalyptic promise, described by Sacvan Bercovitch in *The American Jeremiad*. Puritan culture sought to transfer to the Old World responsibility for the corruption which would usher in a final conflagration, regarding its own nation as the beginning of redemptive, post-apocalyptic assurance. As Bercovitch notes, this was 'a mythic view of history that extended New England's past into an apocalypse which stood "near, even at the door," requiring one last great act, one more climactic outpouring of the spirit, in order to realize itself'. America was on 'an errand to the end of time'.[14] What is remarkable is the flexibility of this myth: it escaped conventional conceptions of linear, developmental history in that it was able to claim not only to come before decadent civilisation and so promote an organic closeness to life's essentials, but also to succeed such decadence in acting as a purging deconstruction of it. The first and final utopias of Old Eden and the New Jerusalem were simultaneously present and valid, and New England historiography was explicitly moulded to buttress such an unempirical principle of progress. In 'On the Progress of Civilization', published in the *Boston Quarterly Review* in 1838, America's pre-eminent nineteenth-century historian George Bancroft asserted the claim for inevitable amelioration. Like a number of his peers, including Edward Everett and Jared Sparks, Bancroft had brief experience of the Unitarian pulpit, and the rhetoric of American manifest destiny informs his writing: 'The world cannot retrograde; the dark ages cannot return. Dynasties perish; cities are buried, nations have been victims to error, or martyrs for right; Humanity has always been on the advance; its soul has always been gaining maturity and power.' Axiomatic to this theory of American history was the assumption that material change served to verify spiritual progress; the establishment in America of commercial expansion, internal peace, democratic principles of government, all provided the strongest possible proof of the inevitability of collective American spiritual development. The *Review*'s editor, Orestes Brownson, offered a bluntly inductive methodology for future chroniclers of the nation:

'Man was made for progress... The historian should always assume man's progressiveness as his point of departure, and judge all the facts and events he encounters according to their bearing on his great theme.'[15]

Emerson's own inclination towards ahistoricism ensured that the theological concept of the fall of man reverberated problematically for him. The fall was structured upon an insistent linearity which rendered impossible the opportunity of returning to a time prior to its happening. In maintaining the potential of man's perfectibility and a nostalgia for the simplistic vision of childhood, Emerson adhered, as Oliver Wendell Holmes succinctly remarked, to 'dreams of Paradise regained'. Emerson's counter-myth 'was a kind of New England Genesis in place of the Old Testament one'.[16] When we come to look at the world with 'new eyes', we shall, Emerson claims in the final section of 'Nature', find 'the phenomenon perfect' (*CWE*, i, 76). The emphasis which he places here on vision (Emerson had an abiding interest in the science of optics, one no doubt with personal resonances, given his own fragile sight) has its literary ancestry in Milton's *Paradise Lost*. In Book xi, the archangel Michael is charged with expelling Adam and Eve from the garden and then rehearsing the story of mankind's eventual salvation, culminating with the Flood and its aftermath. Michael takes Adam up on to a mountain top:

> So both ascend
> In the Visions of God: It was a Hill
> Of Paradise the highest, from whose top
> The Hemisphere of Earth in clearest Ken
> Stretcht out to th' amplest reach of prospect lay.
> (Book xi, 376–80)

From this high vantage point, 'Michael from Adams eyes the Filme remov'd' (412), revealing the secrets of God's redemptive programme. His sight 'Purg'd with Euphrasie and Rue' (414), Adam declares Michael to be the 'True op'ner of mine eyes' (598), a 'Heav'nly instructor' (871).[17] This role of interpreter is one which Emerson now assumes for himself as Poet (Michael's elevated position in Milton chiming with Henry James's assessment of Emerson's 'high, vertical moral light'). As Joel Porte reminds us,[18] Emerson borrowed Milton's phrasing in a journal entry from January 1828 in which he writes that although 'Christianity... takes off the film that had got on the human eye' it nevertheless failed in 'the obvious interest & duty of cultivating the mind'. With tentativeness (this was, after all, written before his 1832 abandonment of orthodox Unitarianism) Emerson rhetorically asks, 'Shall we say then that Ch[ristiani]ty neglected the improvement of the intellect?' His conclusion is that 'the oculist did not wish the blind man to see the sun because he only removed the film & left him no directions what to do with his eyes' (*JMN*, III, 101). Emerson implies that *he* is now providing the directions for his own refocused vision: his reworking of Milton takes the bestowal of sight away from a heavenly external agent (Michael) and relocates it in an internal agency.

That Michael is God's ambassador is indicative of the degree to which the authority of the divine has been transferred from an objective entity to a subjective realm. Encouraged by biblical higher criticism of the late eighteenth and early nineteenth centuries that sought to relativise the significance of the Bible and the oracular authority of Christ, the liberal Unitarian theologian Theodore Parker had famously preached in 1842 that 'the heresy of one age is the orthodox and "only infallible rule" of the next'. Given such reversal, he continued, 'it seems difficult to conceive any reason why moral and religious truths should rest for their support on the personal authority of their revealer, any more than the truths of science on that of him who makes them known first or most clearly'.[19] Cyrus Bartol, another Boston Unitarian whose theology drifted towards the transcendental, declared: 'Here is the real, in your mind. You worship no outward object, but your thought. [God] is the thought of your thought.'[20] For Emerson, explicit relocation of this kind confirmed his belief in intuitive faith, for as higher criticism resulted in a form of comparative religion, it served to place the onus on the individual creative spirit whose own truths were as valid as any of those proclaimed by the representatives of established creeds. Milton's Michael could be replaced, as man's imperative now was to construct a personal mythology for himself and his times. The goal, Emerson noted in his journal, was the writing of 'a bible that should be no provincial record, but should open the history of the planet, and bind all tendencies and dwarf all the Epics & philosophies we have' (*JMN*, VIII, 438).

William Ellery Channing was much taken by Milton's depiction of Paradise and its inhabitants. Together they 'form a scene of tranquil bliss, which calms and soothes, whilst it delights, the imagination', he wrote in a review for the *Christian Examiner* in 1826. Adam and Eve are 'serene' in their 'innocence', excluded from any 'thought of jealousy and shame': 'Their new existence has the freshness and peacefulness of the dewy morning.'[21] There is no record that Emerson read Channing's essay (although it is unlikely that he would have missed it, as the *Examiner* was the mouthpiece of American Unitarianism and in 1826 Emerson was still firmly in the denominational fold); yet in our rush to accept Emerson at his own estimation as an original and deracinated writer, the language employed by Channing is what we might now, in an unconscious reversal of chronology, call Emersonian. Emerson's 1838 Dartmouth College Address on 'Literary Ethics', for example, echoes Channing's description of the Garden. Of the 'new man' of America (the new Eden) he declares, 'The sense of spiritual independence is like the lovely varnish of the dew, whereby the old, hard, peaked earth and its old self-same productions are made new every morning' (*CWE*, I, 159) – Milton's and Channing's paradise thus relocated to Emerson's and New Hampshire's America. Milton was the subject of one of Emerson's six lectures on 'Biography' from 1835. Here Milton's independent spirit is praised as Emerson insists on the poet's enduring relevance: 'The aspect of Milton, to this generation, will be part of the history of the nineteenth century. There is no name in literature between his age and ours, that rises into any approach to his own.'[22] Emerson's preference for Milton's pre-fall Adam is also plainly stated, as he asserts that 'by [Milton's] sympathy with all nature; by the proportion of his powers; by great knowledge, and by religion' the author of *Paradise Lost* is amply qualified to 'reascend to the height from which our nature is supposed to have descended'. Quoting directly from the poem a passage which emphasises Adam's manly and unadorned stature (Book IV, 300–3), Emerson glosses approvingly that 'the soul of this divine creature is excellent as his form. The tone of his thought and passion is as healthful, as even, and as vigorous, as befits the new and perfect model of a race of gods' (160). Adam and Milton are finally interchangeable ('when we are fairly in Eden, [they] are often difficult to be separated' (161)), with Milton conforming to Emerson's later insistence that all true writers should take advantage of the new Eden: 'To the poet the world is virgin soil; all is practicable; the men are ready for virtue; it is always time to do right. He is a true re-commencer, or Adam in the garden again' ('Poetry and Imagination' (*CWE*, VIII, 31)). As Jerome Loving has remarked, Emerson's Milton 'achieved what the Virgil of Dante's *Commedia* could not: he escorted man through the wall of flames back into the Garden of Eden'.[23] Certainly Emerson attaches less importance to the episode of the fall than to the possibility of Adam returning to his Edenic existence.

Emerson's discomfort with the fall is everywhere felt in his first book of *Essays* (1841). In 'Compensation' he maintains that 'the soul always refuses limits, and always affirms an Optimism, never a Pessimism', that man's potential growth will only prove alarming if he rests motionless, content to maintain a 'lapsed estate' (*CWE*, II, 122). In 'Spiritual Laws' he famously addresses the concept of original sin as one of the afflictions to which the adolescent mind is susceptible:

> Our young people are diseased with the theological problems of original sin, origin of evil, predestination and the like. These never presented a practical difficulty to any man, – never darkened across any man's road who did not go out of his way to seek them. These are the soul's mumps and measles

and whooping coughs, and those who have not caught them cannot describe
their health or prescribe the cure. *A simple mind* will not know these enemies.
(*CWE*, II, 132; my italics)

Here a familiar but decaying theological inheritance is likened to germs
infecting and sullying the purity of childhood. The 'problems' of which
Emerson writes are not inevitable curses inflicted upon all, but affect
only those curious enough to give them any credence. Yet, as Porte
notes, it is worth pausing to remember, given the tendency of critics of
Emerson (including both Henry Jameses) to characterise his life and work
as oblivious to the reality of evil, that in this passage he is not denying
the effects of human depravity *per se*, but only warning against certain
doctrinal diseases to which the young, in their excitable analytical state,
are uniquely exposed. It is the 'simple mind', one prior to, or immune
from, the outbreak of youthful self-consciousness, that, Emerson suggests,
can escape the infections of burgeoning adulthood.[24]

It is an oversimplification to claim that Emerson managed to reject totally his theological ancestry. His aunt's coffin-shaped bed and her habit
of wearing a funeral shroud by day and night were powerful and lasting
images of family Calvinism. Yet Phyllis Cole's recent work has thoroughly
demonstrated that Aunt Mary was far from being the unreconstructed
Calvinist of the popular imagination; she embraced many of those characteristics which would come to define her nephew's withdrawal from
orthodox denominational Christianity. Cole describes this acute balancing act as the 'holding on with one hand to New England's religious
tradition in the midst of the Unitarian–Calvinist controversy' while at
the same time 'reaching with the other toward an enthusiasm of the
solitary soul that was universalist, idealist, and eclectic. Saving Puritan
piety from the "times" meant infusing it with energies not its own.'[25]
This precarious inclusiveness is at work in Emerson too, for at times he
could mourn the passing of a certain religious hardiness and austerity
that compared favourably to the 'frivolous' habits of his own age and the
'pale negations of Boston Unitarianism'. Seventy years ago, he writes in
'The Sovereignty of Ethics' (1878), religion was 'an iron belt to the mind,
giving it concentration and force'. Now though 'men fall abroad, – want
polarity, – suffer in character and intellect. A sleep creeps over the great
functions of man . . . If I miss the inspiration of the saints of Calvinism,
or of Platonism, or Buddhism, our times are not up to theirs, or, more
truly, have not yet their own legitimate force' (*CWE*, x, 204, 205). Yet
pitted against this nostalgia for a past tradition of spiritual purposefulness
and direction, Emerson could be thoroughly dismissive of that selfsame
rigour. 'Sixty years ago', he writes in 'Immortality' (first delivered as
a lecture in 1861), 'the books read, the sermons and prayers heard, the

habits of thought of religious persons, were all directed on death. All were under the shadow of Calvinism and of the Roman Catholic purgatory, and death was dreadful ... A great change has occurred. Death is seen as a natural event, and is met with firmness' (*CWE*, VIII, 328). Elsewhere Calvinism influences an early journal entry (1827) in which he states that 'we can copy from our own memories the fatal history of the progress of sin. There is a tremendous sympathy to which we were born by which we do easily enter into the feelings of evil agents, of deep offenders in the hour of their temptation & their fall.' He concludes the passage by affirming that mankind 'falls from innocence & like Adam in Eden is ashamed & seeks to hide himself' (*JMN*, III, 67–8, 70). Such a bias is as important an element of Emerson's philosophy as the more familiar, self-affirming characteristics that might be said to describe the general tenor of his sensibility. Readers of Emerson should pay heed to Joel Porte's remarks that 'though he might come to conceive of evil as being merely privative – the absence of good – that absence, or emptiness, would always yawn somewhere at the bottom of Emerson's consciousness'.[26] Although Emerson attempted wherever possible to minimise the significance of the fall, transforming it into something less ominous and more everyday, his process of transformation does not ignore the strength of the concept. If anything his efforts to escape its Calvinist implications indicate a profound awareness of its power.

Emerson's strategy of recognising the fact of the fall while attempting to reformulate it in as positive and as unthreatening a light as possible is evident in a journal entry of August 1837. He begins by stating the stark elements of the Calvinist creed – 'Man is fallen; Man is banished; an exile; he is in earth whilst there is a heaven' – before proceeding to interrogate them in the hope of achieving liberation from their gloomy prognosis. He considers the conventional interpretation of man's fall as a concluded event: 'We say Paradise was; Adam fell; the Golden Age; & the like. We mean man is not as he ought to be; but our way of painting this is on Time, and we say *Was*.' Trapped in linear history, one in which there is seemingly no return to the golden age, the consequences of the fall are 'traditions of memory' which have become embedded in the collective consciousness. But for Emerson there is the possibility of escape from the inevitable *pastness* of this situation. The powerful Calvinist statements of depravity and human distance, he maintains, can be read in another way, as 'whispers of hope and Hope is the voice of the Supreme Being to the Individual' (*JMN*, V, 371). The fall is thus reimagined, no longer a prior event which still inhibits all men, but a present and internal condition of the individual self which acts as a spur for spiritual improvement. In a letter of 1839 this rereading of the fall as offering the opportunity for personal readjustment is again expressed: 'the true Fall of man is the

disesteem of man; the true Redemption selftrust' (*LE*, II, 213). Through
self-reliance, it seems, one can be absolved from the stain of original
sin; one can escape its historical consequences altogether by situating its
effects and importance in the on-going Emersonian project of internal
growth.

Consistent with this rejection of the burden of history, the fall as
a theological convention became attached to images of advanced age
and physical decrepitude against which Emerson's culturally youthful
American sensibility could shine. The fall acts as an agent of contrast, but
one which renders itself insignificant: it is 'a shade which adds splendor
to the lights' of those basking 'in God's eternal youth' (*JMN*, VII, 250).
This eulogising of the young at the expense of old age finds an extreme
manifestation in 'Circles', in which Emerson is at his most polemical and
transcendentally optimistic:

> Nature abhors the old, and old age seems the only disease; all others run into
> this one. We call it by many names – fever, intemperance, insanity, stupidity and
> crime; they are all forms of old age; they are rest, conservatism, appropriation,
> inertia . . . Whilst we converse with what is above us, we do not grow old, but
> grow young . . . In nature every moment is new; the past is always swallowed up
> and forgotten; the coming only is sacred. Nothing is secure but life, transition,
> the energizing spirit.   (*CWE*, II, 319–20)

The fall is equated here with an attachment to the customs and habits
of a worn-out past. Opposed to this is the forward-looking embodiment
of youth, existing outside of historical time and continually reinventing
itself. The structuring image of the expanding circle represents both
enclosure and, at its border, the continual creation of new horizons to be
conquered. The natural state has, literally, no time for history (it 'abhors
the old'), such that the fall becomes reinterpreted in terms of stance and
direction of vision. One lapses, Emerson is saying, by looking continually
downwards and backwards, by succumbing to the ageing process; the
correct pose should encourage ascension, continual forward and upward
movement. 'The man and woman of seventy' can become 'lovers' with
'their eyes . . . uplifted' and 'their wrinkles smoothed' (*CWE*, II, 319).
Man's fall, although something to be regretted, is something from which
he can escape: 'There is recovery from this lapse & awaking from this
haggard dream' (*JMN*, VII, 250; my emphasis). The etiology of the fall, its
theological genesis as a historical event, is of less importance to Emerson
than its phenomenology; as Barbara Packer notes, his emphasis is on 'how
the fallen world presents itself to the senses, how a redeemed one might
appear'.[27]

Emerson's outlook darkens significantly in the second series of *Essays*,
published in 1844. 'Experience' begins with a question that undermines

the engaging (although sometimes bludgeoning) certainty of the Emerson of 'Circles': 'Where do we find ourselves?' This immediately signals a change, and Emerson's answer suggests a place of endless indeterminacy: 'In a series of which we do not know the extremes, and believe that it has none' (*CWE*, III, 45). The circumferences which offered potential in 'Circles' are no longer visible, and the author's confusion and doubt are underscored by the employment of a metaphor last used in that essay to proclaim affirmative ends. There Emerson had described the project of individual self-formation as one of ascension and the attainment of fresh sight: 'Step by step we scale this mysterious ladder; the steps are actions, the new prospect is power' (*CWE*, II, 305). Three years later the steps return in a more disquieting manifestation: 'We wake and find ourselves on a stair; there are stairs below us, which we seem to have ascended; there are stairs above us, many a one, which go upward and out of sight.' Instead of the certainty of a glorious future through upward vision, of the belief in a benign evolutionary progression, the writer here is stranded in a psychological limbo, unaware that he has ascended thus far and, with an infinity of steps still ahead (steps which, significantly, stretch 'out of sight'), rendered immobilised and impotent. 'All things swim and glitter', as they might do for the sensitive but unacclimatised observer in a Henry James novel. Here the fall supplies confusion and the threat of epistemological destruction:

> Our life is not so much threatened as our perception. Ghostlike we glide through nature, and should not know our place again. Did our birth fall in some fit of indigence and frugality in nature, that she was so sparing of her fire and so liberal of her earth that it appears to us that we lack the affirmative principle, and though we have health and reason, yet we have no superfluity of spirit for new creation? (*CWE*, III, 45)

Worse than the possibility of life's extinction is the danger that such an indeterminate state poses to vision. Such is the bewildering vagueness of Emerson's position that even death is regarded as 'a grim satisfaction', something tangible that would at least mark out a clear boundary, a sense of finitude. But instead of such finality, the writer finds himself adrift in 'this evanescence and lubricity of all objects' (*CWE*, III, 49), desperate to 'anchor' but finding that 'the anchorage is quicksand' (*CWE*, III, 55). The discovery that the fallen state entails a slippery self-consciousness characterised by scepticism and doubt profoundly discomforts Emerson. 'Ever afterwards we suspect our instruments', he writes, as impressions once felt spontaneously and unquestioningly in a prelapsarian state are now encountered via the 'colored and distorting lenses' of our new awareness (*CWE*, III, 75). The clarity of vision obtained via the immediate transparency of the Emersonian eyeball is now obstructed by the interfering refraction of an artificial barrier. Possession of knowledge, of a dangerous self-consciousness that seems at times to equate in Emerson to experiential thought itself, is enough to condemn man to the fallen condition. As reported by Caroline Dall, 'Emerson said [at one of Margaret Fuller's 1841 conversation classes], that to imagine it possible to fall was to *begin to fall*.'[28]

Yet the possibility of escape from this fate might lie in an alternative imagining. Despite the disorientating sense of personal incapacity induced by the fact of experience, even in the midst of such powerful sensations of helplessness Emerson insists on promoting a positive outlook: 'I say this polemically, or in reply to the inquiry, Why not realize your world? . . . since there never was a right endeavour but it succeeded. Patience and patience, we shall win at the last' (*CWE*, III, 85). The appeal can only seem half-hearted in the face of what we have already read, and the language with which it is expressed hardly inspires renewed confidence ('polemically' is a little too insistent, and 'we shall win *at the last*' perhaps signals hope over expectation). But it is characteristic of Emerson that he refuses finally to be drawn into feelings of defeat. The ideal remains, even if somewhat tarnished and seeming less easily reached, and he can close his essay urging the reader not to be disheartened by the fact of the fall: 'Never mind the defeat . . . there is victory yet for all justice' (*CWE*, III, 85–6). As Virginia Woolf once noted, 'what [Emerson] did was to assert that he could not be rejected because he held the universe within him. Each man, by finding out what he feels, discovers the laws of the universe.'[29] For Emerson, the truthfulness of Woolf's assertion, although tested when faced with the sober realisation of the fall, remained ultimately unsupplanted.

II

I have shown how Emerson, although at times preoccupied by the idea of the fall of man, chose to reject the Calvinist etiology of it as a cataclysmic event in history, alienating man forever from his Creator. Instead, in his more optimistic, pre-'Experience' articulations, he came to regard the instance of the fall as of less importance than its aftermath, the possibility of a recovered Eden. The fall was internalised and interpreted as an unbalanced state of mind, a faulty optics, but one which man had the ability to rectify. Even the less polemically optimistic Emerson, panicked by the lack of certainty which he felt was the result of the lapse into self-consciousness, attempted to maintain the possibility of escape and progression from the fallen state. The fall itself was not regarded as useful, but imagined rather as a corruption of that state of sensory immediacy and naturalness which it was hoped could quickly be recaptured.

Nathaniel Hawthorne's tale 'The New Adam and Eve' (first published in 1843 and revised in 1846) offers a subtle counterpoint to Emerson's insistent stance of millenarian optimism. The Emerson–Hawthorne relationship is characterised to a large degree by an awareness on both sides of the different moral emphases placed by both men. Whilst Hawthorne could admire Emerson 'as a poet of deep beauty and austere tenderness' and 'a great original Thinker', he nevertheless 'sought nothing from him as a philosopher'. Questioning Emerson's apparently infallible ability to interpret reality beneath the surface, Hawthorne felt that 'the heart of many an ordinary man had, perchance, inscriptions which [Emerson] could not read'.[30] Emerson in return valued Hawthorne's personality but was never convinced by his work. A journal entry for September 1842, only two months after Hawthorne had come to live in Concord at the Old Manse, encapsulates a judgement which Emerson would consistently hold: 'Nathaniel Hawthorne's reputation as a writer is a very pleasing fact, because his writing is not good for anything, and this is a tribute to the man.'[31] Aside from Emerson's general lack of interest in fiction, his unsympathetic response to his neighbour's work can be attributed to Hawthorne's less than orthodox representation of two of the key ideas of transcendentalism that I have been discussing: the deliberately optimistic accommodation of the fall and, linked to it, the abandonment of historical perspective. Hawthorne's concern that the implications of such an America might be problematic was shared by other writers of the period. Washington Irving and Henry Longfellow both worried over what seemed to be a national preoccupation with future potential at the expense of the cultural past. James Fenimore Cooper's *Leatherstocking Tales* similarly documented a vanishing Eden as historical processes began to intrude upon mythical space. Hawthorne, though, faced the pressures and demands of temporality more soberly and consistently. In 'The New Adam and Eve' all traces of humankind have been destroyed, the earth has been cleansed of its corrupt former inhabitants to make way for the arrival of the tale's eponymous characters, 'created, in the full development of mind and heart, but with no knowledge of their predecessors, nor of the diseased circumstances that had become encrusted around them'.[32] Fully possessing an innate simplicity and goodness, the pair are innocents abroad, encountering the edifices of a now extinct civilisation:

> The squareness and ugliness, and regular or irregular deformity, of everything that meets the eye! The marks of wear and tear, and unrenewed decay, which distinguish the works of man from the growth of nature! What is there in all this, capable of the slightest significance to minds that know nothing of the artificial system which is implied in every lamp-post and each brick of the houses?

In a sequence of episodes Hawthorne places his characters in typical locations at the core of society, recording their incomprehension – a fashion store, a church, a court, a legislature, a prison, a library, and a bank are just some of the scenes. In each instance the reaction of the couple is consistent with an Emersonian rejection of the dehumanising effects of civilisation and its traditions: rather than remain on an abandoned earth, for example, Adam looks upwards, wanting 'to dwell among those gold-tinged clouds, or in the blue depths beyond them' (748). The narrator seems to endorse this attitude, denouncing, in terms reminiscent of Emerson's essay 'Success', the fatal effects of a material wealth that has become 'the mainspring, the life, the very essence, of the system that had wrought itself into the vitals of mankind, and choked their original nature in its deadly gripe' (758). In the library at Harvard College, through Eve's persuasion and in a reversal of the biblical Eden story, Adam vows to ignore the accumulated knowledge of the books in front of him ('the mysterious perils of the library' (761)), a decision which had been urged upon Americans by Emerson in 'The American Scholar' – 'Books are for the scholar's idle times. When he can read God directly, the hour is too precious to be wasted in other men's transcripts of their readings' (*CWE*, I, 91). In Hawthorne's tale the narrator appears to regard the rejection as vital: 'Happy influence of woman! Had he lingered there long enough to obtain a clue to its [the library's] treasures, . . . had he then and there become a student, the annalist of our poor world would soon have recorded the downfall of a second Adam. The fatal apple of another Tree of Knowledge would have been eaten.' Having averted a second fall Adam is, we are told, 'blessed in his ignorance' (761), with the freedom to construct a world in his own image, liberated from the destructive influences of the past. He has managed to escape the historical process.

However such an explicit reading of the tale, one in which the influence of Emerson is viewed unproblematically, is incomplete. In an increasingly direct way Hawthorne's narrator intervenes in his story of apparently renewed Adamism to instil a moment's worry in the reflective reader that humankind's lot may not be so simple. In the fashion store Eve is very taken with the silks and garments she finds there, examining 'the treasures of her sex with somewhat livelier interest'. The seductiveness of culture is not so alien to the pair as the narrator at times would have us believe; Eve is aware of a dormant sensation which undermines the claim of preternatural innocence – 'she handles a fashionable silk with dim yearnings – thoughts that wander hither and thither – instincts groping in the dark'. Adam is also attracted by Eve's enhanced appearance, although his way of expressing this is by gallantly placing the focus on the improvement Eve bestows on the garment rather than vice versa: 'How very beautiful! My loveliest Eve, what a charm you have imparted to that robe, by merely throwing it over your shoulders!' (749). The narrator immediately reverses this emphasis however by remarking that the episode marks Adam's 'first idea of the witchery of dress' (750). Likewise Adam's curiosity in the library, although arrested this time by Eve, leaves the impression that he will not be forever thwarted in his desire to comprehend. The tension implicit in the story between a celebration of a new Edenic innocence and the recognition that such an innocence is continually undermined and eroded finally breaks out into the open when the pair visit a cemetery and walk amid society's methods of commemorating death. The narrator wonders whether 'Death, in the midst of his old triumphs, [can] make them sensible that they have taken up the heavy burthen of mortality, which a whole species had thrown down?' Even in the celestial, primal light of their existence, the narrator proposes that 'there must have been shadows enough . . . to suggest the thought of the soul's incongruity with its circumstances. They have already learned that something is to be thrown aside. The idea of Death is in them, or not far off' (762). This tacitly repeats the thesis of another Hawthorne tale, 'Ethan Brand', where the symbol of the unpardonable sin evolves into a criticism of transcendental theory. In 'The New Adam and Eve' the criticism is less powerful, but its nagging, suggestive quality nonetheless hints that the unalterable condition of human existence is that man will attain truth and knowledge only with difficulty and inevitable hardship, and only within the realm of experience. The ideal of Adamic innocence is impossible to maintain within the context and confines of the real.

Nathaniel Hawthorne and James Senior shared a troubled intellectual relationship with Emerson; both attempted to combine in their work elements of transcendentalist hope with the tempering realities of the Calvinist inheritance. The affinity that James Senior felt towards the novelist is revealed in a letter to Emerson of January 1861. The occasion of the encounter between the elder James and Hawthorne was at one of the meetings of the Saturday Club in Boston, a monthly forum for New England intellectuals and reformers attended by, amongst others, Emerson, Holmes, James Russell Lowell and Henry Longfellow. Writing to Emerson the following day, Hawthorne is described in the following terms:

> [He] is n't a handsome man nor an engaging one anyway, personally: he had the look all the time, to one who did n't know him, of a rogue who suddenly finds himself in a company of detectives. But in spite of his rusticity I felt a sympathy for him amounting to anguish and could n't take my eyes off him all the dinner, nor my rapt attention . . . [He] seemed to me to possess human substance and not to have dissipated it all away as that debauched Charles Norton, and the good, inoffensive, comforting Longfellow. He seemed much nearer the human

being than anyone at that end of the table, much nearer . . . It was so pathetic to
see him, contented, sprawling Concord owl that he was and always has been,
brought blindfold into that brilliant daylight and expected to wink and be lively
like any dapper Tommy Titmouse, or Jenny Wren. How he buried his eyes in
his plate, and ate with such a voracity that no person should dare to ask him a
question!   (*WJ*, 1, 89)

Faced with the glare emanating from a collective combination of complacency and simplicity, Hawthorne's perceived discomfort echoes his
lament in the preface to *The Marble Faun* two years earlier. Writing from
England he despaired of an America 'where there is no shadow, no antiquity, no mystery, no picturesque and gloomy wrong, nor anything but
a common-place prosperity, in broad and simple daylight'.[33] Watching
the author during dinner at the Parker House, James Senior recognised
in Hawthorne, despite the latter's timidity on this occasion, evidence of
a firmer connection to the more complex realities of the human condition than that demonstrated by the more docile and assured members
of the Party of the Future, a grouping to which neither man could fully
subscribe.

The elder James was far from unpatriotic however, proclaiming to
his fellow Newport citizens on Independence Day 1861 his belief that
America had exalted 'man himself unqualified by convention' in contrast to hierarchical Europe, where class lines stifled the 'exquisite honor
which is due to man alone'.[34] Yet his analysis of the state of the nation was
not uncritical, and in an unpublished piece, extant only in manuscript
form, he offers a judgement on both the Old and New Worlds. The
'moral order' of Europe, he suggests, when compared with 'the obscene
despotisms of the East', has made 'an immense stride in the world's destiny': 'Citizenship, now established in Europe past all peradventure, is
the recognition of man's inward freedom or competency to himself in
the sphere of affection and thought.' What Europe is lacking though is
a 'sense of fellowship or equality'; the self-reliance is in place, but (and
of most importance) communality is lacking. America has concentrated
too much on trying to compete with Europe, such that 'the conscious
American himself has been a man of the pettiest aims, with no higher
ambition than to excel Europe, and especially England, in his own futile
way'. What should have been cultivated instead is 'the distinctively social
force of the country, a force so sweet and clean as to make all our ec-
clesiastics mean and trivial'. America is still undeveloped – 'we have by
no means as yet come to our true self-consciousness' – and the Puritan
dream of a New Jerusalem in the New World, although a little nearer,
is still to be achieved: 'We are in an attitude not of despairing inward
contemplation, but of boundless outward expectancy, not feeling that
we have yet received the promises, but seeing them afar off, and being

persuaded of them, and confessing that we are strangers and pilgrims on this worn out ecclesiastical and political earth.'[35]

In one of a series of lectures given in Boston over the winter of 1850/1, James Senior again questioned America's sense of optimism in its own future. In 'Democracy and its Uses' he manages paradoxically to strike both an even more radical position than that espoused by many reformers and a more conservative attitude towards the edifices of the past. He argues in his lecture that democracy as it presently exists in America, despite the fact that the country exhibits the most progressive form of government yet devised by man, is a merely negative force, negative in the sense that it can only act as a corrective to existing institutions of monarchy and aristocracy. Its 'perfect expression'[36] is yet to be given, its present manifestation an intermediate, adolescent stage of development which undertakes a project of wholesale rejection without bothering to construct a superior alternative:

> The urchin has outgrown the jacket and dickey of infancy, but is still a world too small for the standing collar and long-tailed coat of manhood. His actual powers are small, but his instincts are unlimited. He has the thoughts of boyhood, but he utters them with a voice more hoarse than the adult man's. He has the sentiment of freedom, but he knows no positive or manly methods of demonstrating it. He attempts it chiefly by rudeness towards his progenitors, calls his father the old man, and his mother the old woman, and gives out, on every occasion, a suspicion that they have been over-estimated. He renounces the customs and statutes of the paternal mansion, bullies the servants and his younger brothers, and hastens to involve himself in courses which afflict the older people with the saddest auguries of the future man. (4–5)

'The sentiment of freedom' suggests a simulacrum of human liberty, one which cannot hide a potentially problematic future, for in a phrase whose language echoes a transition from the sensibility of Emerson to that of Hawthorne, James Senior writes that 'When compared with the Old World, we present the amoral beauty of the morning emerging from the thick night; but the glowing morning does not always ensure an unclouded noon' (5–6). Unless democracy's sweep could embrace the whole of mankind ('If the rule of a majority be valid as against that of a minority, much more must the rule of the whole be valid as against that of a mere majority' (7)), those institutions serving sectarian interests which America had either curbed or dissolved would re-emerge.

James Senior's attitude towards these institutions, and indeed towards the whole question of America's relationship with the past, is essentially a pragmatic one. Although there is the full recognition that for the nation to be truly divinely redeemed there can be no slavish attachment to the ideas which had so corrupted European civilisations, nonetheless these same ideas hold a purpose for him. The past represents a model of comparison against which America can judge itself; it acts as a reservoir of experience, a substructure on which the country has evolved to its current superior (yet not ideal) situation. As a counter to the ahistoricism proposed by many of the most articulate voices of American Romanticism, James Senior's position is explicit:

> I beg to be fairly understood. I am very far from deficient in a feeling of respect to the past. I could not dare to wish that a single feature of the past legislation had been omitted...Let us therefore not condemn, let us thoroughly justify society in the past. What though her stringent legislation on behalf of persons has become, in the course of time, a shelter for the greatest inhumanity, yet remember the distance between our present position and the chaos out of which we sprang. For all that we now enjoy of goodness, and knowledge, and power, from all the benefits which flow from our intercourse with nature and our kind, we are indebted to past legislation, to past society, and far be it from me accordingly to attempt the slightest disparagement of it. By all the difference between myself and the Hottentot, between my children and his children, I am prevented cherishing any feeling towards *the past* but gratitude.   (25, 27)

The success of Emerson's desire to reinstate a kind of primitivism in American life and letters could only be measured, James Senior argued, against the yardstick of Europe. An inherent naturalness and democratic spirit, something that could refuse to be defined by its relation to its opposite, was an impossibility. Instead the past ought to be regarded in architectural terms as 'the foundation of the future; it is the unhandsome and concealed but still massive and adequate basis upon which the superb columns of our future manhood shall rest' (27).

Consistent with his uneasiness with a rhetoric which preached the elision of historical and ancestral considerations, James Senior was equally averse to the kind of mythologising of the pre-fall Adam figure which symbolised for many the ideal state of humankind. This figure, unfettered by social and temporal restrictions, had, in the nineteenth-century American imagination, been transformed to represent the solipsistic expansionism embodied in Emerson's self-reliant man. Walt Whitman, in lines from his poem 'Ages and Ages Returning at Intervals', had made the link between his own poetic sensibility and that of the first man explicit: 'I, chanter of Adamic songs, / Through the new garden of the West, the great cities calling'.[37] James Senior's reaction to the poet is not extensive, but his suspicions of the kind of self-aggrandisement which Whitman, literally, embodied are undisguised. In an unpublished and undated fragment included among the James family papers, he gives his estimation of *Leaves of Grass*. Although the work was 'vastly less poisonous' than its 'French, English & Italian prototypes', and although its author stood for progress insofar as he seemed less prurient than his European predecessors whose 'clandestine wares ... [were] hawked about in our college days', James Senior finally felt that Whitman was too carnal to be 'savoury', his 'over ripe consciousness' too unattractive – his writing had a distinctly detectable 'stercoracious' smell.[38] Writing in 1860 from Geneva to Caroline Tappan, he further articulates his objections. Whitman's appropriation of the word *cosmos* to describe an individual possessing a systematic, inclusive harmony ('Walt Whitman, a kosmos, of Manhattan the son') draws a sharply satirical response: 'I am not yet a "cosmos" as that gentleman avowedly is, but only a very dim nebula, doing its modest best, no doubt, to solidify into cosmical dimensions.' The superficiality of Whitman's universe, he argued, could not hide evidence of a dearth of transforming self-awareness, of ignorance of the tragic initiation essential to spiritual maturity. Consequently James Senior marked out his preference 'to be knocked about for some time yet and vastated of my natural vigor, than to commence cosmos and raise the barbaric yawp'.[39] The immediacy of Whitman's self-image signified, for the elder James, that obsession with an America rooted in images of youth and self-confidence which betrayed the nation's unwillingness to face its demons in any honest sense. Regenerate man, he insisted, knows that life only 'flowers and fructifies ... out of the profoundest tragic depths'.[40]

For his part, Whitman also remarked upon the difference in sensibility between himself and James Senior, choosing to locate the antagonism in terms of physical health. In conversation with Horace Traubel in 1888, he began with an expression of respect: James Senior 'must have been quite a man: I know several of his companions: they held him in high esteem'. (The same, Whitman felt, could not be said of the younger Henry, whose 'vogue won't last': 'He don't stand permanently for anything.'[41] James's harsh early review of *Drum Taps* presumably had not been forgotten.) Drawn out by Traubel's questioning, Whitman tells how he learned from an unnamed mutual female acquaintance that James Senior did not reciprocate his kind feelings:

> Her great claim for Walt Whitman was that he asserted virility, health, but James used to say to her as to that: 'That's just the trouble: no man can be a great poet who has not known sickness, disease,' and so on. I was always impressed with the idea – it hit me powerful like – impatient as I have always been towards invalidism. James seemed to think that a potentially great poet, before he achieves greatness, must encounter opposition, ostracism, illness: must shed the literal blood from his veins in the cause he upholds. (234)

According to this report, Whitman, the celebrator of self-consciously displayed masculine vitality and beauty, was encumbered poetically by his sheer healthiness. One of the achievements of Howard Feinstein's work on the Jameses is his establishment of a family heritage of physical and psychological disorders. Henry James's nervous breakdown of 1910 followed that of his father (1844), his sister Alice (1868), and brothers William (1870) and Robertson (1881). James Senior, as patriarch of this self-consciously sickly dynasty, chose to assert a paradoxical superiority in suffering. As Susan Sontag and Jean Strouse have both noted, illness in the nineteenth century was often conceived as indicative of a certain elevation of intellect and sophistication of sensibility, to the extent that the suffering of tuberculosis (to take Sontag's example) was transformed into a means of 'affirming the value of being more conscious, more complex psychologically. Health becomes banal, even vulgar.'[42] Writing in the preface to the New York edition of *The Wings of the Dove*, James considers the reasons why he had chosen to create in Milly Theale a character whose fragile physical state is central to the book's construction. Why should such a figure, he asks, 'be disqualified for a central position by the particular circumstance that might most quicken, that might most crown with fine intensity, its liability to many accidents, its consciousness of all relations?' 'To be menaced with death or danger' provides 'the very shortest of cuts to the *interesting state*' (*EWP*, 1288; my emphasis). We are back with James's curious valorisation of his 'obscure hurt' discussed in an earlier chapter, where injury is reimagined as an enabling force offering both the impression of human connection and the rewards of detached observation – elements essential for creative endeavour. Whitman's vibrant well-being, a condition seemingly so facile to James Senior's mind, recalls William James's characterisation in *The Varieties of Religious Experience* of those disciples of the religion of healthy-mindedness, for whom 'the capacity for even a transient sadness or a momentary humility seems cut off from them as by a kind of congenital anaesthesia'.[43] Not surprisingly perhaps, Whitman appears in William's account as a classic example of the kind of optative mentality he has been atomising. The poet, he remarks, 'owes his importance in literature to the systematic expulsion from his writings of all contractile elements. The only sentiments he allowed himself to express were of the expansive order' (83). For James Senior, Whitman's benign expansiveness was of a kind that required curbing by an outbreak of self-consciousness. Adamic man needed to encounter complication, to divest himself of a sham naturalness.

Swedenborg provided the skeletal framework around which James Senior elaborated his response to Whitmanian and Emersonian transcendental optimism. The eighteenth-century Swedish scientist and theologian had systematically set out to interpret the Bible in terms of its symbolic, psychological importance, with the creation story of Genesis signifying the internal history of Everyman: Adam was identified as the creature before the advent of moral consciousness; and Eve as that consciousness itself. Thus, in a reversal of the traditional handing out of blame, the episode of the fall was interpreted as the bringing of Adam to self-consciousness by Eve, a self-consciousness essential to his spiritual survival. In James Senior's scheme the fall ensured that man was given enough confidence to choose between good and evil, without leaving this to God. In the twelfth book of *Paradise Lost* Adam reflects on his fallen condition with a surge of optimism which he finds disconcerting:

> O Goodness infinite, Goodness immense,
> That all this good of evil shall produce,
> And evil turn to good – more wonderful
> Than that which by creation first brought forth
> Light out of darkness! Full of doubt I stand,
> Whether I should repent me now of sin
> By me done or occasioned, or rejoice
> Much more that much more good thereof shall spring –
> To God more glory, more good will to men
> From God – and over wrath grace shall abound.
> (Book XII, 469–78)[44]

These lines articulate the paradox which lies at the heart of James Senior's philosophy. Although the eating of the forbidden fruit represents a direct challenge to an instruction from God, and although such a challenge results in an everlasting sinfulness which corrupts the entire race and distances it from its creator, Adam is required to fall before salvation can be achieved. In an essay tracing the development of this idea back from Milton to the earliest Christian thinkers, A. O. Lovejoy remarks that 'no devout believer could hold that it would have been better if the moving drama of man's salvation had never taken place; and consequently, no such believer could consistently hold that the first act of the drama, the event from which all the rest of it sprang, was really to be regretted'.[45]

In *Society, The Redeemed Form of Man*, James Senior comments on the liberating effect of tragedy and its ability to disorientate and displace the sublime certainties of the self-reliant individual: 'my sense of selfhood must in some subtle exquisite way find itself wounded to death – find itself *become death*, in fact, *the only death I am capable of believing in* – before any genuine resuscitation is at all practicable for me'.[45] The contemporary ideal of man as Adam ensconced in an American paradise was to exist in debilitating isolation. In attempting to manufacture an exemption from the consequences of the fall, the condition which humankind would consequently enjoy would no doubt be benign but also fatally lacking in either focus or drive. In *Christianity the Logic of Creation* (1857), a series of letters addressed to his friend and fellow Swedenborg scholar

James Garth Wilkinson, James Senior describes the Adamic condition as 'a state of blissful infantile delight unperturbed as yet by those fierce storms of the intellect which are soon to envelope and sweep it away, but also unvisited by a single glimpse of that Divine and halcyon calm of the heart in which these hideous storms will finally rock themselves to sleep'.[47] Following Swedenborg's apportioning of the roles of creation, he continues that without the presence of Eve 'we should never have emerged from our Edenic or infantine gristle: we should have remained for ever in a state of Paradisiacal childishness and imbecility: in a word, we should have been destitute of our most human characteristic, which is history or progress' (121). Here then he links his opposition to the two strands of transcendental thought which I outlined earlier. Only by being thrust into the chaos of experience and history can humankind escape 'the Adamic clutch' (122) and hope to achieve the condition of 'the second and sublimer Adam' (127), one whose true selfhood has been formed through a process of maturity, or, as he phrases it, through 'the sacred narrative' (123). The Romantic conception of the self-sufficient isolate is firmly rejected, as he maintains that 'only by voluntarily compelling himself against the inspiration of his selfhood, and frankly obeying the inflowing instincts of fellowship or society which alone unite him with his kind' can 'a very disgusting animal' become 'for the first time a man'.[48] Elsewhere James Senior had written that 'the lion is born the lion, and the horse is born horse. But no man was ever born man; only and at most he *becomes* man.'[49] This notion of the formation of the individual through transforming episodes, sufferings and mistakes, through the 'sacred narrative', points clearly in the direction of fictional narrative and Henry James. Although James Senior was realistic enough to question the assumption that a state of innocence was the last word on the American character, he nevertheless remained an idealist in the sense that he believed that the redemption of humankind was ultimately achievable, and that once achieved a divinely ordered social utopia would result. This fact marks a fundamental difference between his philosophical treatises, in which theoretical constructions of the human process can remain untested, and James's narratives, in which his characters are situated in the muddied waters of the real and unpleasant and attempt to achieve their own kind of private redemption. James does not share his father's belief in a universal utopian spirit and so his focus is less on the benefits following that redemption than on the difficulties of achieving it in the first place – and then of accommodating the changed personality which results in the enslaving historical and social worlds of his novels. Isabel Archer's story is one of Emersonian youthful certainty and self-containment gradually replaced through the trials of experience with a mature awareness of that certainty undermined and that self-containment shown to be illusory.

The novel's notoriously ambiguous ending ensures that, whatever reading we may wish to propose, James can only echo his father's ideas up to a point – the possibility of a transparently utopian denouement cannot be sustained in a shifting and opaque fictional world.

III

One of the criticisms levelled at the Adamic myth is that it perpetuates, through the credence afforded it, a misleading impression of the degree to which even its most ardent proponents were engaged in the social and historical issues of their time. Anne C. Rose, in her 1981 book *Transcendentalism as a Social Movement, 1830–1850*, clearly demonstrated the diversity of thought and opinion among the transcendental movement which allowed for both Emerson's and Thoreau's advocacy of social withdrawal and the more practical social and economic programmes of regeneration and renewal sought by, amongst others, Margaret Fuller, George Ripley and Elizabeth Peabody. Moreover, Myra Jehlen has persuasively written on the materiality that substantiates Emerson's life of the spirit, such that 'nature itself [becomes] a sort of commercial enterprise, and establishes enterprise as part of the natural, the cosmic, the divine'. Emersonian ahistoricism is anything but ideologically neutral, but serves rather to legitimate a project of expansion and incorporation (both spiritual and geographical) that is freed from the dialectical pressures of European models of history. By emphasising spatial frameworks over temporal and historical ones, 'the conception of a New World permitted principles that in the old world were rendered relative by their connection to process and growth to become absolute . . . Reconceived as a spatial concept, process did not mean transformation but expansion'.⁵⁰ The shift from Europe to Eden, from history to geography, was indicative of an ideology of individualism that silently transformed issues of historical dispossession into ones of 'natural' appropriation.

Carolyn Porter, in her important contribution to the rehistoricising of Emerson, asserts that the writers of American Romanticism not only gave expression to social issues but were not always able to resist conforming to the hegemony of the ruling orthodoxy in doing so. By perpetuating the idea of Adamic innocence, she argues, critics seriously misrepresent a literature which, although in theory fantasised about historical escape, in practice was rooted in the inchoate complexities of the real. Adamism 'has virtually assumed the status of fiction, fostering our desire to examine the linguistic environment a novelist tries to create while allowing us to dismiss the environment in which he finds himself'.⁵¹ In reality, Romantic ahistoricism co-existed with a mid-nineteenth-century preoccupation with historical narratives, narratives which served to bolster the nostalgic vision of a golden age; an ideal of the past was imposed on the perplexities of the present. What Michael Kammen characterises as the 'quest for republican legitimacy' and validation ensured a continual looking back on an earlier period for future guidance, a strategy which masked both the precariousness of the institutions of the past and the cruelties of the present being perpetrated under the banners of American exceptionalism and manifest destiny.[52] Thus the combination of Emersonian ahistoricism and the practice of highly selective Bancroftian historiography (the difference between the two approaches is not, after all, that wide) could promote and underwrite the political and economic status quo.

Although Porter's argument is effective in tackling a critical tradition which values and defines American literature through its aesthetic sophistication rather than its ideological rootedness – essentially the thesis of much of Richard Poirier's work, as I outlined in the introduction – it is somewhat dispiriting that the argument still requires formulation, assuming as it does a lack of sophistication on the part of both writer and reader to distinguish between prelapsarian aspiration and everyday evidence of and collusion with a postlapsarian world. (Emerson's response to accelerated American capitalism is just one example of this uneasy collaboration.) Porter's revisionist anxiety about the relatively contemporary valorising of the Adamic myth by R. W. B. Lewis at the end of his book *The American Adam* is useful,[53] yet the myth itself is not undermined or invalidated so long as we recognise myths too are subject to historical pressures. They flourish in particular periods *because* of particular cultural and historical factors that grant them powerful resonances. Adamism may have been a vulnerable illusion, as Porter suggests, but it remained for many writers an important means of criticising the limiting compulsions of society. It embodied (and no doubt simplified) a profound philosophical critique of social structures pressurising the uniqueness of the American condition. Theodore Roosevelt's embrace of nativism, for example, his self-fashioning as a 'Rough Rider', can be read as an embrace of mythical Adamism in response to an anxiety about very real changes in the economic and racial complexion of America at the end of the nineteenth century. His ideal of the 'sinewy, hardy, self-reliant' cowboy possessing 'to a very high degree . . . the stern, manly qualities that are invaluable to a nation' responded to a nation undergoing accelerated industrialisation and immigration, both processes viewed by Roosevelt as threatening to male Anglo-Saxon models of American identity.[54] For Henry James in *The Portrait of a Lady*, the Adamic myth provided a character framework which, although open to systematic dismantling by social compulsions, nevertheless indicated an initial unwillingness on the part of its adherent to be read by prevailing customs and habits. Although recognisably precarious and prone to deconstruction, Adamism in James's novel represents one possible response to a particular set of social and moral circumstances.

Situating James within this dialogue on cultural innocence, which I have broadly characterised as being represented by Emerson on the one side and by James Senior on the other, results in a distinctly secular shift in emphasis. The *religious* significance of America as a New Jerusalem, a reinhabited Eden, formulated by the Puritan colonists and still the major emphasis of the transcendentalists, assumed less relevance for James, just one generation later. The religious ferment of the Second Great Awakening in the first third of the nineteenth century, and the growth in the number of denominations, sects and schisms over this period, reinforced the impression that the country was still attempting to create for itself a spiritual identity, that man's relationship with God was still the prime consideration. For James the religious importance of an Edenic innocence was replaced by an understanding of its cultural significance. American innocence now allowed the author to place his well-meaning characters in an environment in which their values would be tested against those of another, less benign culture, in much the same way that James Senior had earlier insisted that American goodness could only be validated by its relationship to its European opposite. The religious archetype of the fall, anxiously circumvented by Emerson and fully embraced by James Senior but nevertheless for both men concerned with humanity's relationship with the Divine, was repositioned by James as a narrative model facilitating character self-revelation and mature moral decision-making. The relationships which counted for the novelist remained human ones.

For James, the influence that America exerts upon Isabel Archer is perhaps best summarised by the narrator of the tale 'An International Episode', written in 1878 during the early composition of *The Portrait of a Lady* and published in book form the following year. The impressions gained by two English visitors to Newport are described as 'a train of harmonious images – images of brilliant mornings on lawns and piazzas that overlooked the sea . . . of infinite lounging, and talking, and laughing . . . of occasions on which they knew every one, and everything, and had an extraordinary sense of ease'.[55] James reinforces this atmosphere of idyllic simplicity in his 1908 revision of this passage for the New York Edition, where we are told 'of a confidence that broke down, of a freedom that pulled up, nowhere . . . It was all the book of life, of American life, at least; with the chapter of "complications" bodily omitted'[56] – the final few words here echoing his observation in *A Small Boy and Others* of 'the old local bonhomie, the comparatively primal innocence, the absence of complications' which characterised James's own childhood (*A*, 134). The plot of *The Portrait of a Lady* represents Isabel's 'chapter of complications', for as soon as she decides to leave the book of American life, as represented by Albany and the dull, comfortable world of her sisters, at the beginning of the story, her estimation of herself becomes vulnerable. The progression of the story entails a rewriting of Isabel's book to incorporate these complications in the recreation of her character. Of course Isabel's Albany and the Newport of 'An International Episode' are dissimilar in many ways: the blissful nature of the entertainment offered in the latter has no equivalent to the prison-like Archer family home. Albany is not an Eden in any concrete sense, but the state of mind that has been fostered in Isabel both there and presumably during her travels abroad with a restless father (shades of James Senior here) is one understood by Emerson to be a prerequisite to recovering Eden. The sense of a Newport 'freedom which pulled up . . . nowhere' might be taken as Isabel's defining credo for the first half of the novel. Yet Robert Weisbuch is wise to draw our attention to *The Portrait*'s opening words, 'Under certain circumstances', which establish the operation of an environment which introduces barriers and limitations, which may insist upon conditions that have to be met, myths that require puncturing. Despite Isabel's assertions of unfettered independence, this first phrase 'acknowledge[s] the reality of a world not created by the self but independent and sometimes governing'.[57]

Millicent Bell has argued that James's American characters, lately landed in Europe, bring with them little of the inconvenience of past history and relationships. For example, the past represented by Caspar Goodwood is viewed by Isabel, at least initially, as inessential to the freedom of her narrative present. In *The American* Christopher Newman's native land is an unclear, symbolic space out of which he emerges with little evidence of its potential deleterious influence; American City in *The Golden Bowl* is similarly a remote and unrealised place; and Milly Theale's New York past in *The Wings of a Dove* is never presented to the reader. Bell goes on to note that only in *Roderick Hudson* did James attempt to detail the history of his Europeanised American by representing Roderick's home-life in Northampton, Massachusetts. Significantly the author came to feel that this had been a mistake, for in the novel's preface James confessed that his story had merely 'nestled, technically . . . in the great shadow of Balzac': 'I yearned over the preliminary presentation of my small square patch of the American scene, and yet was not sufficiently on my guard to see how easily [Balzac's] high practice might be delusive for my case' (*EWP*, 1044). Reversing the journey from the Old to the New World, James's American characters more usually retain the spirit of expectation of a condition where nothing is determined by what may already have happened to them. As Bell comments, 'Displaced from their native background and past in both the scenic and historic sense, they seem newborn.'[58] James's single glance back at Isabel's Albany life is not without importance however, for regardless of his central character's wish to renounce her past, James's representation of it, although brief, provides the groundwork for a reading of Isabel during the first half of the novel. The sense of the self's newness, of its escape from both historical and social entrapment, has specific cultural and historical references which resonate in these early pages. Mrs Touchett first encounters her niece in the 'office' of the Albany house, a secluded room to which access was originally intended via a now bolted door that, if unlocked, would open out on to the street. Isabel has no desire to use this portal, and her reason is significant: 'she had no wish to look out, for this would have interfered with her theory that there was a strange, unseen place on the other side – a place which became to the child's imagination, according to its different moods, a region of delight or of terror' (23). Instead of risking an encounter with circumstantial living in all its variety, Isabel is alone and engrossed in a book – a symbolic withdrawal from the uncomfortable world of reality into a theatre of the inner life governed by her imagination. The book she is reading is revealed to be a history of German philosophy.

This small but significant detail locates Isabel in a deliberately specific Romanticist context. The influence of German philosophy on Emerson and his own notion of transcendental thought has been well documented.[59] Central was an article by the Unitarian minister Frederic Henry Hedge which outlined the 'transcendental method' in philosophy as developed by Kant and others. In rejecting an empirical (Lockean) tradition built upon a reliance on the senses, Hedge described Kant's new thinking in these terms: 'Since the supposition that our intuitions depend on the nature of the world without will not answer, [let us] assume that the world without depends on the nature of our intuitions.' By shifting the focus and location of understanding to intuitive and inherent Reason, Kant was able to free the process of accumulating knowledge from a slavish dependence on the unreliable sensory acquisition of the phenomenal world. Hedge summarises this in terms remarkably prescient of Isabel's conception of herself: 'the very essence . . . consists in proposing an absolute self as unconditionally existing, incapable of being determined by anything higher than itself, but determining all things through itself'.[60] Kant's definition of Reason thus makes up the fundamental basis of Emerson's self-reliance – the necessity of trusting the basic, essential self. James Senior held a very different conception of Kant and the whole tradition of European Romantic philosophy. His 1863 volume *Substance and Shadow* contains an attack on Kant's ideas, suggesting that the German thinker had erroneously elevated the phenomenal to the realm of the intuitive, so placing man at the centre of the philosophical universe and denying philosophy's true vocation, an examination of the divinely ordered spiritual world. Opposing the primacy given to the ideas of Reason, James

Senior writes that 'every fact of life or consciousness proceeds in other words upon the implication of a strictly conjugal tie between a sensible organization and the outlying world'.[61] Kant's apparent lack of interest in the phenomenal and ordinary is his failing, for such realms, James Senior argues, provide a testing ground enabling the mature emergence of the spiritual and eternal:

> Philosophy is nothing, if it be not a recognition of the Infinite in the finite, of the Absolute in the relative; and if therefore you eliminate the finite and the relative from knowledge, you *à fortiori* vacate the infinite and absolute, and so reduce Philosophy, with Fichte, Schelling, and Hegel, on the one hand, into a rabid glorification of our natural Egotism; or else, with Sir William Hamilton [a disciple of Kant] on the other, into the protracted howl of man's inveterate impotence and despair.   (344)

That the book which so engrosses Isabel in her study contains ideas which James Senior would consider to be pernicious is felt in the answer he provides to his own question regarding Kant's influence. He asks of it 'What has been the result to Philosophy?', replying that 'She has gone stark staring mad in Germany' (334).

James's description of Isabel's life before she is removed by Mrs Touchett to Europe is thus important in establishing the nature of her 'absolutely undiminished ... American consciousness', a phrase James uses in *William Wetmore Story and his Friends* (1903) to describe the American expatriate artist's permanently grafted native character, discernible in the midst of even the most familiar foreign influences. Such a description of Story applies equally as well to Isabel's continuing and prominent Americanness: 'This property he carried about with him as the Mohammedan pilgrim carries his carpet for prayer, and the carpet, as I may say, was spread wherever the camp was pitched.'[62] Isabel's approach to knowledge through intuition and feeling, the assumption of a benevolent universe, the highly self-conscious dedication to the spontaneous realisation of the self, all resemble Emerson's doctrine of self-reliance as interpreted by James in the chapter devoted to 'Brook Farm and Concord' in *Hawthorne* (1879). James's gloss on Emersonianism there serves as a useful character summary of his fictional heroine: 'Emerson expressed, before all things, as was extremely natural at the hour and in the place, the value and importance of the individual, the duty of making the most of one's self, of living by one's own personal light and carrying out one's own disposition' (*EAE*, 382). Emerson's obliviousness to the fact of evil (whether actual or otherwise is, as I have shown, a moot point) is echoed in Isabel's conception of her own childhood, a time when 'in a world in which the circumstances of so many people made them unenviable it was an advantage never to have known anything unpleasant' (32). Later the narrator reinforces Isabel's estimation of herself and confirms the impression we have received of her at Albany: 'With all her love of knowledge she had a natural shrinking from raising curtains and looking onto unlighted corners. The love of knowledge coexisted in her mind with the finest capacity for ignorance' (213). Isabel, lacking any substantive knowledge of evil, prefers to conceive of its existence in pictures of 'dusky pestiferous tracts, planted thick with ugliness and misery' (55), romanticised imagery redolent of the gothic novel that serves to aestheticise the unpleasant, distancing it from felt experience and thus reducing its impact.

James's understanding of evil is based on, or is equivalent to, an imaginative appreciation of sin that, if not 'original' in the strictly didactic Calvinist sense, is certainly fundamental to the human situation. Writing of Ivan Turgenev in 1874, perhaps the writer he admired above all others, this sober recognition is made explicit. 'Life *is* in fact, a battle,' he asserts. 'On this point optimists and pessimists agree. Evil is insolent and strong; beauty enchanting but rare; goodness very apt to be weak; folly very apt to be defiant; wickedness to carry the day; imbeciles to be in great places, people of sense in small, and mankind generally unhappy' (*EWP*, 998). Robert Weisbuch has argued that James's American sensibility, one chronologically distant but not emotionally disconnected from a Puritan past, accounts for the metaphysical tone of his imagination of evil. Reinscribing a theological tradition in secular or psychological terms, James 'stakes out his postcolonial claim as an American writer' at the same time as he inhabits fictional territory that is characteristically European.[63] In an 1876 essay on Charles Baudelaire, James compares the French poet's sense of evil with that understood by Hawthorne, locating his preference firmly with the internalised focus of the American writer. James's lack of comfort with the literary practice of 'art for art's sake' (something to which he directly refers in the essay) is evidenced by his coolness for Baudelaire's deliberate but controlled apprehension of *mal*, as 'something outside of himself, by which his own intellectual agility was not in the least discomposed'. For James's taste, Baudelaire's insistence on 'the nasty' has an overpowering sensory quality to it; the effect, he writes, is of being confronted with 'a rhapsody on plumcake and *eau de Cologne*' (*EWP*, 155, 156) where the appeal is not to one's moral sense but 'to our olfactories'. The Frenchman's lurid but 'passionless' imagination contrasts with the more metaphysical Hawthorne, whose experience is more valid because he 'felt the thing at its source, deep in the human consciousness' (*EWP*, 155).

Arnold Kettle famously commented of *The Portrait of a Lady* that 'it would not be outrageous . . . to call it a nineteenth-century *Paradise Lost*'.[64] Indeed although *The Portrait of a Lady* is far from being simply a moral fable, the Miltonic echoes of the Genesis story serve as a helpful, if imperfect, context for understanding James's characters. By imperfect I mean that Miltonic understanding may be appropriate for the allegorical purposes of the seventeenth century and for the philosophical meditations of James Senior, but for the novelist its danger lies in a too close identification with the limitations of the 'scientific criticism' that the narrator of the novel warns us to avoid in judging Isabel ('she would be an easy victim of "scientific criticism" if she were not intended to awaken on the reader's part an impulse more tender and more purely expectant' (53)). The Miltonic perspective is 'insufficiently flexible in its allegorical understandings, too impoverishing of a full consciousness'.[65] Moral culpability is too firmly assigned in allegory for the form itself to be of transparent use to James. We are not encouraged to denounce Madame Merle as wicked, for example, for viewed within the human focus of the novel she becomes a centre for Isabel's sympathy and understanding – '[B]efore Isabel returned from her silent drive she had broken its silence by the soft exclamation: "Poor, poor Madame Merle!"' (566). The importance of religious literatures, as one might expect of the son of a strictly non-denominational father, is finally one of artistic stimulus rather than of dutiful adherence: in a review of Taine's *History of English Literature* (1871) James refers to 'the great Scriptural *inspiration* of Bunyan and of Milton' (*EWP*, 846; my emphasis). Given this significant caveat, the Miltonic/biblical echoes nevertheless serve to reinforce the reader's understanding of James's characters. Isabel chooses to conceive of herself in terms of Edenic imagery perfectly consistent with the impression that we have gained of her delight in the beautiful and unthreatening. The narrator instructs us that Isabel's 'nature had, in her conceit, a certain garden-like quality, a suggestion of perfume and murmuring boughs, of shady bowers and lengthening vistas, which made her feel that introspection was, after all, an exercise in the open air, and that a visit to the recesses of one's spirit was harmless when one returned from it with a lapful of roses' (55). The intoxicating and balmy nature of this kind of selfhood is felt to be untouched by the existence of other gardens, other fallen Edens. Isabel remains so detached from these less agreeable vistas that her inability to incorporate them is readily admitted: 'What should one do with the misery of the world in a scheme of the agreeable for one's self?' (56). Perfectly attuned to the Emersonian delight in America as a new Eden, Isabel enthuses to Ralph over her native country 'stretching away beyond the rivers and across the prairies, blooming and smiling and spreading till it stops at the green Pacific! A strong, sweet, fresh odour seems to rise from it' (98). Emerson in 'The Young American' is similarly eulogistic about his homeland and its potential for offering both physical and spiritual succour to the perceptive consciousness. 'The bountiful continent is ours,' he writes, 'state on state, and territory on territory, to the waves of the Pacific sea ... The land is the appointed remedy for whatever is false and fantastic in our culture. The continent we inhabit is to be physic and food for our mind, as well as our body' (*CWE*, I, 364–5). In her attempt to transplant this assured, somewhat complacent interpretative strategy to the exciting new realm of Europe, Isabel experiences a profoundly disabusing awakening. Her 'naturalness' (Ralph confesses to his mother that 'She strikes me as very natural' (44)), signifying that freedom from deterministic 'natural laws', comes up against the socially conditioned and sanctioned behaviour of Osmond and Madame Merle. Of the latter Isabel perceptively remarks that 'she was not natural – she had rid herself of every remnant of that tonic wildness which we may assume to have belonged even to the most amiable persons in the ages before country-house life was in fashion' (205),[66] a warning which, at this stage of the novel, Isabel overlooks in her determination to see good in everything, her insistence that 'a charming surface doesn't necessarily prove one superficial' (206).

Isabel's encounters with Merle are central to a discussion of selfhood and the dialogue on the subject which had preoccupied the generation prior to James's own. Isabel's transcendentalist-like belief in her own perceptual abilities is demonstrated in her first encounter with the mysterious stranger at Gardencourt, shortly before Mr Touchett's death. Listening to Merle at the piano, Isabel initially decides that she is French, a romantic thought which 'made the visitor more interesting to our speculative heroine'. On learning that she is in fact a native of Brooklyn, this information only serves to heighten Isabel's favourable impression of her new acquaintance ('rarer ... seemed it to be American on such favourable terms' (185)). Moreover Isabel chooses to ignore Mrs Touchett's half-joking observation of Merle ('She's too fond of mystery' (187)) for a determined character assessment of her own: 'It was a face that told of an amplitude of nature and of quick and free motions ... Experience ... had not quenched her youth; it had simply made her sympathetic and supple. She was in a word a woman of strong impulses kept in admirable order. This commended itself to Isabel as an ideal combination' (187–8). Isabel's insistence on not only the validity of her own interpretation but also its accuracy reminds us of Emerson's comment that for the transcendentalist 'experience inclines him to behold the procession of facts you call the world, as flowing perpetually outward from the invisible, unsounded centre in himself' (*CWE*, I, 334).

The pivotal encounter in the novel's representation of selfhood is the much discussed philosophical colloquy between the two women in chapter 19, where James seems to be encroaching upon his father's preferred literary territory. Certainly James here is engaging with the same ontological questions that preoccupied both James Senior and Emerson. But by embedding those references within the dynamic form of the novel, in which held opinions are not able to crystallise into rigidity, he ensures that overall moral approbation and condemnation are much harder to determine. Merle states her side of the argument first:

> There's no such thing as an isolated man or woman; we're each of us made up of some cluster of appurtenances. What shall we call our 'self'? Where does it begin? where does it end? It overflows into everything that belongs to us – and then it flows back again. I know a large part of myself is in the clothes I choose to wear. I've a great respect for *things*! One's self – for other people – is one's expression of one's self; and one's house, one's furniture, one's garments, the books one reads, the company one keeps – these things are all expressive.

To which Isabel responds, 'I don't agree with you. I think just the other way. I don't know whether I succeed in expressing myself, but I know that nothing else expresses me. Nothing that belongs to me is any measure of me; everything's on the contrary a limit, a barrier, and a perfectly arbitrary one' (216). Isabel's assertion of the inviolability of the autonomous self, of its total independence from anything which may attempt to identify and circumscribe it, is as Emerson's in 'The Transcendentalist': 'You think me the child of my circumstances: I make my circumstance' (*CWE*, I, 334). Merle of course is far from being the embodiment of James Senior's philosophy – her entrapment within the world of social mores and pressures would indicate for him her still unregenerate state. Nevertheless her refutation of Isabel's romanticism in favour of the realisation of an inevitable accommodation that the self makes with the 'NOT ME', to use Emerson's phrase in 'Nature', is, as I have indicated, a central component of the elder James's dynamic of spiritual rebirth. Isabel's dismissal of the notion that the clothes which she chooses to wear are any measure of her is a defence of the hypothetical self divorced from the phenomenal world (and also a restatement of the romantic celebration of the naked state, as described for example in Whitman's poem 'As Adam Early in the Morning').

Isabel repudiates her own good taste as a criterion for judgement, the same Isabel who commends her future husband with 'You've such adorable taste' (261). She then proceeds to contradict herself on the matter of choice, claiming that her clothes are forced on her by society – she has no choice but to wear them. This backing down indicates, I think, a realisation on her part that to admit choice in the phenomenal realm is to admit that the phenomena chosen are to some degree indicative of one's nature. Merle counters and effectively closes the debate by asking Isabel whether she should 'prefer to go without them [i.e. her clothes]' (216), for if the choice of any clothes is not expressive of Isabel's self, would the only possible alternative, the *reductio* of a Whitmanesque nakedness, be any more so? This not only takes us back to Isabel's premise that 'nothing else expresses me', but also provides an answer to her 'I don't know whether I succeed in expressing myself'. If no possible choice within the context of actuality, even the choice *not* to choose, is relevant to the nature of the self, then the self is ultimately inexpressible and unknowable – an inner reality existing within the context of, but totally unrelated to, an external reality that passes for the manifestation of it. This line of thinking results in an absolutism that inevitably becomes a disabling solipsism. For James, as for his father, the self is not a philosophical abstraction or a transcendental ideal, and Merle, despite her social conditioning, displays a maturity in realising this. That this is a novel and not an exercise in dialectic ensures that James is able to go on to qualify and refine the impressions which the reader receives of the two characters involved in the debate. Positions held are not final ones, certainly not in the case of Isabel, and the presentation of Merle here allows James to test an argument held by his father by presenting it through a character seemingly trapped in that intermediate stage of development (the construction of a socially reactive selfhood) between naïve innocence and final individual (and thus, for James Senior, social) regeneration. That Merle is regarded finally as a pathetic figure deserving of sympathy is an indication both of Isabel's maturity and of the novelist's realistic appraisal of the difficulties of achieving even a private utopia in a much more complex and demanding world.

James structures his story in such a way that the reader is presented with two different types of plot. The first, present until chapter 36, is a variation on the marriage narrative of the nineteenth-century novel, with Isabel reminiscent of the independent-minded heroines of Jane Austen. The variation of course lies in her determined rejection of those suitors who could provide her with financial and social status: Isabel refuses both Caspar Goodwood, the embodiment of capitalist Young America, and Lord Warburton, that of aristocratic good-breeding, because their positions within their respective social structures would necessarily compromise her independence. Of marriage to Warburton, Isabel remarks that 'the idea failed to support any enlightened prejudice in favour of the free exploration of life that she had hitherto entertained or was now capable of entertaining' (117). Isabel's eventual choice of husband is consistent with her idealistic principles, for in the same way that she values her own ability to remain outside the grasp of society's demands and expectations, she chooses to see in Osmond a similar independence, a choice no doubt aided by Merle's listing of her former lover's qualities: 'No career, no name, no position, no fortune, no past, no future, no anything' (211). Because Osmond is an aesthete and seems to stand apart from a material culture of manufacturing and respectability, Isabel assumes that he is liberated from all forms of dependency. He suggests to Isabel 'no stamp nor emblem of the common mintage that provides for general circulation' (247), but rather 'the image of a quiet, clever, sensitive, distinguished man, strolling on a moss-grown terrace' (299). This pastoral image of a figure embodying a unique, unfettered negativity is what attracts Isabel, despite the fact that Osmond is a collector of objects and a cultivator of appearances. His appreciation of Beauty is as an appropriator and custodian of it: 'he perceived a new attraction in the idea of taking to himself a young lady who had qualified herself to figure in his collection of choice objects by declining so noble a hand [as Warburton's]' (328).

The first half of the novel ends with Isabel's choice of suitor made, and chapter 36 opens with Isabel married to Osmond for some three or four years and the relationship now turned sour – Merle tells Ned Rosier that they 'think quite differently' (390). This elision of detail is audacious on the author's part: in addition to omitting the facts of the breakdown James has also earlier chosen not to portray Isabel's acceptance of Osmond's proposal. He proposes in chapter 29, Isabel accepts some months later, between chapters 31 and 32, and the marriage takes place and time passes between chapters 35 and 36. James's refusal to chart his heroine's decline into unhappiness makes sense if we realise that the careful reader has already been provided with enough information about the agents involved not to be surprised at Merle's disclosure to Rosier. But it is not only because of narrative economy that James has no interest in filling these gaps. His concern ultimately is not with plotting the causes of a failed marriage but with describing the process by which Isabel evaluates her situation maturely and, in any real sense, encounters for the first time that experience of the tragic deemed essential by James Senior for human development. The plot of the marriage novel has ultimately failed Isabel, and the rest of her story is akin to a *Bildungsroman* in which the heroine comes to interpret herself and others in a more realistic manner.

The images of brightness and sunshine that had described Isabel in the first half of the novel now give way to a Hawthornian preoccupation with darkness and the soul's depths: 'Isabel, as she grew older, became acquainted with revulsions, with disgusts; there were days when the world looked black and she asked herself with some sharpness what it was that she was pretending to live for' (435). The justly praised chapter 42 of the novel (James himself rated the vigil scene as 'obviously the best thing in the book' (*EWP*, 1084)), in which Isabel approaches a greater knowledge of herself and thus of Osmond, can be read as her own vastation experience, the 'mystic conversion' (*EWP*, 1083) to which James refers in the novel's preface. Like James Senior's episode at Windsor in 1844, the outcome of Isabel's contemplation is one of supreme disillusion in which her previous notions of identity and purpose are undermined by a sense of inadequacy. The imagery of shadows and depths accumulates as Osmond's home becomes 'the house of darkness, the house of dumbness, the house of suffocation. [His] beautiful mind gave it neither light nor air' (466). The idea of vastation, of Isabel's confrontation with and rejection of a deficient selfhood, is reinforced by a use of language borrowed from the supernatural: 'her soul was haunted with terrors which crowded to the foreground of thought as quickly as a place was made for them' (460). And again: 'Her mind, assailed by visions, was in a state of extraordinary activity, and her visions might as well come to her there, where she sat up to meet them, as on her pillow, to make a mockery of rest' (472). Isabel realises that, despite her previous Emersonian confidence in her powers of perception and interpretation, 'she had not read [Osmond] right' (463), and her appropriation of Edenic imagery now incorporates the presence of evil: '[Osmond's] egotism lay hidden like a serpent in a bank of flowers' (466). The importance that James attached to the idea of transforming the everyday into the artistic and meaningful is not shared by Osmond, for whom the base reality is enough: 'one was to keep it for ever in one's eye, in order not to *enlighten* or *convert* or *redeem* it, but to extract from it some recognition of one's superiority' (467; my italics). The realisation of fallibility, attained during a night of quasi-religious intensity, signifies Isabel's transformation.

Recognising that she has been the victim of an elaborate scheme of manipulation, perpetrated by Merle, Osmond and the Countess Gemini, Isabel is prompted to consider her own moral naïvety: 'She knew the idea [of wickedness] only by the Bible and other literary works; to the best of her belief she had had no personal acquaintance with wickedness . . . Isabel had flattered herself at this time that she had a much richer view of things' (565). This understanding occurs while she is driving alone through Rome, a city which, like the Venice of James's preface, draws thoughts away from the personal and immediate to wider, historical concerns. Of Venice, where James was attempting to write his novel, he admits that the 'romantic and historic sites . . . are too rich in their own life and too charged with their own meanings merely to help him out with a lame phrase; they draw him away from his small question to their own greater ones' (*EWP*, 1070). For Isabel, Rome is similarly powerful. Its surroundings offer her spiritual succour, 'for in a world of ruins the ruin of her happiness seemed a less unnatural catastrophe. She rested her weariness upon things that had crumbled for centuries and yet still were upright; she dropped her secret sadness into the silence of lonely places' (563–4). From a solipsistic assertion of her own individuality, Isabel comes to recognise that her self is a social issue as well as a private concern. As David Minter has suggested, 'to become a responsible social agent she must master worlds, customs, conventions, mores and institutions that possess histories of their own that preclude their ever becoming wholly hers'.[67] This represents a movement from a lyrical desire for transcendence to a strategy of social involvement: Isabel, we are told, 'had grown to think of [Rome] chiefly as the place where people had suffered'; it offered to her 'a companionship in endurance' (564). What Isabel approaches is that which James characterises in his preface to 'The Lesson of the Master' as 'the high and helpful public and, as it were, civic use of the imagination' (*EWP*, 1230). The previous decade James Senior had articulated a similar conception of collective support:

> No man has been great in history with a truly *human* greatness, who has not won his way to it through suffering; that is, by painfully subjugating the rampant hell of his merely *personal* ambition and aspiration to a tranquil inward heaven of just and equal relations with his fellow-man. And to be blind to this great fact is to be blind in my opinion to the total divine worth and significance of human nature.[68]

Ross Posnock writes that we must be careful to distinguish between James's technique of centre-of-consciousness and transcendentalism's belief in *centred* consciousness (Emerson declares, for example, that the Poet is 'a sovereign, and stands on the centre' (*CWE*, III, 7)). Writing on Guy de Maupassant in 1888, James commends the Frenchman's recognition that the novel 'is simply a vision of the world from the standpoint of a person constituted after a certain fashion'. Hence it is 'absurd to say that there is . . . only one reality of things'. The world which we perceive is merely 'our particular illusion about it', an illusion which we mistakenly brandish as the manifestation of a 'universal consciousness' (*EWP*, 523). In his letter to the Deerfield Summer School the following year, James celebrates the democratic potentiality of this relative perspective: 'any point of view is interesting that is a direct impression of life. You each have an impression colored by your individual conditions; make that into a picture, a picture framed by your own personal wisdom, your glimpse of the American world' (*EAE*, 93). *The Portrait of a Lady* is structured around the disparity between theoretical/imagined epistemological centrality and the realisation by the narrating centre of increasing (and inevitable) marginality. By peeling away the protective layers of Isabel's powerful self-confidence James uncovers her fundamental ontological insecurity. As Posnock notes, Isabel Archer takes on the role of central consciousness in the novel only after the pivotal vigil scene and the sobering understanding which accompanies it: 'her structural centrality coincides (negatively) with her dawning sense that her centered consciousness is actually decentered'.[69] Isabel's proudly declared individualist sensibility is shown to be at risk, off-kilter – she is no longer upright, as Emerson might lament.

The supremacy of the individual is, for both James and his father, not an essentialist given, as it is for Emerson and Stephen Pearl Andrews. Rather, selfhood is contingent upon, and affected by, numerous and changing extraneous factors – cultural, economic, political. Although the *I* may still attempt to maintain its autonomy in the face of such apparently uncontrollable pressures, an assertion of unique identity serves only to re-enforce rather than to diminish the power of those same impinging elements. Writing of his impressions of the guests at the Waldorf–Astoria hotel in New York, James acutely points out the widening gap between the persistence of individuality as it manifests itself in forms of opulent display and performance ('this ubiquitous American force') and the some-what sinister but unrecognised presence of a larger force allowing such theatricalities to take place – corporate business, Wall Street, the capitalist economy. James, of course, is not so materially specific, choosing instead to imagine this presence as 'some high-stationed orchestral leader, the absolute presiding power, conscious of every note of every instrument, controlling and commanding the whole volume of sound, keeping the whole effect together and making it what it is'. Yet the implication re-mains that the conspicuous consumption enjoyed by the clientele of the hotel world is something which is on loan, at the mercy of this governing figure who may at some point choose to lavish his attention elsewhere. Certainly he 'understands his boundless American material', but the fact that he '*plays with it* like a master' (my emphasis) hints at a potential precariousness. Displays of individuality under such compromised con-ditions seem foolish rather than brave, because enacted from a position of ignorance. Obliviousness rather than proud defiance characterises, for James, these 'puppets' who mistakenly 'think of themselves as delight-fully free and easy'.[70] Isabel Archer's rejection of this kind of misplaced self-aggrandisement is evident in the novel's ending. Having defied her husband and travelled back to England for a final reconciliation with the dying Ralph, Isabel's encounter with Goodwood at Gardencourt offers the temptation of a return to America and the embrace of unbounded possibility. Caspar asserts:

> 'We can do absolutely as we please; to whom under the sun do we owe any-thing? . . . If you'll only trust me, how little you will be disappointed! The world's all before us – and the world's very big. I know something about that.'
> Isabel gave a long murmur, like a creature in pain; it was as if he were press-ing something that hurt her. 'The world's very small,' she said at random; she had an immense desire to appear to resist. She said it at random, to hear herself say something; but it was not what she meant. The world, in truth, had never seemed so large; it seemed to open out, all round her, to take the form of a mighty sea, where she floated in fathomless waters.   (643)

Caspar's insistence on their unlimited potential echoes a sentiment Isabel had articulated to herself much earlier in the novel after watching her rather dull relatives leave London to return to America: 'The world lay before her – she could do whatever she chose' (347). The reference to the end of *Paradise Lost* is explicit ('The World was all before them, where to choose / Thir place of rest, and Providence thir guide' (Book XII, 646–7)).[71] But by the end of the book, Isabel is unable to participate in Goodwood's words – she cannot repeat his belief in the world's largeness, even though, at this moment, she feels it to be her own experience. Recoiling from the highly sexualised manner of Goodwood's plea ('[I]t wrapped her about; it lifted her off her feet, while the very taste of it, as of something potent, acrid and strange, forced open her set teeth' (642)), Isabel fears that to vocalise agreement is to be overpowered by her suitor's discourse. Her response to such geographic immensity, after all, is of a very different register. Where for Caspar it signifies (as does Isabel) the incentive for exploration, conquest and mapping, Isabel's own location in this panorama is less assured – as with Emerson's sense of anxious drifting in 'Experience', the 'fathomless waters' on which she feels herself to be floating cannot be measured. They are beyond the reach of both empirical standards and means of comprehension. For James, Goodwood's kind of benign boundless freedom is illusory. As Jonathan Levin has noted, although many of James's central characters are 'distinctively individual', their individualities are confronted 'with the irreducible relationality of social experience'. The concept of freedom can only be entertained within inevitably delimiting conditions. The 'fine intelligence' on display in a James text 'does not transcend its environment but is rather attentively responsive to that environment'.[72]

Readings of the novel and its heroine have implied that Isabel is finally the subject of her creator's scorn: Juliet McMaster, for example, has argued that Isabel has a perverse desire for unhappiness and that James wishes us to see her that way; and Mary S. Schriber insists that, from the outset, Isabel is a consummate Victorian lady who understands the subtle use of power and manipulation.[73] The first of these critiques ignores the very sympathy which the narrator feels for Isabel and her process of maturity, whilst the second chooses to elide those specifically American antecedents discussed earlier. Isabel's rejection of Goodwood's bastardised and economic Emersonianism (in which the pioneer dream of untrammelled individuality is reduced to ruthless entrepreneurism) and her return, presumably, to Osmond, is far from the cold defeat of renunciation described by, amongst others, Arnold Kettle and Alfred Habegger.[74] Isabel returns to the scene of her error, for recognition of her own complicity enables her to retain a form of freedom, freedom not of the absolute variety but one exerted against the limits of chosen circumstance. The world of 'lengthening vistas' is ultimately a wide vacuity, and although James does nothing to minimise our sense of Isabel's future unhappiness, he suggests that the acquired wisdom and the expansion of consciousness represents a development far higher than either her life in America with Goodwood or with Warburton at Lockleigh would have attained. Roslyn Jolly has contended that Isabel's 'plot', the romantic assertion of her individuality, is characteristically defeated by the expectations of history, by the faceless force of its responsibilities and social conventions: 'In most of the novels of this period', Jolly writes, 'the characters' plots are unable to make a lasting impression on reality, and in the end are defeated by the immutable facts and incontrovertible truths represented by the narrator's historical record.'[75] Regardless of the fact that the term *history* (as Jolly chooses to use it, implying an *ex machina* power) overlooks the fact that Isabel is defeated not so much by this as by *other* characters' plots, the destruction of the romantic impulse is not, finally, James's intention. In his preface to *The American* he writes that the ideal interest of the author is 'when he commits himself in both directions [i.e. to romance and to reality]; not quite at the same time or to the same effect, of course, but by some need of performing his whole possible revolution, by the law of some rich passion in him for extremes' (*EWP*, 1062). His characters' romanticism thus remains an essential component of his art. Only a type of inquisitive mind like Isabel's is capable of the kind of self-knowledge required to adjust those youthful and ardent feelings into something more pragmatic and adult. The novel ends with a tentative beginning, for Isabel is on the threshold of a decision which the reader does not actually witness being taken. Escape from the uncharted and unchartable 'fathomless waters' involves a return to the co-ordinates of her marriage and a provisional sense of solidity beneath her ('In the movement she seemed to beat with her feet, in order to catch herself, to feel something to rest on' (644)). The kind of freedom on offer at the end of the book is not romantic or heroic independence. Instead it is predicated upon boundaries, con-cessions and 'circumstances' – the particular demands of modern social interaction. If this appears renunciatory and restrictive, it nevertheless sig-nals a more sophisticated conception of autonomy in complex societies and James's refusal to be seduced by impossible alternatives.

James Senior had warned that American idealism was prone to cor-ruption. It depends upon an egotism that, unless tempered by sobering understanding, destroys any initial noble aspirations. He had affirmed the possibility, indeed the necessity, of a life beyond tragedy by virtue of the self-transcendence that only the tragic can initiate. Opposed to what he considered to be the trite affirmations of transcendental think-ing, tragedy offered the promise of a full, divinely redeemed humanity; engagement with the complexities of living was an essential component in the development of this utopian state. James shared this understanding of the importance of immersion in experience, of a secular fall. But his refusal of the notion that experience of tragedy *necessarily* moves one into a sphere of existence beyond tragedy in any final sense marks the significant difference between the two men, their sensibilities and their generations. The transition from James Senior's predominantly religious culture to his son's aesthetic and secular one is revealed in the shift from millenarian aspiration to realistic accommodation and compromise. James places his characters in a modern social world where epistemological uncertainties and precarious identities have problematised the nature of human comprehension. Self-transcendence is limited, achieved within the confines of these rapidly shifting and partial perspectives. Isabel's 'freedom' is the ability to brave future hardship, for, James seems to suggest, humanity is embodied in this process of ceaseless confrontation.

4

Doing 'public justice': New England reform and The Bostonians

Henry James Senior died on 18 December 1882. Neither of his two eldest sons was present: Henry was travelling back to America from England; William was staying in Henry's rooms in London when news of the death reached him. On 26 December Henry wrote to William giving him an account of their father's final hours, as told to him by Alice and then refracted through his embellishing consciousness to evoke a pious image of melancholic romanticism. James Senior had faced death with calmness and determination: 'Father had been so tranquil, so painless, had died so easily &, as it were, deliberately, & there had been none – not the least – of that anguish & confusion which we imagined in London.'[1] His final illness could most comfortably be understood as something 'as full of beauty as it was void of suffering' (339). The old philosopher had finished with the temporal world with which he had been burdened and death was to be embraced: 'the "softening of the brain" was simply a gradual refusal of food, because he *wished* to die. There was no dementia except a sort of exaltation of belief that he had entered into "the spiritual life" ... He prayed and longed to die' (339).

The brothers were preoccupied with the question of respectfully dealing with their father's intellectual legacy. William was the first to respond, prompted by feelings of ignorance of James Senior's philosophy, an ignorance felt to be closely aligned with ingratitude:

> I must now make amends for my rather hard non-receptivity of his doctrines as he urged them so absolutely during his life, by trying to get a little more public justice done them now. As life closes, all a man has done seems like one cry or sentence. Father's cry was the single one that religion is real. The thing is to "voice" it that other ears shall hear, – no easy task, but a worthy one, which in some shape I shall attempt.   (William to Henry, 9 January 1883, p. 344)

The outcome of this task would be the publication of *The Literary Remains of the Late Henry James* in 1884, but of more immediate concern to Henry was his father's financial legacy, which he had been asked to oversee as executor. This was to prove a troubling task, for James Senior had decided to omit Wilkie from his will altogether, curiously disinheriting one of his sons as he himself had been disinherited by *his* father back in 1832. Although Wilkie had recently received $5,000 from his father, in addition to earlier payments, his exclusion naturally enough angered him. Writing to Robertson James on 26 December 1882, the sense of his and Bob's felt separateness from the two elder, and more obviously intellectual, brothers is strongly conveyed: 'It was a base cowardly act of father's, . . . a death stab at the only two of his children who dared fight through the war for the defense of the family and the only two who attempted while very young to earn their own living and have earned it steadily since [there had also been some fuss over a deduction from Bob's inheritance as stipulated in the will].'[2] The brothers who had shared none of Henry's intellectual and emotional contortions surrounding issues of action and vocation, choosing instead enlistment during the Civil War and more conventional, if unsuccessful, entrepreneurial careers, had inexplicably been penalised. The episode succeeded in provoking a disagreement between William and Henry that focused their minds on the issue of filial honouring. William soon came to feel that the wishes of their father should be adhered to fully as part of the memorial process. Writing to his brother he insisted: 'I know that he [James Senior] kept the feeling that Wilky in some way ought to remain responsible for the money thus lost, & this foolish wholesale will was the expression of that feeling . . . For us absolutely to ignore that element in father's will would be to cast rather a dishonourable slur on *him*, would it not?' (22 January 1883, pp. 352–3).

For his part, Henry was insistent on an equal redistribution of the estate, marshalling the family in support of his cause in a letter of typical hesitancies, written to William a fortnight later: 'So, I say, Alice feels, & so does Bob, & I therefore (as it is my own earnest feeling) again express the sincere hope that you will by this time have signified to me you assent to the division *pure & simple* (as I say), making no differences between us on account of money supplied in the past' (5 February 1883, p. 360). Where William could advance the idea of complete acceptance of the will as the best way of honouring his father, Henry was left in the uncomfortable position of feeling the document's unfairness and yet not wishing to be thought of as anything less than dutiful. To regard the terms of the legacy as a *test*, he wrote to William, was one way in which he too could claim to understand his father's wishes. 'I think we had better abide by the fact that having Wilky equal with us & not insisting on the forfeit in order to justify Father . . . The will was unfortunate, in its wholesale character, & the best way to justify Father is simply to assume that he expected us, (as he *did* expect us) to rearrange equally' (11 February 1883, p. 365). Hinting that the will may not actually have reflected James Senior's final intentions at all, James could propose the argument that an equal division of the spoils was the only way of remaining true to the memory of their father. Doing what James Senior would 'expect' rather than what he actually instructed was the justification for Henry's stance. As Richard Adams has noted, the role of legal executor becomes reimagined as one of textual interpreter, as Henry 'transforms the process of arranging his father's legacies into a grand composition, a work of translation and commemoration'.[3] The will becomes, for Henry, a document to be 'read' creatively, in much the same way that William's correspondence would be reimagined for *Notes of a Son and Brother*, as discussed in the first chapter. Before receiving the 11 February letter, William had reluctantly already given in ('division by simple fifths is by far better than my proposal' (23 January 1883, p. 356)). No doubt his initial anxieties had been motivated in part by a desire to protect the family's interest – Wilkie and Bob had indeed squandered money and both men were married to affluent women. Yet the concern not to act in any way that could have been interpreted as a criticism of their father, a concern which the handling of this financial and practical matter highlights, was the final appeal of both brothers and indicates the degree to which they were intent on safeguarding the paternal reputation from sullying from within and outside the family.

The matter of the tangible, economic legacy settled, William worked steadily for eighteen months on his tribute to the elder James's thought, completing it with a concentrated period of activity during the summer of 1884 and announcing that he 'had never been as intimate with father before'. He composed a long prefatory essay which he hoped would present his father to contemporary readers in a more accessible manner, and as editor of his work chose to regard James Senior's final writings as representative of his entire output, allocating most of the selection to the one volume, *Spiritual Creation*, on which he had been working prior to his death. Two shorter pieces were also included, the popular 1864 lecture on Carlyle (the significance of which in terms of *The Bostonians* I shall examine) and the unfinished fragment of autobiographical fiction presented in the form of a memoir of Stephen Dewhurst which I discussed in the opening chapter. The memoir had already been published in the *Atlantic Monthly* in the hope of attracting some advance publicity for the book. 'I thought it would advertise somewhat the book and in this age of publication would on the whole be no sacrifice of dignity', William wrote to Henry (18 October 1884, p. 385). The concern about the reception of *The Literary Remains* was felt even prior to its appearance.

That William chose to focus almost exclusively on the latter part of his father's intellectual career is disappointing but not altogether surprising. What is elided is the period of approximately ten years from the mid-1840s during which James Senior had enjoyed his greatest successes and popularity as a lecturer, journalist and author. For a year he contributed weekly pieces to the Fourierist newspaper the *Harbinger*, prior to its closure in 1849; and his association with Horace Greeley, editor of the influential Whig reformist newspaper the *New York Tribune*, ensured that the columns of the paper were made available for his lengthy discursions on such topics as spiritualism, American democracy and gender roles. For a few years at least James Senior was a familiar presence in the intellectual circles of New York and New England, so much so that in 1852 Greeley's *Tribune* could link him with no less august a figure than Emerson, announcing that they were 'the two profoundest and most sweeping radicals of our time'.[4] Yet despite such prominence, James Senior's position at the centre of his cultural circle was to prove relatively short-lived, a fact partly of his own making and partly a result of historical circumstance. The passing of the major phase of reformist agitation coincided with the nation moving into a more prosperous and expansionist new decade. Utopians in the 1850s refrained from advocating broad structural reform, preaching instead changes in personal lifestyle. The communitarian nature of the millennial future that James Senior had embraced became scaled down to one centred on select circles of liberated middle-class individuals. Broad cross-class experiments gave way to mildly individualistic solutions, and patience with the notion of the dissenting utopian community waned as a coalition of reformers rallied against Southern slavery.[5] James Senior was marginalised by this transformation, but also managed to marginalise himself by taking his family to Europe for three years in 1855. Aside from occasional essays on European life and character which he wrote for the *Tribune* during this period, he was largely exiled from those outlets that had allowed him as a journalist to focus on issues of specifically American importance.

The extent to which James Senior managed to isolate himself from the main currents of progressive and reformist thought can be illustrated by his response to the slavery question. Writing in the leading abolitionist newspaper *The Liberator* prior to the outbreak of war, he conceded that although the current moves for reform were well intentioned, they should be considered only as 'harbingers' of an ideal state: 'If all these specific reforms of yours claimed the authentication of some more universal doctrine . . . they would be greatly enhanced in importance to the popular conscience.'[6] In 1863 (after the Emancipation Proclamation had been issued) he was even more explicit in his doubt about the value of abolition:

> Though I have a great respect for the 'Abolitionists' personally, based upon their thorough truth and manliness as contrasted with the sordid and skulking crew who had always formed the bulk of their assailants, I yet have never been able to justify philosophically their attitude towards slavery. They attack slavery as an institution rather than as a principle; that is, on moral grounds rather than spiritual; making it primarily a wrong done the slave rather than one done the master... *The practical working of the institution has been on the whole, I doubt not, favorable to the slave in a moral point of view;* it is only the master who from recent developments seems to have been degraded by it, spiritually, out of every lineament of manhood.[7]

The idea that slavery was ultimately only truly harmful to the slave owner corresponded perfectly with James Senior's repeated warnings about the danger of an inflated selfhood. By exaggerating his power through the possession of another, the slaveholder forgot that selfhood is illusory and transient. Elsewhere (in an undated lecture probably written prior to the outbreak of fighting as no reference to the conflict is made) the elder James had sought to minimise the degree to which slavery might be regarded as a defining factor in the political hostilities by characterising the national tensions as the playing out on a grand scale of a psychic battle that would result in the formation of a spiritually mature humanity. Specific issues were merely incidental:

> I am perfectly persuaded myself that the crisis we are now passing through is not a whit more accidental than a man's arriving at manhood is accidental. I am persuaded in fact that the actual crisis is only a reproduction on a grander scale and in a public sphere of that interesting crisis in everyone's individual experience. It is a symptom of the advancing complete manhood of the race.[8]

Wilkie James, badly injured fighting alongside the 54th Massachusetts regiment, had, James Senior felt, 'become manly and exalted' as a result of his exertions: 'It is literally quite incomprehensible to me to see so much manhood so suddenly achieved.'[9] The progress towards *abolition* remained unmentioned. In his 1915 tribute to James T. Fields, editor of the *Atlantic Monthly*, and his wife Annie, Henry James would describe the Civil War in similar terms of personal development, as being the discarding (even the excreting, or *vastating*, to use his father's terminology) of impurities in a process necessary for the achievement of healthy adulthood. 'We had exactly *shed* the bad possibilities,' he wrote, 'were publicly purged of the dreadful disease which had come within an inch of being fatal to us, and were by that token warranted sound forever, superlatively safe' (*EAE*, 161).

Yet despite the consistency of James Senior's position, the unpopularity among some abolitionists of such a conservative Northern stance as his was recalled years later by James in his biography of William Wetmore Story. In remembering those people during the war who held similar views to those of his father, James described the dilemma of their situation in terms not inapplicable to that of the narrator of *The Bostonians*. It was, he writes in 1903, 'thus impossible, in looking back on the "quiet" people of that time, not to see them, as rather pitifully ground between the two millstones of the crudity of the "peculiar institution" on the one side and the crudity of impatient agitation against it on the other'.[10] Caught between the last dregs of the reformist movement (after its 1840s apogee) and the predatory and reactionary manoeuvrings of Basil Ransom, James's narrator is similarly reluctant to adhere to partisanship, reluctant, to borrow T. S. Eliot's phrase, to have his mind violated by ideas. As I will suggest, rather than being 'ground between the two millstones', the narrator resorts to a satire which is aimed at both parties, progressive and conservative, with a voice which is uncertain of its authority, leaving the question of narrative endorsement in doubt and the notion of a romantic resolution undermined.

William's omission of any record of his father's more controversial and radical essays and journalism of the late 1840s ensures that any shifts and modifications in the elder James's thinking are not traced in the book. William achieves what he set out to do as described to Henry in the letter of January 1883. *The Literary Remains* is the devoted attempt at posthumously winning for his father the 'public justice' which he had been denied when alive. But as a representation of the life of an intellect the volume is inadequate. F. O. Matthiessen's assessment of William's introductory remarks as 'an objective portrayal by the leading philosopher of one generation of the dominant philosopher of the generation preceding him' is wide of the mark both as a judgement on William's words and on their subject.[11] Henry's response to his brother's book is to be found in a letter written three days after he had received copies of it. It contains no indication that he found it incomplete and thus inadequate as a record of a lifetime's work. Instead James's concern is the attempt to combine eulogy and a continued romanticised image of his father with guarded and almost apologetic attempts at differentiation (of himself from James Senior and perhaps by implication from James Senior's devoted editor). Admitting that he had only read the Introduction thus far, he nevertheless felt that it was 'admirable, perfect' and that the extracts from his father's writings were 'beautiful and extraordinarily individual'. Like William, Henry too felt that he was at last doing justice to his father, appreciating him 'more than ever before', struck by 'how intensely original and personal his whole system was'. Alice and he had together conjured up the melancholic image of the spurned seer, turning his face to the wall and 'fading away into silence and darkness, the waves of the world closing over this System which he tried to offer it, . . . [H]ow we were touched by this act of yours which will (I am sure) do so much to rescue him from oblivion.' The generic vagueness of the phrase 'this System', combined with an attempt to instil it with a sense of significance through capitalisation, embodies the problem that Henry faces in trying to respond both to his father's ideas and to William's tribute. He tentatively distances himself from having to grapple with its intricacies (note the parenthesis in 'I can't enter into it (much) myself'), suggesting that this inadequacy is to do with his own inability to think like his father – 'I can't be so theological nor grant his extraordinary premises' – where the meaning of 'extraordinary' is delicately ambiguous. Are these premises unusually great or outlandishly bizarre, or a combination of the two? Ambiguity also permeates James's admission that he is not 'sure that the keynote of nature is humanity'. Is James's lack of certainty a failing in him, or is James Senior's absolute conviction, *his* sureness, the limitation? Perhaps sensing this tension, he resorts in the next sentence to a more reassuring image, that of 'poor Father, struggling so alone all his life, and so destitute of every worldly or literary ambition, [but] . . . yet a great writer'. James could more truthfully conceive of the relationship as one of influence and suggestion than of wholesale understanding and appropriation, one in which the general intellectual aura surrounding his father was the tangible element: 'I can enjoy greatly the spirit, the feeling & the manner of the whole thing' (*Letters*, III, 62).

Writing in March 1885 to Edwin L. Godkin, whose magazine *The Nation* had published a critical review of William's edition, James maintained that the book had 'a real literary importance' and continued to depict his father in the role of doomed and misunderstood genius:

> I have a tenderness for my poor Father's memory which is in direct proportion to the smallness of the recognition his work was destined to obtain here below and which . . . fill[s] me with a kind of pious melancholy in presence of the fact that so ardent an activity of thought, such a living, original, expressive spirit may have passed into darkness and silence forever, the waves of time closing straight over it, without one or two signs being made on its behalf.
>
> (*Letters*, III, 72–3)

If James could not feel entirely enthusiastic with the 'sign' that William had made on his father's behalf, a collection of dense, mostly theoretical, argument which did little to reflect the living 'spirit' which had so animated the family home, *The Bostonians* was his attempt at a novel that would depict the cultural and intellectual milieu of his father, linking two subjects which had preoccupied James Senior, sexual politics and spiritualism. That the original plan for the novel was recorded in James's notebook only four months after his father's death suggests the degree to which thoughts about his father's life and interests had prompted James's decision to write 'a very *American* tale, a tale very characteristic of our social conditions'. His fiction would centre on 'the so-called "woman's movement"' (James Senior too had insisted on embedding this phrase in sceptical quotation marks), a grouping whose adherents he characterised as 'old abolitionists, spiritualists, transcendentalists, etc.'.[12] James's satiric portrayal of reformers, a broad church of individuals and specialities which Mrs Luna labels in the novel as 'mediums, and spirit-rappers, and roaring radicals' (*B*, 37), draws on his father's writings (although like William, in a highly selected and edited manner) and, in a broader sense, on the literary and intellectual tradition which demonstrated a scepticism towards spiritualism and the reform impulse, often (like James) conflating them.

I

In 1852 James Senior published a collection of writings, *Lectures and Miscellanies*, which was to prove his most commercially successful volume. One of the miscellanies was the essay 'Spiritual Rappings', in which he addressed the issue of the growing popularity in New York of spiritualism and its associated arts. The so-called 'Rochester rappings' emanating from seances at the home of the Fox sisters, Margaret and Katherine, in New York in 1848 (and generally considered to mark the advent of American spiritualism) had greatly interested James Senior's frequent employer Horace Greeley. In the columns of his newspaper Greeley had announced, with a seriousness that now seems ludicrous, that he had made contact with a dead friend who had disclosed that the recently deceased Edgar Allan Poe was happily living in 'the third society, second sphere'.[13] 'Spiritual Rappings' was James Senior's response to Greeley's announcement. He begins thus: 'I understand that these rappings are on the increase in this city, and are devoutly attended by scores of people soliciting intelligence of their trans-sepulchral friends and cronies.'[14] Doubtful of the significance attached to the phenomenon from the beginning, James Senior very quickly drops the pretence of disinterested and second-hand knowledge ('I understand that') in favour of mock grandeur (the deceased are in a 'trans-sepulchral' state) and backstreet commercial seediness (the living are 'soliciting' their dead 'cronies'). As a devotee of Swedenborg he was not sceptical about the existence of a spiritual realm, but instead was concerned at the extent to which 'certain unscrupulous knaves in the world of spirits' (424) had been granted oracular status by those in the world of the living. Irritated by the way in which spiritual communication had been corrupted in the service of cheap publicity and salacious scandal-mongering ('the abject personal gossip which they deal out to us' (418–19)), he mocks the vogue of celebrity manifestations and the sense of gravitas surrounding them:

> I am told that a communication was lately received from Tom Paine and Ethan Allen, saying that they were boarding at a hotel kept by John Bunyan, and I can readily fancy the shaking of sides, and the rich asthmatic wheeze, wherewith that communication was launched by the inveterate wags who projected it. But we are also told very seriously, that the Apostle Paul and other distinguished persons, have each a chosen medium in our neighborhood, on whom to dump his particular wisdom, and so establish a depot for that community. And I learn besides that Dr Franklin, Dr Channing, and several other well-behaved persons, are turning out mere incontinent busy-bodies, and instead of attending to their own affairs, have actually turned round again in the endeavor to instruct and regulate a world, which had previously seen fit to discharge them.   (419–20)

A year later in 1853 he was repeating his belief that the genuine faculty of 'second sight' had been perverted, 'its place . . . supplied, so far as it might be, by deceit or simulation, more or less conscious, until finally the whole degenerated into sheer craft or imposture'.[15]

James Senior's response to the advent of American spiritualism was not atypical. Emerson too was amazed at the publicity granted to spiritualists during the 1850s, commenting in a journal entry that it is 'the peculiarity of this sorcery that it has stood in the teeth of the press, nay, uses the press largely for its own propagandism' (*Journals*, x, 62). Such was the success of this campaign to make respectable the practice of the occult that in 1855 Emerson included many of its devotees under a list of new professions that he felt had established themselves that year. Along with the landscape gardener, the railroad man and the daguerreotypist could be found 'the sorcerer, rapper, mesmerist, medium' (*Journals*, VIII, 574). The decline of traditional denominations, he believed, had encouraged this growth of spurious beliefs and practices under the guise of religion. In 'The Man of Letters', a lecture given at Dartmouth College in 1863, he identified spiritualism with superstition and charged his countrymen with vainly seeking refuge in an unholy trinity of 'Rome, Mesmerism, Spiritualism . . . as if for want of thought' (*CWE*, x, 245).

William Dean Howells, in his 1916 memoir of his youth, noted that in his hometown of Ohio spiritualism was 'rife in every second house in the village, with manifestations by rappings, table-tippings, and oral and written messages from another world through psychics of either sex'.[16] Ten years earlier Howells, still recalling his years on the Western Plain, described the connection which quickly formed between spiritualism and social radicalism, whereby the advocates of socialism, abolition, women's rights, and free love felt that they received angelic sanction for their programmes. Such people 'tested more new religions and new patents than have ever been heard of in less inquiring communities. When we first came among them they had lately been swept by the fires of spiritualism . . . They were ready for any sort of millennium, religious or industrial, that should arrive.'[17] Horace Greeley's role in popularising spiritualism has already been mentioned; Albert Brisbane, the bringer of Fourierism to America, attended trance sessions in New York in 1847, pronouncing that spiritual manifestations 'contained a reality'; and George Ripley and Parke Godwin, one-time members of Brook Farm, were so impressed by the then popular medium Andrew Jackson Davis that they endorsed his book of revelations in the *Harbinger*, Ripley proclaiming Davis 'the most surpassing prodigy of literary history'.[18] The connection between spiritualists and certain kinds of reformers was not accidental, both parties sharing certain ideological and emotional affinities, notably the view that humans were perfectible and that nature was benign. Their common interest in the writings of Swedenborg reflected not simply a fascination with a Protestant alternative to Dante's paradise but a belief that there existed demonstrable 'correspondences' between spiritual and material worlds. Like Fourierists, spiritualists viewed the world as a divine machine whose material and spiritual parts operated according to the same principles of natural law. Yet the marriage between the two movements was brief, for as spiritualism became more commercialised, showing little interest in a formal alliance with a waning utopian movement, it alienated many of the writers and professionals previously drawn to it. By the mid-1850s nothing in its favour was heard from Ripley, Godwin or William Henry Channing (another one-time supporter), and Horace Greeley too became wary of defending mediums. Yet despite the brevity of the relationship, social reform and spiritualism were thought of as closely connected by the reading public, and for many writers of the mid-nineteenth century this pernicious combination proved a productive target for satire and sensationalised exposé, creating a literary tradition to which Henry James would himself contribute three decades later. Both Orestes Brownson's *The Spirit Rapper: An Autobiography* (1854) and the pseudonymous Fred Folio's *Lucy Boston; or, Women's Rights and Spiritualism, Illustrating the Follies and Delusions of the Nineteenth Century* (1855) make the link between reform and the occult explicit.

Brownson, a one-time member of the Brook Farm community, had converted to Catholicism in 1844, convinced that 'true American literature will be the product, not of Protestant, but of Catholic America'.[19] Rome was the last stop on a promiscuous religious journey which had seen him reject his strict Puritan upbringing in favour of, successively, presbyterianism, universalism and unitarianism. This theological restlessness led one contemporary chronicler to describe Brownson as 'an experimenter in systems, a taster of speculations, [who] passed rapidly from one phase to another, so that his friends ascribed his steadfastness to Romanism, to the fatigue of intellectual travelling'.[20] The narrator of Brownson's novel similarly occupies a state of religious restfulness, sliding from an interest in mere amateur mesmeric activity into apocalyptic spiritualistic demonism, before finally embracing Catholicism on his deathbed. In the preface the reader is informed that spiritualism's early spokesmen affirm the connection with 'modern philanthropy, visionary reforms, socialism . . . revolutionism'. The narrator declares that such movements – with their hoards of 'seers and seeresses, enthusiasts and fanatics, socialists and communists, abolitionists and anti-hangmen, radicals and women's rights men of both sexes' (a list which surpasses James's own 'mediums, and spirit-rappers, and roaring radicals') – are the 'spirit of the age'.[21] Encouraged by an inquisitive and philanthropic sensibility, he places his occult gifts at their disposal (specifically at the disposal of Priscilla, a married feminist with whom he forms an intellectual alliance). Believing that the spread of rappings throughout America and Europe has successfully 'set afloat a system which . . . would supplant Christianity' (67), humankind's real foe in the process of reform, the narrator sits back to admire his achievements only to be stabbed (fatally, as it turns out) by Priscilla's husband, who with his wife has converted to Catholicism. The final third of the book is devoted to deathbed debates on the nature of spiritualism between the narrator and a Mr Merton in which all points of view are considered: that the phenomenon is hallucinatory, mesmeric, truly angelic. Of course each argument is won by Merton, the author-manqué, who convinces the narrator that the influence is demonic, prompting his embrace of Catholicism. The novel concludes with the comforting assertion that 'good is greater than evil, and love stronger than hell' (234).

Brownson's book is something of a hybrid, attempting to combine elements belonging to the novel, the romance, biography, and the theological treatise, elements which the author admitted had been 'thrown together' (1) in the cause of presenting his case. More conventional in terms of a fictional narrative form is Folio's *Lucy Boston*. Aiming a satirical swipe in its title both at the city of reformers and at one of reform's prominent enthusiasts, the feminist Lucy Stone, Folio's work warns against a conspiracy of female spirits plotting to extend the rule of women to earth through spiritualism, 'the talisman under which woman, casting her banner to the breeze will bear it onward from victory to victory, till it floats proudly in the noontide blaze of political power'.[22] The author's preface, like Brownson's, makes clear the book's purpose: 'Written, as it is, to expose to public contempt the two greatest humbugs of modern times, it will be read by all sensible people, who are both disgusted with the follies and pained by the evils of Spiritualism and Women's Rights' (viii). With his hitherto serene and uncomplicated life invaded by wild rappings and spectral presences, Amaziah Badger, through the prompting of a mermaid-like manifestation which tells him of the coming dominance of women, is suddenly transformed into an appreciator of all things feminine – 'a new era in his existence now dawned upon him' (27). At a women's convention (satirically based, perhaps, on the Seneca Falls meeting of 1848), Badger is impressed by the mannishly clad, short-haired Lucy Boston. She it is who pens the declaration which, after much squabbling among the other women (including a Mrs Peabody, surely no coincidence – Elizabeth was later a controversial target in *The Bostonians*), defines the convention's position: 'As woman was evidently the mainspring to human activity, she must of course be regarded as the normal force, not only of the first impulse, but also of its continuance . . . [W]oman is the motive power of the world' (99). The narrator's reaction to this exhibition of female stridency is thoroughly dismissive, acidly derogating the meeting as merely a symptom of summer madness: 'The hour for the assembling of congregated wisdom, philanthropy, and injured innocence, was at that precise moment when the sun was highest, and shone the hottest' (74). Boston and her crudely named male associates (the clairvoyant Fungelhead, Dr J. Socrates Nozzelman and Judge Addlehead) prove unable to govern. Lucy resigns her office in order to embrace conformity and marriage, and Nozzelman is arrested for murdering his patients.

Although there is no evidence to suggest that James had read either *Lucy Boston* or *The Spirit-Rapper*, both novels are important for their participation in the development of the intellectual and cultural currency from which *The Bostonians* emerged.[23] But whereas Brownson and Folio had written in response to what they perceived to be a current danger, Bayard Taylor's *Hannah Thurston: A Story of American Life* was written in 1863, looking back – like James's novel – on the reform movements of a previous decade. Taylor's plot, like that of *The Bostonians*, recounts the liberation of the eponymous heroine, a young Quaker feminist, from an apparently successful career in public speaking on reform issues by one Max Woodbury, a wealthy man with a distinct aversion to the two most popular enthusiasms of the day, 'Spiritualism and Women's Rights'.[24] Taylor characterises these as 'peculiarities' of an American culture that placed more value on intellectual 'activity' than on intellectual 'development' (I, vi; I, 192), much in the same way that James satirises the ineffectual sediment of a once-golden era of Bostonian reform. Although Taylor had selected sincere Quakerism rather than the less respectable world of the trance medium as the peculiar aspect of his heroine's background, Ransom's outspoken scorn of women's capacity for public life and his elevation of their domestic role is only a more aggressive and ironically conceived version of the views of Taylor's gentlemanly but inflexible Woodbury. There is one further correspondence: James's Selah Tarrant, Verena's father, bears a close resemblance to the itinerant magnetic medium of Taylor's novel, Dyce, whose powers are similarly based more on showmanship and opportunity than on genuine occult possession:

> [Dyce] led a desultory life, here and there, through New York and the New England States, presiding at spiritual sessions in the houses of the believers, among whom he had acquired a certain amount of reputation as a medium. Sometimes his performances were held in public (admittance ten cents), in the smaller towns, and he earned enough in this way to pay his necessary expenses. When he discovered a believing family, in good circumstances, especially where the table was well supplied, he would pitch his tent, for days or weeks, as the circumstances favoured. (II, 55)

A drifting entertainer, Dyce had preached the doctrine of perfectionism at Aqueanda, a utopian enclave which many of Taylor's readers would have associated with the Oneida Community founded by John Humphrey Noyes in 1848, a communitarian enterprise practising 'complex marriage' derived from Noyes's interpretation of primitive Christianity. At Aqueanda, so Dyce enthuses to a potential female convert, 'those selfish institutions, marriage and the right of property' had been replaced by 'free love and communal labour' (II, 52). In *The Bostonians* Selah Tarrant's experience of a utopian community had been at Cayuga, now less than enthusiastically defined by Selah's wife as a place 'where there were no wives, or no husbands, or something of that sort'. There Selah had been '"associated" with a celebrated medium'. James's highlighting of the word in this passage of free indirect speech is suggestive of both Mrs Tarrant's unspoken disapproval and James's own ironic slant (*B*, 93, 94).

James makes no reference to *Hannah Thurston* in his writings, yet the fact that he was familiar with at least three other of Taylor's works invites speculation that he may have been acquainted with the novel. He had dismissingly reviewed Taylor's second fiction, *John Godfrey's Fortunes* (1864) in the *North American Review*, deciding that its author lacked 'that union of good sense and good taste which forms the touchstone of the artist's conceptions' and concluding with the observation that 'to write a good novel is a work of long labour, of reflection, of devotion; and not in any degree an off-hand piece of business' (*EAE*, 625). Taylor's work evidently fell far short of these criteria, but this judgement was felt to be too strong by the *Review*'s editor, Charles Eliot Norton, and the review went unpublished.[25] Although Taylor was reviewed by James only once more (a dismissive estimation of his 1874 drama-manqué *The Prophet*, a thinly veiled account of the birth of Mormonism),[26] James makes reference to his translation of Goethe's *Faust* (1870–1) in *The Bostonians*. Olive Chancellor, encouraging Verena's growing enthusiasm for the women's movement, asks her new disciple if she understands German: 'Do you know "Faust"?' said Olive. ' "*Entsagen sollst du, sollst entsagen!*" ' This however is a misquotation, for Faust's line is actually 'Entbehren sollst du! sollst entbehren!', and the distinction is crucial. Both *entsagen* and *entbehren* are verbs meaning to renounce or to refrain, but their emphases are quite different. Grimm's *Deutsches Wörterbuch* defines 'entbehren' (in the sense in which Goethe uses it) as 'zuweilen ohne casus', to give up without cause, without reason (definition 1). Olive's 'entsagen' has a much more proactive, less helpless bias, with little of the despair associated with Goethe's choice of word. That Olive manages to both misquote Goethe and Taylor's translation of Goethe ('Thou shalt abstain – renounce – refrain!' is Taylor's line, not Olive's renounce, refrain, abstain ordering) has suggestive significances. Olive misunderstands the dejection behind Faust's line (he is lamenting the world's denial of possibility for him, not announcing a regime of denial essential to the achievement of social reform!). Moreover, if we accept for a moment that James was familiar with *Hannah Thurston* and its dismissal of the women's movement, there is an intertextual irony in Olive's ignorance of that novel if she is able to cite Taylor here with such approval (*B*, 107).[27]

Spiritualism and reform had thus been linked in the imagination of writers in America since the 1850s – James's novel evolves out of a tradition of twin-pronged satire already well established. His father too had consistently warned of the dangers of spiritualism and of its practice by manipulative charlatans. But whereas James Senior's anxieties about both the source of spiritualism and its exploitation in the service of entertainment were unwavering, that other issue of much public debate which seemed to be for many dangerously coupled to the occult, the proper role of women, proved to be a less stable (and more embarrassingly controversial) topic for him. By the late 1840s, with utopian communitarian reform movements already on the wane, interest in Charles Fourier's social philosophy became focused less on his discredited economic blueprint than on those aspects which proposed the theory of 'passional attraction', liberating the individual from bourgeois family structures and the sterility of unhappy marriages to a realm of sexual freedom in which the wishes of that individual took precedence over societal fetters.[28] James Senior was responsible for the American publication of the first Fourierist tract that concentrated solely on such sexual theories, his anonymous 27-page translation in 1848 of Victor Hennequin's *Love in the Phalanstery*. (An article in the *Harbinger* revealed the identity of the translator.[29])

Existing relations between the sexes, Hennequin argued, were defined by societal fetters and restrictions that undermined the possibility of marital success from the outset: 'Nous pensons, ou plutôt nous savons que les relations entre les sexes sont actuellement un foyer de mensonage, de déception, de maneuvres cupides, une occasion de marchés infâmes; nous savons qu'elles engendrent l'adultère, la prostitution, la contagion, l'avortement, l'infanticide, la paternité fictive.'[30] In the utopia of Fourier's imagination, Hennequin suggests, 'on refuse de s'enchaîner par des liens exclusifs, indissolubles', with relations dictated not by material considerations but by personal feeling ('jouissances du cœur') (37). Writing in the preface to his translation, James Senior disclosed his hope that the volume would replace lurid rumour with facts, to 'provoke the attention of honest minds to the truths involved in these views'.[31] In an essay 'Free love – marriage', extant only in manuscript form, he could further assert that 'No reasonable man I think will deny that free-love is far more consonant with the heart's instincts than enforced marriage':

> Thus at this day we are confronted with the free-love speculation, and invited to assist at the new gospel it offers of the world's renovation through an equalization of love and marriage, or the release of concubinage from any further control of the conjugal sentiment. These reformers are bold enough to maintain in fact that love is its own end, its own sufficient justification, and should be held to the sole responsibility of its proper issues... [Free love is] an enormous expansion of the social force in humanity.[32]

Yet James Senior's support for the movement was quickly diluted, for in a newspaper article written after his identity as Hennequin's translator was revealed, he discloses the strictly theoretical nature of his endorsement: although anticipating the day when 'the private will of the parties' will be the only consideration in sexual contact, a time when society will approve either an 'exclusive' or a 'varied alliance', depending upon an individual's wishes, nevertheless (and with some relief) he states that the sexually liberated future must wait for a 'superior social order'. A later article further indicates his wavering commitment, for although depicting love in a future society he nevertheless professes himself 'unconscious... of any desire after greater passional liberty in any sphere, than the present constitution of society affords'.[33] Reaction to the Hennequin book was immediate and, from conservative New York, harsh – James Senior was involved in an often fierce debate in the pages of the *Harbinger* with an evangelical minister, A. E. Ford, which lasted until the paper's closure in February 1849.[34] He was stung too by being linked in the eyes of the reading public with the ideas of his more radical acquaintance Marx Edgeworth Lazarus, who, in his uncompromising book *Love vs. Marriage* (1852), had not only declared the arrival of sexual utopia but had offered an intimate physiological analysis of how it was being enjoyed. James Senior and Albert Brisbane shared his views, Lazarus claimed, 'although considerations entirely personal may prevent them from taking openly the same ground'.[35] The elder James frequently managed to give the impression of being a lately arrived fellow-traveller, enthusing for people and ideas before realising either his lack of sympathy for them (his relationship with Emerson is a good example of this) or the full implication of his support of them (as in this brush with the anarchic world of the free-love advocates and the radical fringes of sexual politics). That a position he seemed to have expounded not from any real sense of conviction but rather from ideological duty should attract such uncomfortable publicity, caused him to pull back from an embrace of social radicalism: this period effectively marks the point at which his thinking began to turn in the direction of sexual conservatism, of woman offering man spiritual succour rather than enjoying the benefits of a relationship based on absolute equality and her own desires.

James Senior had met with the leaders of Oneida community, which had advocated free love, in the late 1840s. Noyes had written approvingly of James Senior's apparent support of its sexual practices, declaring that he 'handled his weapons with great ability, and exhibited powers of logic and analysis which we have rarely seen surpassed'.[36] However, recollecting in 1852 his encounter with Oneida's 'leading men', the elder James was keen to distance himself from these '*ultra* – that is to say, consistent – Calvinists' whose fanaticism had led them beyond 'common sense'. His visit had been merely to lecture them on their 'disorderly lives'.[37] Although in 1870 Noyes would maintain in his *History of American Socialisms* that James Senior had 'continued faithful to both Swedenborg and Fourier, *to the present time*' (my emphasis), the elder James's advocacy of Fourier, especially once the Frenchman's theories on sexual conduct became the central focus of attention, was by then less than wholehearted.[38] His flirtation with sexual anarchism was firmly a thing of the past by 1875, when Henry James reviewed Charles Nordhoff's *The Communistic Societies of the United States* for the *Nation* magazine. The book, an idealising account of nineteenth-century American utopian communities (James felt that Nordhoff tended to 'dip his pen into rose-color' (*EAE*, 560)), interested its reviewer with a 'most curious' section on the Oneida community (*EAE*, 566). Reading about this enterprise, where the 'ladies and gentlemen are all indifferently and interchangeably each other's husbands and wives', James felt that 'morally and socially it strikes us as simply hideous'. He considered Noyes to be 'very skilful' in engineering economic prosperity, yet also toyed with the word '"magnetic"' as applied to Oneida's leader by his followers, a word whose association with spiritualism James must have been aware of and whose power he undermines by surrounding it with doubting quotation marks (*EAE*, 567). In 1875 James Senior's earlier interest, however fragile, in a fundamental reorganisation of sexual conduct is forgotten, as the family view on Oneida is confirmed as consistent from one generation to the next, prior to the disparaging reference made to the community in *The Bostonians*.

The elder James's earliest published articulation of his newly embraced conservative views on the woman question appeared in 1853 (less than a year after Lazarus had named him as a fellow-radical) in the March volume of *Putnam's Monthly*. 'Woman and the "Woman's Movement"' ('"the woman's movement," as it is somewhat ambitiously called', he sceptically notes[39]) illustrates its author's adherence to the popular mid nineteenth-century conception of woman as spiritual instructor of man. Whereas individual women may (ineffectually) 'read lectures, or write paragraphs and pamphlets upon the sufferings of the poor maidens who lack suitable and healthy employment', woman (in the generic sense) is to be valued for 'her disinterested affection, her cheerful self-denial, her blithe and genial activity, and the power which these things give her to redeem the longest day from tedium' (281). Women's reformist aims are 'vagaries' (282) when compared to the role of nurturing man during his respite from the process of nation-building: she 'comes to pitch the white tent of her innocence beside him, and make his otherwise inevitable wilderness blossom like the rose' (283). Essentialised difference between the sexes is fundamental for James Senior, indeed the writer Madame de Staël (so beloved of the transcendentalists) is criticised for her 'essential masculinity': despite her 'force of passion, and even greater variety of intellectual endowment' she has repressed her true femininity (287). De Staël would have found 'both her truest happiness and her truest dignity in fulfilling the part of wife, or ministering angel to man' (285).

A description of the well-bred woman of 1830, published in the bible of female decorum, the *Ladies' Magazine*, encapsulates in a breathlessly devotional manner the ideology to which James Senior now subscribed:

> See, she sits, she walks, she speaks, she looks – unutterable things! Inspiration springs up in her very paths – it follows her foot-steps. A halo of glory encircles her, and illumines her whole orbit. With her, man not only feels safe but is actually renovated. For he approaches her with an awe, a reverence, and an affection which before he knew not he possessed.[40]

Here was a sentiment which sought to obscure or elide women's economic function, a sentiment which defined femininity always in terms of its effects on man. Woman is something to be perceived and reacted to (note the injunction to the reader to 'See'), an angelic being pleading for value, worthy because she is able to initiate moral change by offering protection and spiritual succour. An article published seventeen years after his initial essay in *Putnam's* showed that James Senior had now firmly appropriated such thinking. The appearance in America in 1869 of two books taking polar views on the subject of women's role in society, John Stuart Mill's plea for female liberty *The Subjection of Women* and Horace Bushnell's anti-feminist tract *Woman's Suffrage: the Reform Against Nature*, were the ostensible subjects of the elder James's review written for the *Atlantic Monthly* in January 1870. Although praising Mill's work as 'the one best worth reading that the controversy has called forth', he nevertheless felt that Mill was fundamentally in error in suggesting that, other than physiological differences, there was inherently nothing to discriminate man from woman (and vice versa).[41] Mill's argument, as James Senior summarised it, was that 'the distinction between man and woman . . . is purely organic. There is really nothing corresponding to it in either the rational or moral plane. Sex is an attribute of matter, not of mind' (68). For the elder James the dissimilarity of the sexes was essential, a belief based on his reading of the biblical Eden story in which the fall is necessary for the gaining of spiritual maturity, and in which Eve, far from being demonised as the temptress responsible for Adam's expulsion from the garden, is man's saviour. Thus '[Eve's] seed and not his [is] the pivot upon which the redemption of the race from the hardships imposed upon it by his credulity or unbelief is appointed to turn' (67). The reformist aspirations of woman in the temporal world will necessarily end in failure, he maintains, unless first she realises the importance of her 'inward and spiritual qualities which lift [man] above the brute' (68). The marriage tie offers the ideal opportunity for the exertion of this spiritual, civilising influence, 'abasing the male sway in our nature, and exalting the feminine influence to its place' (69). Free love is no longer a possibility for James Senior, for men and women 'have no right' to live together 'without the amplest previous social authorization'; 'the welfare of society is primary', taking precedence over 'the welfare of persons' (71).

Henry James had read Mill's book during the summer of 1869, describing getting to the end of it to William (who also reviewed it and Bushnell's title for the *North American Review* in October that year) as his 'own intellectual feat'.[42] His response to his father's review indicates a degree of shared sentiment. Writing to him from Geneva in January 1870, he enthuses, 'Your *Atlantic* article I decidedly like – I mean for matter. I am very glad to see someone not Dr Bushnell and all that genus insist upon the distinction of the sexes. As a mere piece of writing moreover I enjoyed it immensely' (*Letters*, I, 187–8). Bushnell, belonging to the 'genus' of Congregationalism, would be expected to articulate anti-feminist views; the elder James's piece is more credible, Henry seems to be implying, coming as it does from a non-denominational voice. Other reactions to James Senior's writing followed: in March Henry tells

William that 'among the things I have recently read is Father's *Marriage* paper in the Atlantic [a reference to the article 'Is Marriage Holy?', a copy of which William had sent the previous month] – with great enjoyment of its manner and approval of its matter. I see he is becoming one of our prominent magazinists' (*Letters*, I, 212); and later that month he commiserated with his father on the 'rather flippant' nature of the *Nation's* review of his January article (*Letters*, I, 217).

Certainly, then, James was aware of and receptive to James Senior's ideas on the relationship between the sexes, and his satire of the reform movement in *The Bostonians* fictionalises to a degree his father's scepticism about the efficacy of temporal and secular agitation. In Basil Ransom too are incorporated many of the ideas that James Senior proclaimed after his radical interlude. Yet in an attempt to write a book with a distinctly American locale and subject, James produces a novel which is uncertain of its position with regard to its principal ideological players. Far from being a crude satire on spiritualism and reform, with its targets easily identifiable, as is the case with Brownson's, Folio's and Taylor's efforts, James's attempt to validate his father's memory through fiction is finally undermined by the competing pressures of fiction itself – pressures in which various voices jostle for the reader's attention and between which the narrator is somewhat apologetically unable (or unwilling) to choose. *The Bostonians* is far from being merely a narrative constructed around an ideological position based solely on James Senior's post-1850 analyses of gender difference, as argued most recently by Alfred Habegger in his book *Henry James, and the 'Woman Business'*. James's appropriation of his father, while at times supporting a reading of the novel that stresses its satire of women reformers, also encompasses an awareness of James Senior's recently republished (and less than flattering) views on Thomas Carlyle. Such Carlylean elements serve to complicate any reading that proposes that the novel's author was motivated solely by the desire to honour his father through anti-feminist satire.

II

Alfred Habegger's analysis of *The Bostonians* is founded upon present-day assumptions about the nature of the relationship between the sexes. In reading the text ahistorically he loads on to it late twentieth-century feminist expectations which are committed to a progressive liberalism or to a more enlightened sexual politics. James's apparent approval and use of his father's ideas on gender separateness, ideas which (as I have suggested) were hardly controversial at the time, causes him to become 'an unwilling medium', preaching a reactionary message until finally reaching 'the nasty end of a novel few readers seem to have followed'.[43] Habegger's work is useful in highlighting for the first time those influences that do exist between the novelist and his father: James's endorsement of James Senior's marriage papers and his picking out from them the idea of 'the distinction of the sexes' are relevant to the novel he would later come to write. The subject of difference – of clearly demarcated boundaries of class, sex, function – pervades the book. North and South, freedom and slavery, speech and writing, public and private – these oppositions are linked to the difference between masculine and feminine in the narrative, most obviously voiced by Basil in a diatribe revealing his desire to save his own sex 'from the most damnable feminization!':

> I am so far from thinking, as you set forth the other night, that there is not enough woman in our general life, that it has long been pressed home to me that there is a great deal too much. The whole generation is womanized; the masculine tone is passing out of the world; it's a feminine, a nervous, hysterical, chattering, canting age, an age of hollow phrases and false delicacy and exaggerated solicitudes and coddled sensibilities, which if we don't soon look out, will usher in the reign of mediocrity of the feeblest and flattest and the most pretentious that has ever been.   (B, 327)

Fearing, like the narrator of Fred Folio's crude story, a society dominated by women in which the differentiating presence of the strong male has been dissipated, Basil's project is the displacement of his lost authority as a Southern man over the slave on to the New England woman, herself a symbol (at least in the figure of Miss Birdseye) of the golden age of abolition. He articulates the protest of the individual figure against the levelling tendencies of all democracies. Here though, a certain (or rather, uncertain) distance is maintained between the linking of individualism with Basil's character, based as it is on the Southern gentleman, by the 1880s already established in the North as a cultural image of dubious worth. In 1862 Emerson had declared that 'in the Southern States, the tenure of land and the local laws, with slavery, give the social system not a democratic but an aristocratic complexion' (*CWE*, XI, 324–5). Mark Twain's *Life on the Mississippi* (1883) built on this observation in its lengthy protest at the South's assimilation of the aristocratic romanticising found in Walter Scott's novels. As John Fraser has remarked, Scott's Saxon culture, of 'a supposedly primitive but in fact proud, sturdy, and morally admirable slaveowning people' that 'refused to acknowledge any inferiority to the ostensibly more sophisticated Normans', was appropriated by the South, which saw its own plight mirrored in this recreation of the Middle Ages.[44] Twain accused Scott of dressing up reactionary social systems in the guise of pastoral idylls, idylls that were no more than 'dreams and phantoms; with decayed and degraded systems of government; with the sillinesses and emptinesses, sham grandeurs, sham gauds, and sham chivalries of a brainless and worthless long-vanished society'.[45] Although much of the world may have progressed beyond this state, not so America's South which, for Twain, displayed a disabling mixture of progressive ideas and 'the inflated speech, and the jejeune romanticism of an absurd past that is dead, and out of charity ought to be buried' (500). So pernicious was Scott's influence on the formation of Southern character that Twain insisted 'he is in great measure responsible for the war' (501).

Ransom's speech, while consistent with the antipathy to gender sameness and dilution which had characterised James Senior's statements, also embodies a distinctly imperial and hierarchical strain nowhere present in those articles. It continues, piling clause upon clause with a syntax consistently disrupted as it strives for the final exclamation mark: 'The masculine character, the ability to dare and endure, to know and yet not fear reality, to look the world in the face and take it for what it is – a very queer and partly very base mixture – that is what I want to preserve, or rather as I may say, to recover; and I must tell you that I don't the least care what becomes of you ladies while I make the attempt!' (*B*, 327). Habegger contends of Ransom that 'the novel wants us, in spite of everything, to *like* this man – to wish his career and courtship well, to sense real distinction in his opinions, to take him seriously as a conservative intellectual . . . The reality James fabricates says that Basil is right' (191). Sandra Gilbert and Susan Gubar had voiced a similar matching the previous year, arguing in *The War of the Words* that 'Basil's aesthetic is an essentially Jamesian one.'[46] Such a position is strengthened if we turn to James's article of 1906/7, 'The Speech of American Women', in which Ransom's objections to the deleterious effects of feminisation are replayed by his creator. In submitting to the crude speech of women (most evident for James when combined with political ambition), America is in danger of social breakdown: 'the word, stripped for action . . . [will] become an inexpensive generalized mumble or jumble, a tongueless slobber or snarl or whine, which every one else would be free, and but too glad, to answer in kind . . . "Don't let us have women like that . . . in the names of our homes, our children, our national honor, don't let us have women like that!"'[47] Caroline Field Levander has noted that for James, as for other late ninteenth- and early twentieth-century theorisers of language, 'the link . . . create[d] between women's correct tonal enunciation and "our national honor" allows them strategically to rework their figuration of woman's language as dissociated from content-oriented public speech'.[48] Language that was 'stripped for action', that is to say ready for practical/political usefulness, was a vulgar infringement on the more appropriate feminine quality of language as pure sound, as unencumbered vocal tone. Listening to Verena speak, Ransom decides that 'the necessity of her nature was not to make converts to a ridiculous cause, but to emit those charming notes of her voice'. She was 'a vocalist of exquisite faculty, condemned to sing bad music' (*B*, 85). With the evidence of James's article before us, expressive of sentiments clearly rehearsed by Basil in the novel, it may appear that James stands convicted of Habegger's charge of loading his narrative too heavily in favour of reactionary sentiment. Perhaps we are required to approve of Ransom after all. The critical debate surrounding the narrator's endorsement (or otherwise) of Ransom has been a lengthy one: both Philip Rahv and Lionel Trilling claimed him as a conservative hero challenging a culture of publicity, mediocrity and vulgarity; Charles R. Anderson read the novel as a 'fable championing the institution of marriage' and thus lauds Basil's decisive final action; and more recently both Kenneth Graham and Elsa Nettels have concurred with this bias, stating that James 'can be felt basically to endorse Ransom's position' and that 'James locates his standard of judgement . . . in the speculative scrutiny of Basil Ransom.'[49] Yet a note of caution should be introduced, for James's novel is a more complex and less consistent text than his later unmediated polemic against the contamination of feminine language. From the point of view of the reader of *The Bostonians*, the issues are less clear-cut. Certainly Ransom's opinions represent a widely held nineteenth-century view of gender relations, one that James Senior, for all his early radicalism, was swift to endorse. But the ideological waters are muddied when we turn to consider that other figure who looms behind Basil – Thomas Carlyle. Habegger's argument that James wholeheartedly approves of the figure of Ransom is based, I suggest, on an only partial understanding of James's response to Carlyle, whose own lack of sympathy with reform and whose image of brusque, energetic masculinity informs the novelist's characterisation. Indeed the link is at one point rendered explicit, the narrator advising the reader that Basil 'was an immense admirer of the late Thomas Carlyle, and was very suspicious of the encroachments of modern democracy' (*B*, 199).

James was certainly preoccupied with Carlyle at the time of his composition of *The Bostonians*. In 1883, when the initial plans for the novel were taking shape, he was reading and reviewing the Emerson and Carlyle correspondence (the review was published in June of that year), and during the writing of the book was immersed in the final two parts of James Anthony Froude's monumental three-volume edition of the Scottish writer's *Letters and Memorials of Jane Welsh Carlyle*. Froude's work was something of a *succès de scandale* (revealing the unhappy nature of Carlyle's marriage and his keen sense of guilt at his wife's death), and had come in for much criticism from a reading public on both sides of the Atlantic more used to maintaining a veneer of propriety and the illusion of domestic harmony. James also felt that Froude had gone too far, confessing to a friend in 1883 that 'we find Mrs Carlyle rather squalid, but a great one for saying things well, and we thirst, generally, for the blood of J. A. Froude' – Froude's vampiric intrusion, as James saw it, neatly turned back on himself (*Letters*, II, 421). Elsewhere Froude was denounced as 'unspeakable' in a letter to Charles Eliot Norton in 1886, whose own edition of Carlyle's letters James had just read (*Letters*, III, 145).

Yet these anxieties about the intrusion of the reading public into the private misfortunes of the Carlyles are not intended to suggest that James had any great instinctual liking for Froude's subject. Indeed in the same letter to Norton he insists of Carlyle that 'he remains the most disagreeable in character of men of genius of equal magnificence ... it appears to me even striking how his disagreeableness comes out more and more in proportion as his talent develops' (*Letters*, III, 146). James's review of the Carlyle and Emerson correspondence is similarly strident, noting how natural it was that 'Carlyle's philosophy should have aristocratic premises, and that he should call aloud for that imperial master, of the necessity for whom the New England mind was so serenely unconscious', a contrast fictionalised in the encounter between Basil and Olive Chancellor (*EAE*, 245). Like that of Ransom, Carlyle's disdain for reformers is explicit, with James quoting a letter in which he complains, 'I am terribly sick of all that; – and wish it would stay at home at Fruitland, or where there is good pasture for it' (a reference to Bronson Alcott's short-lived utopian experiment) (*EAE*, 241). Carlyle's sense of inalienable individuality pitted arrogantly against the democratic mass (an inflated selfhood which Ian Bell links usefully with James's harsh early estimation of Walt Whitman in his 1865 review of *Drum Taps*[50]) is matched in the novel by the way in which Ransom's patrician disdain is described during his climactic approach to the Music Hall and Verena's public lecture: 'He was not one of the audience; he was apart, unique, and had come on a business altogether special.' His stratagems to capture Verena recall John Wilkes Booth's stalking of Lincoln. Indeed Basil explicitly likens himself to a young man who 'he could imagine ... waiting in a public place, [having] made up his mind, for reasons of his own, to discharge a pistol at the king or the president' (*B*, 414). The venue is a vulgar democratic spectacle which he transforms into a Roman gladiatorial arena in which his 'rescue' operation is a challenge to 'all his manhood' (*B*, 425). Imagining himself as a knight errant in an age grown timorous, Basil notes the 'tremendous entreaty' (*B*, 426) in the faces of Olive and Verena. Before these weak women and the emasculated male contingent represented by the two publicity-mongers Selah Tarrant and Mr Filer, Basil's sense of the power of his individual selfhood grows. From his elevated position everything else 'looked small, surmountable, and of the moment only' (*B*, 425). Verena herself is dwarfed and ineffectual: he 'notice[d] her strange, touching tone, and her air of believing that she might really persuade him' (*B*, 428). Yet Basil is by this stage convinced of his own triumph, sure that she had 'evidently given up everything now – every pretence of a different conviction and of loyalty to her cause' (*B*, 428).

Far from transforming Basil in this scene, as Habegger suggests, 'from a reactionary fool into a noble hold out' whose action is 'all the finer in that the public at large is too depraved to respect it – the stupid, gregarious, gullible public to which the contemporary reader evidently belongs',[51] James's 1883 review of the Carlyle and Emerson correspondence serves to illustrate how his consideration of the dangers of Carlyle's authoritarian self informs Ransom's monomania here. Praising the truthfulness of Carlyle's style (how it is 'in complete correspondence with the feeling of the writer'), this approval is tempered by the worrying aspect that Carlyle 'had invented a manner, and that his manner had swallowed him up. To look at realities and not at imitations is what he constantly and sternly enjoins; but all the while he gives us the sense that it is not at things themselves, but straight into this abysmal manner of his own that he is looking' (*EAE*, 249). Note the vocabulary of ingestion employed by James here. Carlyle's literary style, what was already termed 'Carlylelese' (the *OED* cites first usage in 1858), had taken him over, to the extent that he had ceased to exist independently of it. The printed page offered Carlyle the best opportunity to express this style in its most concentrated and influential form, and in *On Heroes, Hero-Worship and the Heroic in History* (1840) he registers his preference for the written over the spoken word. Although 'everywhere in the civilised world there is a pulpit' from where 'a man with the tongue may, to best advantage, address his fellowmen', Carlyle celebrates the advent of a print culture that has initiated a radical change in the composition and nature of one's audience: 'The writer of a Book, is not he a Preacher preaching not to this parish or that, on this day or that, but to all men in all times and places?'[52] Basil Ransom shares this enthusiasm for the printed page: we first meet him at Olive's, 'already absorbed in a book' which he had picked up as soon as he entered the drawing-room, now 'lost . . . in its pages' (*B*, 35); in another instance Basil is preoccupied by a book 'which, according to his habit at such times, he had mechanically taken up, and in which he speedily became interested' (*B*, 113); and his own sense of intellectual worth is validated by the forthcoming publication of his anti-reform views in the appropriately titled *Rational Review* (*B*, 359). To be published is the pinnacle of Basil's achievement, something which he regards as superior to Verena's public speaking and which he assumes with amusement will appear 'pitiful' to someone who merely publishes herself through her voice (*B*, 360). Basil implies that Verena cannot understand the importance and power of the printed word, cannot understand that the act of writing itself is an inherently masculine activity working in competition with the massed (and hysterical) female voices of the reform movement. Basil 'speaks with the pen' (*B*, 360), one of those 'gentlemen in plenty who would be glad to stop your mouth by kissing you' of which Olive warns Verena (*B*, 151). Ransom's Carlylean sense of the power of the written word through its ability to communicate intimately and directly feeds into his felt sense of apartness and superiority at the Music Hall, the forum of the public speaker. Ian Bell notes how James, through other, peripheral characters, attempts to set up an opposition to Basil's insistent reduction of the community represented at the Music Hall to the role of mere audience, a gathering of passive spectators waiting to receive the dubious benefits of Verena's inspired oration. Through these various voices human collectivity is expressed as 'the public', 'the multitude', 'the people', yet even Olive finally projects herself as the victim of a mob: 'I am going to be hissed and hooted and insulted!' (*B*, 432). Bell makes the point that such a proliferation of terms has the effect of rendering the concept of the 'public' irrevocably unstable, worrying for James because 'it suggests not only an elitist fear of social disorder but a fear of a more radical kind: if "public" is shorn of its human, civic meaning, then how will any form of social commentary be possible?'[53]

It would be an insensitive reading that easily dismissed Ransom's patrician stance as it is informed by James's reading of Carlyle. Certainly the distinction that James makes between the democratic openness of Emerson and the aristocratic superiority of Carlyle is to the political credit of the former, yet this apportioning of praise is far from uniform as James judges both men on a number of criteria. One example of this shifting of approval involves his consideration of the presence or absence of literary colour:

> The fine touch in [Emerson's] letters, as in his other writings, is always the spiritual touch. For the rest, felicitous as they are, for the most part they suffer a little by comparison with Carlyle's; they are less natural, more composed, have too studied a quaintness ... The violent color, the large, avalanche-movement of Carlyle's style ... make the effort of his correspondent appear a little pale and stiff. (*EAE*, 246)

The strength of Carlyle's stylistic colour, and its accompanying capacity for expressive feeling and artistic specification, is here cause for comparative approval. Although Ransom's style is used for manipulative ends, his rhetoric is similarly the most colourful in the novel. To state this is not to defend his style (although many critics have), but rather to point to the complexity of James's borrowings in the construction of his character.

Not only are negative and positive aspects combined, but in significant ways James offers an exaggeration of Carlyle and important divergences from his thought, divergences that serve to undermine Habegger's confident assertion that Basil '*is* a transatlantic Carlyle'.[54] Ransom's concern with 'royalists and cavaliers', signifying a period of history during which 'his pedigree' had 'flowered' so that 'he revered his forefathers, and he rather pitied those who might come after him' (*B*, 199), directly opposes Carlyle's lauding of Cromwell. James quotes Carlyle's lament for his own and future generations, which proposes very different candidates for the ushering in of an optimistic future: 'my heart is sick and sore on behalf of my own generation . . . I feel withal as if the one hope of help for it consisted in the possibility of new Cromwells and New Puritans' (*EAE*, 243). It is as if James, in creating Basil, has given him a political and historical bias consistent with the patrician pretensions he shares with Carlyle, attempting to iron out the contradictions (or perhaps, more accurately, the duality) in the Scot's thinking that often convey republican sentiment through an aristocratic, conservative rhetoric. That Ransom's point of view is revealed as 'narrow' (*B*, 328), that Verena 'didn't suppose you could hear anyone say such a thing as that in the nineteenth century, even the least advanced' (*B*, 321), suggests that his conscious modelling of himself on Carlyle is of an extreme kind, which, although teetering just the right side of parody, is nevertheless prone to an effective dismantling when tested.

As Bell notes, the ease with which the figure of Carlyle might be put to excessively exaggerated use was something of which James was very conscious. In an essay on Anthony Trollope, written for the *Century Magazine* in July 1883 (again, the date seems significant in terms of the composition of James's novel), he regarded as a 'blemish' the author's conscious parody of Carlyle in the figure of Dr Pessimist Anticant in Trollope's novel *The Warden* (1855): 'for certain forms of satire (the more violent, doubtless), he [Trollope] had absolutely no gift'. Similarly, Swinburne's vituperative attack on Carlyle's support of tsarist Russia in its conflict with the Turks, ('cruelty', Swinburne had declared, 'has naturally provoked the stigmatic brand of [Carlyle's] approbation'),[55] also earned James's criticism: in an 1877 review of the pamphlet *Note of an English Republican on the Muscovite Crusade* (1876), James noted the melodramatic 'thunderous style' which, taking its cue from the excesses of Carlyle's prose, had over-dramatised the depiction of his reactionary politics (*EAE*, 1342, 1285). James, as one might expect of a writer for whom the epithet Jamesian (*OED*, 1905) would be coined as a mark of distinction and as one of belittlement and pastiche, was highly aware of how style could quickly become frozen into inflexible affectation. But although Basil Ransom in James's novel resists caricature, nevertheless his intellectual pretensions are revealed to be flimsy. His nostalgic reverence for women in traditional roles (a preference, like that of James Senior, for those found 'in the realm of family life and the domestic affections'; those who are, quite appropriately, 'perfectly weak and second-rate' in a public role (*B*, 332)) is undermined by the demographic and economic realities then crystallising the women's movement. Reminding Basil of those women without families, Verena asks, 'What are you going to do with *them*? You must remember that women marry – are given in marriage – less and less; that isn't their career, as a matter of course, any more. You can't tell them to go and mind their husband and children, when they have no husband and children to mind' (*B*, 329). Given that Basil's home is female-dominated, comprising a mother and unmarried sisters suffering the aftermath of the Civil War, Verena's point seems particularly apt. The women's movement, she is implying, responds to profound changes in society – changes in the marriageabilty of women, and especially in women's need for new *economic* roles (and not merely the limiting status of domestic spiritual saviour). Basil's chivalric scheme fails to take account of this demographic shift in the complexion of the population – he brushes it off with a nonchalant 'that's a detail!' (*B*, 329). Although many of the reformers in the novel may be ripe for satiric representation, Basil's own ideological convictions are less than considered, seeming to be more instinctual adversarial responses than well-argued, 'rational' articulation.[56]

Up to this point I have concentrated on the ways in which James, in creating the figure of Basil Ransom, draws on a selection of attitudes based partly on his father's conception of women and partly on his own understanding of Thomas Carlyle. Whereas James may feel sympathy with his father's worry about the erosion of difference between the sexes, he complicates what would be a straight endorsement of James Senior's views by having them professed by a character schooled in the rhetoric of Carlyle, a rhetoric whose dangers James was sensitive to. Alfred Habegger argues that James deliberately chose not to engage with some of Carlyle's more brutal views, opting instead to recognise his aesthetic genius: 'This way of salvaging the cranky Sage of Chelsea came to James, I believe, from his father.'[57] This is a misreading, but a misreading with a perfectly consistent logic if it is to fit into Habegger's overall thesis that *The Bostonians* is a celebration of James Senior's less than enlightened sexual politics. For if Basil is a figure of whom we are asked to approve (as Habegger suggests), the fact that he is linked both implicitly and explicitly with Carlyle entails that both Jameses are required to display a benign appreciation of the 'Sage of Chelsea', and that James's was derived in large part from his father (whose views Basil rather crudely expounds). Even a cursory reading of James Senior on Carlyle reveals that such a perspective of blinkered appreciation is far from accurate. Moreover the elder James's words need be placed in the context of an American response to Carlyle at the time, one increasingly polarised between North and South, critical and favourable.

The essay of his father's on Carlyle which William James included in *The Literary Remains* was first delivered as a lecture in New York in the autumn of 1864. Charles Eliot Norton seems to have expressed an interest in publishing it in the *North American Review* at this time, but James Senior was reluctant for it to appear in print while its subject was still living. 'It is not a literary criticism of the writer,' he wrote to Norton, 'but a sketch of the man himself illustrated by facts of observation, and though these are all creditable to Carlyle in the way he seeks to be accredited, they are still not exactly what one would care to publish so long as he survived.'[58] Despite these reservations about publication, the lecture became a staple in James Senior's repertoire, with William informing his brother Henry in 1872, eight years after its first delivery, that 'Father read his paper on Carlyle yesterday at the Radical Club very successfully'.[59] That Henry read the lecture himself is fairly certain: it eventually surfaced as the lead article in the May 1881 edition of the *Atlantic Monthly*, separated by a matter of pages from the latest instalment of his own *The Portrait of a Lady*. (James Senior was true to his word about refraining from publication. Carlyle had died in February of that year.) The Scot's reputation in America by this time had diminished. In 1843 James Senior was looking forward to reading the American edition of Carlyle's dissection of English society, *Past and Present*, finding in him a refreshing moral directness and latent Puritanism which he compared favourably to what seemed to be the more ethereal articulations of Emerson and his fellow transcendentalists. 'Carlyle is the very best interpreter of spiritual philosophy which could be devised for this age', he wrote in a letter to Emerson (*WJ*, 1, 47). Many American readers believed that the muscularity of Carlyle's prose corresponded with their own sense of themselves and their country as unconventional and defiant. His expansive style seemed to match the nation's spatial extremes, its cherished exceptionalism, and a religious sensibility free of established religion. Carlyle's praise of Cromwell – 'that last glimpse of the Godlike vanishing from this England'[60] – appealed to an anti-monarchical republic whose strongest spiritual identification was with Puritan dissent. But it was Carlyle's reaction to the issue of slavery which caused many of his American admirers among the Northern intelligentsia to revise their estimation of him. Both his 'Occasional Discourse on the Nigger Question' (an article in *Fraser's Magazine* in 1849 and widely distributed as a pamphlet in 1853) and 'Shooting Niagra: And After?' (published in *Macmillan's Magazine* in 1867) displayed Carlyle's aristocratic and hierarchical sentiments at their most polemical, sentiments which had always been in his work but which had seemingly been ignored by an American readership enamoured of his accompanying strains of republicanism.[61]

The volte-face undertaken by many of his erstwhile admirers from the North highlighted the political fault line running through America, for influential voices in the South continued to insist on Carlyle's prescience. An example of the North's response comes from John Greenleaf Whittier, who in 1854 registered his disgust at Carlyle's *Occasional Discourse*: 'It is difficult to treat sentiments so atrocious and couched in such offensive language with any thing like respect. Common sense and unperverted conscience revolt instinctively against them.' Carlyle, Whittier condemns, 'mercilessly consigns an entire class of the children of his Heavenly Father to the doom of compulsory servitude'.[62] Four years earlier, a reviewer in *DeBow's Review*, a journal offering economic analyses of the antebellum South and acting as a platform for pro-slavery advocates, had articulated a different response to Carlyle's essay: 'The West India question is, for the first time, put in its true light before the English people, and it will much surprise us if a reaction, in favor of common sense, is not the result' (310). The *Atlantic Monthly* published 'A Letter to Thomas Carlyle' in its October 1863 edition. The writer, David A. Wasson, encapsulated (albeit hysterically at times) the shift from admiration to opprobrium felt by many abolitionist readers of Carlyle. Wasson had been an early disciple, reading *Sartor Resartus* 'aloof and on horseback, sleeping with it under my pillow and wearing it in my pocket till pocket and it were worn out'. Yet narrating in highly emotional terms the story of a young slave who had been whipped for disobedience because she had refused the sexual demands of her master, Wasson finds Carlyle complicitous: 'Yes, Thomas Carlyle, I hold you a party to these crimes. *You*, YOU are the brutal old man who would flog virgins into prostitution. You approve the system; you volunteer your best varnish in its commendation; and this is an inseparable and *legal* part of it.'[63]

Perhaps the most Carlylean response from the South is the sociologist George Fitzhugh's *Cannibals All: or Slaves Without Masters* (1857). Quoting extensively from Carlyle's *Latter Day Pamphlets*, it accuses the North of a mania for 'Isms' of all kinds. Fitzhugh was alarmed at the increasing political dominance of the North, an alarm which had been 'displayed in full relief, by the single fact, which we saw stated in a Northern Abolition paper, that "there are a hundred Spiritual Rappers in Congress"'.[64] It was not only the vogue for spiritualism which attracted his criticism, for expressing that sense of Southern superiority and disdain which Basil Ransom embodies, Fitzhugh focused his censure on what he regarded as a peculiarly American preoccupation, namely discussion of the relation between the sexes. Europe may have its anarchist movements, but these are almost respectable when compared with America's reformist brashness: Europe 'dare not inaugurate New York Free Love, and Oneida Incest, and Mormon Polygamy. The moral, religious, and social heresies of the North are more monstrous than those of Europe. The pupil has surpassed the master, unaided by the stimulants of poverty, hunger, and nakedness which urge the master forward' (11). Europe may have reason for its revolutions, Fitzhugh's argument goes, because of its inequality and economic instability, but America, especially North America, and (to project Fitzhugh's point onto Basil Ransom) especially a victorious North America after the Civil War, has no need for such agitation.

Although the conflicting reaction to Carlyle during this period broadly reflected the union–confederacy divide, as I have indicated, some responses in the North were less condemning than one might expect. An early draft of Whitman's *Democratic Vistas* (1871), written partly in response to Carlyle's 1867 outburst, had included a sharp attack on its author which Whitman, on rereading *Shooting Niagra* more sympathetically, decided to omit. Carlyle's words, Whitman decided, had nevertheless 'come from an earnest soul'.[65] Emerson too, recording his reaction in a journal entry, decided to tolerate Carlyle's views on the grounds that men of genius should be allowed their idiosyncrasies – 'Each of the masters has some puerility, as Carlyle his pro-slavery whim' (*Journals*, x, 52). James Senior's lecture, written prior to *Shooting Niagra*, displays no such intellectual or moral contortions. It is certainly not uniformly critical of its subject, for the elder James is prepared to acknowledge those qualities which had so attracted him to Carlyle back in the 1840s: 'He was a man of even a genial practical morality, an unexceptionable good neighbor, friend, and citizen.'[66] Moreover he anticipates Henry James's favourable comment on Carlyle's strong sense of literary style: 'having an immense eye for color, an immense genius for scenic effect, he seized with avidity upon every crazy, time-stained, dishonoured rag of personality that still fluttered in the breeze of history, and lent itself to his magical tissues' (600). Habegger quotes the first two phrases of this remark, citing them as the core of their author's thesis in his lecture: that James Senior had substituted the idea of Carlyle as a stylist for any criticism of his less appealing moral and social views. Yet this is a selective reading of these words, undermined by what James Senior goes on to say in the very same paragraph about the *dangers* of such aesthetic flair: 'the habit was tyrannous' because of the 'heartless people who hang, for their own private ends, upon the skirts of every pronounced genius, and do their best, by stimulating his vanity, to make himself feel a god' (600). What may at first seem like a parasitic relationship between Carlyle and his readers turns out to be symbiotic. The vampirism here is mutual: the readers feed on the writer's style, the writer feeds on their feeding. Both sides benefit from operating in a moral vacuum. Anticipating his son's analysis of Carlyle's inflated personality, for James Senior it is exactly this colour and strength of Carlyle's expression which has enabled him to create an image of himself as infallibly unique because admired by so many. Moreover the antipathy to reform noted in James's review is also strongly felt in the father's sketch. Carlyle 'had no belief in society as a living organizing force in history... He saw no possible way of dealing with weak races but by reducing them to slavery; no way of dealing successfully with evil men but by applying lynch law to them, and crushing them out of existence' (601–2). In a passage which directly refutes Habegger's charge that the Jameses chose to separate aesthetic admiration from moral judgement, James Senior likens Carlyle's embrace of goodness and truth to mere pictorial embellishment, painter's pigments which are of no intrinsic value except 'for the effects they lend themselves to in the sphere of production' (603). Carlyle's intense scepticism of existing institutions and dogmas 'obviously meant nothing beyond the production of a certain literary surprise, of the enjoyment of his own aesthetic power', and James Senior shrewdly suggests that the reason Carlyle was so critical of America was because he foresaw a time when its initial enthusiasm for him would begin to wane upon closer inspection: 'He hated us, because a secret instinct told him that our exuberant faith in him would never be justified by closer knowledge' (603–4). The stance of the superior, alienated individual which Basil cultivates so fastidiously in *The Bostonians* is, for James Senior (echoing Emerson's 1862 remark and anticipating Twain's 1883 attack), 'Carlyle's most rustical idea of human greatness', a romanticised pastoralism which belies its foundation in the exercise of autocratic power. The feudal simplicity of his system involved 'the glorification of force, ability, genius' in a process of natural selection whereby 'the strong man [would] grow ever more strong, the feeble man [would] grow ever more feeble, until he is finally extinguished' (606).

James Senior's pages of recollections are far from being the endorsement of Carlyle as an artist (regardless of his other less palatable opinions), and far from being that endorsement then transmitted to James to become the basis for the figure of Basil Ransom. As part of his intention to conflate Carlyle and James Senior into one ideological unit, to smooth out the creative and competing tensions which, I suggest, surround the depiction of Ransom, Habegger quotes from an article of 1880 in a Swedenborgian journal which considered James Senior as 'something of a Carlyle in his mannerisms and trenchant style'.[67] Yet in an earlier portrait of Carlyle from 1864, James Freeman Clarke, Unitarian minister and friend of James Senior, came to the opposite conclusion: the elder James 'is, in his philosophy, the very antithesis of Carlyle... A course of reading in Mr James's books might, we think, help our English [*sic*] cynic not a little.'[68] That Carlyle and the elder James merge into one wholly consistent fictional form is necessary for the thesis that both men shared certain intellectual dispositions and were the blunt, outspoken models for an authorially approved Ransom. Thus Habegger's statement: 'Without assuming that James was the doctrinaire theorist his father was, . . . he [nevertheless] identified his father's views with Basil, and, as commenting author, stepped in to the novel to endorse them' (201). But it is a questionable assertion that James, as narrator, makes his presence felt to bolster the claims for superiority made by the cousin from Mississippi. In fact the narrator's fluctuations between criticism of others and self-deprecation reflect an ambivalence towards the ideological conflict which he has constructed, something evident in his assessments of his ability to control the pace of the narrative. The representation of Basil problematises the issue of authorial control, with the text both claiming the credit for its objectivity and sliding willingly into subjective allegiance with him: 'The historian who had gathered these documents together does not deem it necessary to give a larger specimen of Verena's eloquence, especially as Basil Ransom, through whose ears we are listening to it, arrived, at this point, at a definite conclusion' (B, 268–9). Both a 'historian' and one of the 'we' placed within Basil's consciousness, the narrator cedes authority to a character whose 'definite conclusion' is offered here as definitive.

Elsewhere the narrator insists on reviewing and previewing experience, anxious about his skill in managing a narrative uncertain of the direction of its satiric thrust. The novel's famous qualified conclusion – 'It is to be feared that with the union so far from brilliant into which she was about to enter, these [tears] were not the last she was destined to shed' (B, 433) – is a startling undermining of Basil's sense of himself as Verena's saviour, casting doubt on their imminent union. There are at least three other instances of this anxious prefix in the novel that relate to Basil: meeting Dr Prance for the first time, 'a perfect example of the "Yankee female"' (B, 67), the narrator writes that Basil, 'it is to be feared, had a fund of cynicism' (B, 68); later in the book we read that 'It is to be feared there was no disguise of Ransom's satisfaction at finding himself once more face to face with the charming creature with whom he had exchanged that final speechless smile the evening before' (B, 108); and finally 'It is to be feared, indeed, that Verena was easily satisfied (convinced, I mean, not that she ought to succumb to him, but that there were lovely, neglected, almost unsuspected truths on his side)' (B, 380). In all of these examples the attempt to remain in control of the narrative by offering the reader privileged insights into the minds of his characters is qualified by the manner in which this information is introduced. 'It is to be feared' is not simply a rhetorical device or narrative nicety, but the expression of the narrator's own distrust. Basil represents a powerful force which cannot be evaded or underestimated, and the attempt at asserting control by anticipation and insightful revelation is revealed as feeble by this admission of apprehension. The paradoxically tentative assertion of the book's conclusion can be read as a final attempt by the narrator to wrest control of his narrative from Basil's magnetic charm and strident simplicities. It predicts a future scenario, which, while offering the reader the opportunity to reassess his or her opinion of Basil one last time, cannot confidently be considered as the authoritative judgement on him. It only seems as if the novel closes with the balance of sympathies tipped in Verena's direction, for 'It is to be feared' not so much guides the reader as lets the narrator off the narrative hook on which he has been caught.

I have suggested that the composition of *The Bostonians* was initiated in part by Henry James's reaction to the death of his father. The novel is on a different scale to James's earlier story of New England life, *The Europeans* (1878). The brief scenes of the earlier work, vignettes almost, with their emphasis on the telling phrase or gesture, give way in *The Bostonians* to extended dialogue, much of it in the form of debate and argumentation, and frequent narrative commentary. Delicacy of method is superseded by a thorough familiarity with the art of Balzac and the requirements of the naturalist novel. Yet the public and political subject matter were not only a result of James's admiration of the French master; James Senior's interests were almost exclusively those debated in the public sphere, and the two on which his son chose to focus, spiritualism and women's rights, needed an appropriately large canvas to do them justice. There existed a strong satiric literary tradition to which James was contributing with this novel, but *The Bostonians* is more complex than any of its precursors, a complexity founded on the shifting nature of James's fictional world, which refuses to appropriate ideological positions, either James Senior's or Thomas Carlyle's, in any form of neat synthesis. By combining in Basil Ransom James Senior's ideas on women and their shared estimations of Carlyle, James created for himself a character who, despite the legitimacy of some of his observations on the eccentricities of the reform movement of 1870s Boston, nevertheless could not be wholeheartedly endorsed. Alfred Habegger's argument, while forcefully made, projects onto the novel a wished consistency of authorial stance, one which depends upon too high a degree of partial reading.

In a letter to William James in 1885 Henry lamented the recent bankruptcy of the publisher of *The Bostonians*, James R. Osgood, and the lack of critical success his novel had received ('This deathly silence seems to indicate that it has fallen flat'). James Senior's *The Literary Remains* was also on the Osgood list, and James's own failure prompted a lament for the absence of interest in his father's work:

> But how can one murmur at one's success not being what one would like when one thinks of the pathetic, tragic ineffectualness of poor Father's lifelong effort, and the silence and oblivion that seems to have swallowed it up? . . . It is terribly touching and, when I think of the evolution of his production and ideas, fills me with tears.
>
> (*Letters*, III, 102)

Both attempts at filial respect had proved unsuccessful. For Henry, as I have shown, it was not until the writing of *A Small Boy and Others* that he attempted to respond in a direct and personal way to the figure of his father. In that autobiographical volume ideological engagement is stripped away, so that the troublesome aspect (at least for James's fiction) of the specific elements of James Senior's intellectual history could be erased in favour of a typically late James focus on personal dynamics and the workings of the sensitive mind. *The Bostonians* engages most directly with the cultural milieu of New England intellectuals in which the elder James operated and with the social issues that preoccupied him. Aside from *The Princess Casamassima*, it is James's most explicitly political novel, one in which the discourse of public affairs provokes the very characteristic Jamesian interest in power relations and emotional possession. However the novel is, I have been arguing, unstable in its satirical allegiances, critical at times of the campaign for female suffrage and at others of the book's principle opponent of that campaign. Finally, such oscillation at the heart of this narrative incapacitates any reading that attempts to transform James's text into something that unproblematically advocates an ideological position. For sure, this is a conclusion perfectly consistent with the pragmatic framework of indeterminacy that James's texts have been seen to embody, but it is a position accomplished almost through narrative sleight of hand, where ideological indecision is achieved as if with relief rather than by design.

5

Breaking the mould

In 1884, as Matthew Arnold was engaged on a lecture tour of America, the *English Illustrated Magazine* published an essay on the critic and poet by the expatriate American Henry James. A previous estimation of Arnold by James, one of his earliest published pieces (1865), showed him arriving at an acute understanding of Arnold's conception of criticism. There James had written: 'We said just now that its duty was, among other things, to exalt, if possible, the importance of the ideal. We should perhaps have said the intellectual; that is, of the principle of understanding things' (*EAE*, 717). Choosing not to follow his first impulse to assign criticism to an ideal realm, James instead approves of Arnold's insistence on making it serve the everyday world of living. For Arnold, James declares, the world is not simply a given; in order to make sense of it we need to engage in a 'labour' of interpretation. In his 1884 judgement James characterised Arnoldian criticism as the bridging of historical and cultural gaps – an essential service (and one he felt to be particularly necessary in America), for if the human mind has difficulty in understanding its own culture, so much greater are its problems when faced with those of others. James posits the situation of a foreigner confronted with a world he does not know. As he explains, those who have always lived within one culture display an 'unconsciousness of the people [i.e. those encountered] concerned' and tacitly assume that 'their form of life is the normal one':

> This unconsciousness makes a huge blank surface, a mighty national wall, against which the perceptive, the critical effort of the presumptive stranger wastes itself, until, after a little, he espies, in the measureless spaces, a little aperture, a window which is suddenly thrown open, and at which a friendly and intelligent face is presented, the harbinger of a voice of greeting. With this agreeable apparition he

175

> communes – the voice is delightful, it has a hundred tones and modulations; and as he stands there the great dead screen seems to vibrate and grow transparent.
>
> (*EAE*, 721)

This is typical James in its use of architectural metaphor to describe a state of consciousness, its hint at the supernatural (the amiable presence is an 'apparition'), and its preoccupation with a sensitivity to welcome vibrations. The voice causing the wall of national isolation and preconceptions to become transparent is, James suggests, Arnold's, the visitor's 'intellectual companion' (*EAE*, 720). He it is who meets the visitor 'half way', acting as a guide to English life and culture, as an aid to understanding and interpretation:

> He discharges an office so valuable, a function so delicate, he interprets, he explains, illuminates so many of the obscure problems presented by English life to the gaze of the alien; he woos and wins to comprehension, to sympathy, to admiration, this imperfectly initiated, this often slightly bewildered observer; . . . he appears to understand his feelings, he conducts him to a point of view as gracefully as a master of ceremonies would conduct him to a chair.
>
> (*EAE*, 720–1)

That James here uses terms of his own theory of fiction (bewildered observer, point of view) in his description of the function of Arnold's criticism attests to the close affinity between the two writers. Indeed recalling in his autobiography a childhood visit to the theatre to watch a stage production of *Uncle Tom's Cabin*, James tells how his young self 'got his first glimpse of that possibility of a "free play of the mind" over a subject which was to throw him with force at a later stage of culture, when subjects had considerably multiplied, into the critical arms of Matthew Arnold' (*A*, 94).

The Arnoldian influence is present in one of James's last essays, 'The New Novel' (1914), in which he describes the ideal critical sensibility as one no longer reliant upon 'instinctive' judgements, but instead receptive to 'the great flood of awareness' by which the mind 'wanders further and further for pasture'. Any 'reversion to instinct', he warns, will 'block up the ingress' of productive unfamiliarity, leaving us 'sit[ting] in stale and shrinking waters' (*EAE*, 125, 124, 125). James's understanding of Arnold's notion of criticism has relevance not only for James's own theory of fiction but also for that fiction itself. The situation of the exasperated foreigner in need of guidance closely resembles that of the protagonists in James's international novels, where a coherent, but ultimately fallible, perspective is confronted by unfamiliar forces that provoke ontological fragmentation. A character, whose behaviour is usually determined by the conventions of one environment, is set down in another, where he or she must employ all his or her individual resources to find an intelligent accommodation with certain new practices and expectations. In his preface to *The American* James writes admiringly of those writers who have the 'largest responding imagination before the human scene' (*EWP*, 1062). The protagonists of the international novels, generally Americans, confront the 'human scene' of a European country and are usually baffled. Only if they are prepared to enter into an interpretative relationship with the other culture will that culture be disclosed to them; and in the process (for 'process' is what it is) their conception of selfhood is also reinterpreted and comprehended anew. In an 1877 essay, 'Occasional Paris', James remarks that although one set of national customs, 'wherever it may be found, grows to seem to you as provincial as another', the process of relating them may nevertheless be instructive and entertaining. The essay contains a defence of the comparativist perspective of the cosmopolite, defined as an informed observer who thinks 'well of mankind': 'The consequences of the cosmopolite spirit is to initiate you into the merits of all peoples, to convince you that national virtues are numerous, though they may be different, and to make downright preference really very hard.'[1] For James the cosmopolitan individual marks a standard against which to set both the extremes of the proud Rooseveltian patriot and the exile devoted exclusively to a foreign culture.

James's depiction of the 'unconscious' observer of alien environments, of that preference for the complacency and safety of the 'huge blank surface' of national prejudice, brings to mind the at times deliberately isolationist self-sufficiency of Emerson, who, even in his travel writing, is a conspicuously uncomfortable tourist. In a letter to Samuel and Sarah Ripley from Paris in July 1833 he describes the city as an unimpressive 'vulgar superficial unspiritual marketing community'. Although Paris offers that potential for the aesthetic and material enjoyment that Lambert Strether discovers during his visit (Emerson describes the theatres, the botanical gardens, the café society, all offering a 'boundless domestic liberty'), he is nevertheless soon tired of a place that he feels unable fully to appreciate: 'But whilst I see the advantages of Paris they are not very great to me. Now that I have been here fifteen days I find I spend most of my time in the reading room & that I can do at home.' The life of the mind proves to be more endurable and rewarding than the passing pleasures of a society of which, Emerson admits with admirable self-awareness, he may be an 'ill conditioned' observer (*LE*, I, 389, 390, 391, 389). In a journal entry made two months later while waiting at Liverpool for the ship to take him back to America, he muses on why European travel must inevitably disappoint him. Neither men nor things are ultimately satisfying, he concludes, because they cannot live up to his *idea* of them. The effect of having met Landor, Coleridge, Carlyle and Wordsworth – 'the men I wished to see' – is merely to have 'thereby comforted and confirmed me in my convictions': 'To be sure not one of these is a mind of the very first class, but what the intercourse with each of these suggests is true of intercourse with better men, that they never *fill the ear* – fill the mind – no, it is an *idealized* portrait which always we draw of them' (*Journals*, III, 185). Emerson is happy, almost relieved, to have had his idealist suspicions confirmed, happy therefore to have seen Europe, and particularly happy that, at the age of thirty, he feels that his 'travelling is done' (*Journals*, IV, 79). A later journal comment emphasises his low expectations of journeying beyond the boundaries of Concord. One should not anticipate discovering anything new in one's explorations, he asserts, explorations which at best serve only to confirm what is already known about the self. Employing a Coleridgean image, he declares:

> Travel I think, consists really & spiritually in sounding all the stops of our instrument. If I have had a good indignation and a good complacency with my brother, if I have had reverence & compassion, had fine weather & good luck in my fishing excursion & profound thought in my studies at home, seen a disaster well through; and wrought well in my garden, nor failed in my part at a banquet, then I have travelled though all was within the limits of my own fenced yard. (*JMN*, VIII, 18)

What is missing from the experience is the possibility of a truly productive or enlightening (or, in Jamesian terms, bewildering) encounter with the not-me, the different. The constant factor for Emerson is always the self and the ways in which it can be revealed. The historical other, the geographical other, the cultural other, all are valuable only insofar as they provide a commentary on the already written text of the self.

In examining the pose of omniscience struck (and problematically insisted upon) by the narrator of James's novel *The Sacred Fount* (1901), Carolyn Porter has suggested, in terms strikingly reminiscent of Emersonian aesthetics, that the limitations of such a method of observation are revealed when 'the contemplative posture of the observer becomes so entrenched as to seem to constitute his identity... When observation is carried to this point, reified consciousness behaves as if it were a disembodied eye, only to be faced with its own presence in the world it presumes to observe.'[2] At one point in *The Sacred Fount* the narrator alludes to his 'transcendent intelligence', that faculty of 'preposterous acuteness' which can read into others 'an interest so much deeper than mere human things were in general prepared to supply'.[3] The solipsistic vision of the narrator insists upon its own interpretative accuracy; but his premise that romantic attachments deplete one party, vampire-like, only to strengthen another is arrived at via only very limited information (certain characters seem younger or cleverer, others appear older and less intellectually nimble). Once the theory is formulated however, evidence is marshalled through the monomaniac perception of the 'I'/eye. The challenge for the reader is to effect a withdrawal from this epistemological prison, to raise an objection to the claustrophobic and enclosed system of meaning once propositions advocated as infallible are shown to be vulnerable and open to revision. The narrator, I am suggesting, embodies attitudes which characterised for James some of the limitations of transcendental thought. But not only for James. Theodore Parker, that sober judge of the interpretative excesses of his younger disciples, warned in his essay 'The World of Matter and the Spirit of Man' (*c.* 1850 but unpublished during Parker's lifetime) of men who 'have scorned observations, have taken but a few facts from which to learn universal laws, and so failed of getting what is universal, even general'. Danger lies, he notes, for one who takes 'a transient impulse, personal and fugitive, for a universal law'.[4] Of Emerson in particular, in an otherwise admiring review of his writing, Parker had the perspicacity to add the qualification that his subject 'is sometimes extravagant in the claims made for his own method, and maintains that ecstasy is the natural and exclusive mode of arriving at new truths *while it is only one mode*' (195; my emphasis). Ecstasy is certainly the impression cultivated by *The Sacred Fount's* narrator, whose self-congratulatory prose luxuriates in its own heady Romanticism: 'The beauty perhaps was only for *me* – the beauty of having been right; it made at all events an element in which, while the long day softly dropped, I wandered and drifted and securely floated. This element bore me bravely up, and my private triumph struck me as all one with the charm of the moment and the place' (76). Emerson, of course, should not be read as the model for James's embodiment of the excesses of transcendental epistemology; the novel's narrator and its reader are immersed in an aesthetics of Romanticism pushed almost to the point of absurdity, well beyond anything Emerson might have advocated. Yet, as Parker's comments serve to illustrate, transcendental theory and its application held dangers for even the most sober-minded. Emerson's apparent fleeting reliance on observation (on 'the transient impulse'), and then only on observation which serves to confirm a universal truth already firmly held, was for Henry James indicative of that myopic serenity of thought that had abandoned intellectual rigour and the pleasures of surprise. His less than flattering recollections of visiting the Louvre and the Vatican with Emerson in the winter of 1872/3 resonate with a sense of baffled disappointment: '[Emerson's] perception of the objects contained in these collections was of the most general order. I was struck with the anomaly of a man so refined and intelligent being so little spoken to by works of art. It would be more exact to say that certain chords were wholly absent; the tune was played, the tune of life and literature, altogether on those that remained. They had every wish to be equal to their office, but one feels that the number was short – that some notes could not be given' (*EAE*, 269). From an initial criticism of Emerson's lack of appreciation of European art, James finds himself having to widen the scope of his companion's lack of engagement to a vaguer but simultaneously more inclusive obliviousness. Emerson's music is lacking in richness and complexity.[5]

Although Ford Madox Hueffer would align Emerson with Matthew Arnold when commenting on the latter's American lecture tour (Hueffer writes of 'the restrained muse of Matthew Arnold, whose temperament, in its rarefied way, was as "New England" as was ever that of Emerson or James Russell Lowell'[6]), Arnold himself worried about the reaction his American audience would have to a talk he was planning to give on the recently deceased philosopher. 'I only trust that I may get through the first half of it without being torn to pieces', he confided.[7] Although his estimation was broadly sympathetic, it did provoke angry reaction from certain quarters – 'it roused the provincial ire of the pure disciples', was how Charles Eliot Norton described the fuss in a letter to Lowell.[8] In his lecture, Arnold expressed admiration of Emerson as 'the friend and aider of those who would live in the spirit', a great man who 'will surely prove in the end to have been right'.[9] Yet against this he judged that his poetry 'lacks directness' (154) and his prose could not rank with that produced by such as Cicero, Plato and Bacon, whose writing 'is a kind of native necessity true and sound' (159–60). The aphoristic nature of Emerson's work, its progression by flashes of inspiration and poetic beauty, could not satisfy the more systematic Arnold. Emerson's poems 'have no evolution' (157), and his status as a major philosophical thinker is dubious because 'he cannot build; his arrangement of philosophical ideas has no progress in it, no evolution; he does not construct a philosophy' (169). Indeed it is precisely those less than rigorously formulated principles and biases of Emerson's thought, such as self-reliance and compensation, that characterise, for Arnold, the Concord writer's provincial limitations and the insufficiencies of his perspective: 'With maxims like these, we surely, it may be said, run some risk of being made too well satisfied with our own actival self and state, however crude and imperfect they may be' (186).

I have already shown how James Senior distanced himself from the limitations of a simplistic model of American exceptionalism. Instead of what feels at times like Emerson's wholesale rejection of European influence, the elder James, without disavowing America's sacred potential, was inclined to accept the Old World inheritance, and to use it as a reservoir of experience with which to build the millenarian American society soon to dawn. In an unpublished lecture, principally on the subject of slavery and the South's desire to secede, he conceptualises America's relationship with its European past in these terms:

> We inherit the solution which Europe has already given to her own destructive problems, which are those of religion and government, and start upon our own distinctive career from the basis of her most approved experience . . . We inherit all their ripest culture in these particulars. We inherit Protestantism and constitutional liberty: but there is this great difference between us: we begin where they leave off . . . we enter upon full possession the estate which it cost them their best blood to found and mature.[10]

James Senior's conciliatory language (he writes of Europe's 'approved experience'; its 'ripest culture', which was carefully cultivated at some cost) towards those European institutions that most interest him offers a stark contrast to the Emerson of *English Traits*. There Emerson concludes that 'if the courage of England goes with the chances of a commercial crisis, I will go back to the capes of Massachusetts, and my own Indian stream, and say to my countrymen, the old race are all gone, and the elasticity and hope of mankind must henceforth remain on the Allegheny ranges, or nowhere' (*CWE*, v, 314). Although England may come in for some grudging praise, as a nation it is fatally undermined by the accretion of historical events spanning nearly 2,000 years. The United States, by contrast, has the great advantage of starting afresh and, with it, the possibility of building a national character and identity based on principle and choice, the possibility, at least, of becoming the best of nations. Although both men were grounded in the Puritan utopianism of a New Jerusalem, the elder James did not share Emerson's assertive belief in the simplistic fact of America's superiority. For him, Europe would have to be engaged with, and America would be wise to reap the benefits of a European encounter.

Freed from the limitations of the particularities of his father's intellectual world and continuing the dialogue on the value of that European encounter exemplified by the positions of Emerson and James Senior, in *The Ambassadors* James pursues his analysis of an American selfhood becoming unsettled and transformed by immersion in a cultural 'other'. Paris is an environment of non-self, profoundly disorienting to a mind steeped in a combination of Puritan and genteel Emersonian traditions. De Tocqueville's prescient analysis of the limitations of an American mind satisfied with the Cartesian alignment of thought and identity, an equation embraced by transcendentalism's belief in the imperial mind's interpretative powers, is enacted in James's novel by Lambert Strether. Only by the embrace of difference (as suggested in 'Occasional Paris'), by a willed succumbing to the possibility of error, is James's protagonist able to divest himself of a reliance on the uniformity and consistency of a world thought already understood. He is finally committed to an act of making, to the evolution of an entire process of judging with new criteria for evaluation, and a willing suspension of received conventions.

In the detailed outline of *The Ambassadors*, called simply 'Project of Novel' sent to his publishers in the autumn of 1900, James noted, with Christian diction, the strong sense of mission which both Strether and Mrs Newsome feel at the outset of their plan for Chad's safe return to America. They 'have both fully felt, and in almost equal good faith, that it will have been, on the possible bad issue, but a small honour to them if the boy be lost without some earnest, some practical, personal effort to save him. The case has been virtually as simple for them as that. Perdition on one side, salvation on the other.'[11] James's novel transforms the Puritan notion of an errand into the great wilderness of America into one in which that wilderness is regarded by Strether (at least initially) and Mrs Newsome (consistently) as civilisation, as Europe – a *moral* wilderness. This sense of the salvific potential of America went hand in hand with a complacent moral isolation which James had noted in Hawthorne. Discussing *Our Old Home* (1863), Hawthorne's collection of travel sketches of England, he judged it to be 'the work of an outsider, of a stranger, of a man who remains to the end a mere spectator . . . and always lacks the final initiation into the manners and nature of a people of whom it may be said . . . that to know them is to make discoveries' (*EAE*, 433). The 'wall' of cultural myopia which James would later depict in his essay on Arnold manifests itself here, in familiar Jamesian phrasing, as Hawthorne's 'exaggerated, painful, morbid national consciousness' (*EAE*, 434). James characterises the disorientation of the American traveller in Europe in terms which could serve as a useful gloss on his evocation of Strether's experiences some twenty years later. European experience causes the representative of the New World to re-evaluate his national consciousness, which is now 'placed on the circumference of the circle of civilisation rather than at the centre'. Europe induces a novel sense of uncertainty in the American, 'a sense of . . . relativity . . . [which] replaces that quiet and comfortable sense of the absolute' previously thought unshakeable. Given these comments it may seem surprising that James chose to praise the character of Hilda in another Hawthorne work, *The Marble Faun* (1860). She is, after all, the very representative of starched New England moralism, one who would like to redeem the guilty Miriam and save Donatello's innocence, to say nothing of her own or Kenyon's. But what James admires about this 'pure and somewhat rigid New England girl' is her willingness to abandon her inflexible attitude when she enters the confessional, where she 'deposits her burden . . . and pours out her dark knowledge into the bosom of the Church'. James understands that Hilda's loss of what he calls her 'perfect innocence' (*EAE*, 446) results from her witnessing an act of evil (Miriam and Donatello impulsively murder the enigmatic monk who is linked to Miriam in some mysterious, unspecified manner), an understanding that also informs *The Ambassadors*. Strether's final encounter with Chad and Madame de Vionnet on the river is a witnessing of immorality that destroys the last vestiges of his innocent disposition to regard their liaison as a 'virtuous attachment'.

It is tempting to imagine James's reaction to Hawthorne's fragmentary romance 'The Ancestral Footstep', in which a young, intensely patriotic American goes to England to claim a family estate. He becomes increasingly torn between his missionary patriotism and his longing for the peace and security of a place in the age-old traditions of English culture and society. James makes no reference to the fragment, written at the same time Hawthorne was compiling the notes which would constitute *Our Old Home* but published posthumously in the *Atlantic Monthly* in 1882/3. Yet it would be surprising if he had not encountered it given his close connection with the journal at this time. *The Portrait of a Lady* had appeared in twelve instalments within its covers, and James had initially intended for the journal to publish *The Bostonians*, before the planned six instalments ballooned to thirteen and it finally appeared in *The Century*. Aspects of Hawthorne's story resonate in James's work. Although the notes are far from explicit, Hawthorne seems to have intended his hero Middleton to return to America with his new bride Alice at the end of the story. Her voice articulates the superiority of the New World:

> There is much that is seductive in English life; but I think it is not upon the higher impulses of our nature that such seductions act. I should think ill of the American, who, for any causes of ambition – any hope of wealth or rank – or even for the sake of any of those old, delightful ideas of the past, the associations of ancestry, the loveliness of an age-long home – the old poetry and romance that haunt these ancient villages and estates of England – would give up the chance of acting upon the unmoulded future of America.[12]

Despite the obvious attractions of England – Middleton curiously inverts the Edenic imagery usually associated with America, regarding his 'ancient home' as 'Paradise' and 'Eve's bridal bower' (3) – it is the uncircumscribed potential of America that is finally victorious in this pull of competing forces. She is 'unmoulded'. The idea of moulding as a form of moral and cultural determinism is something which, as I will show, also interests both the elder James and his novelist son. One other literary antecedent should be mentioned. Like Hawthorne's romance, William Dean Howells's *Indian Summer* (1886), a novel with which James was familiar, dramatises the conflict in its protagonist Theodore Colville between Young American practicality and the emergence of an aesthetic

sensibility immersed in Europe. Colville experiences a troubling redis-
covery of youthful European romance (as does Strether in James's novel),
and the tension between the two cultural modes culminates in what Tony
Tanner judges to be an 'epiphanic moment of uncertainty' characteristic
of the expatriate in Europe, as Colville's typically American resistance
to the Old World finds expression.[13] Watching the benignly Emersonian
figure of Mr Waters immersed in his studies of thirteenth-century Italian
architecture, Howells writes that

> Colville stared after him; he did not wish to come to just that, either. Life,
> active life, life of his own day, called to him; he had been one of its busiest
> children: could he turn his back upon it for any charm or use that was in
> the past? Again that unnerving doubt, that paralysing distrust, beset him, and
> tempted him to curse the day in which he had returned to this outworn Old
> World. Idler on its modern surface, or delver in its deep-hearted past, could
> he reconcile himself to it? What did he care for the Italians of today, or the
> history of the Florentines as expressed in their architectural monuments? It was
> the problems of the vast, tumultuous American life, which he had turned his
> back on, that really concerned him.

Colville's 'arrested fate', the sense that 'he had not yet lived his life', is akin
to Strether's own dissatisfaction.[14] Here though, and unlike Strether, the
hero of Howells's novel identifies America as the location for his return
to profitable living. Howells brought a sense of the quotidian and the
tangible to American literature in an attempt to temper an excessive
dependence on the sentimental and romantic, and Colville's preference
for the reality of his American life is to some extent an expression of
Howells's.

In *The Europeans* James had already staged an encounter of expatri-
ated sophistication with home-bred staunchness in a pastoral comedy. By
bringing the Baroness Munster and Felix Young from their Bohemian
splendour to a Woollett-like suburb of Boston to visit their American
cousins, the Wentworths, James assembled some of the elements of his
later novel. Yet the problems that Madame de Vionnet might present at
Woollett are quite unlike the rather vague unsettlings which the Baroness's
ennui causes in the Wentworth's commonwealth. The Baroness returns
to her native exile, and the two lovers, Young and Gertrude Wentworth,
design for themselves a reproachless expatriation. Robert Dawidoff has
characterised this gentler Jamesian strain thus: 'James makes light of [it]
by essentially saying, with a muffled "poor dear things" echoing somewhere, it does fine for the likes of most Wentworths and their friends.
New England has a good and attractive set of local customs, but they
will not really do for everyone... Native allegiance is a mild obstacle
to be removed.'[15] The kind of American thinking about nationality

and selfhood represented rather touchingly in the novel by the reference to a volume of Emerson's essays on a chair beside the bed-bound and 'sweet-faced' Mrs Acton, comes in for more sustained analysis in *The Ambassadors*, where the encounter with an alien culture proves more unsettling and the possibility of smooth expatriation less assured.

I

Dorothea Krook was careful in her judgement of James's intellectual inheritance:

> I have thought it safer, however, to proceed on the hypothesis that [James] did not take it from anywhere, or anybody, in particular: neither from Hegel, nor F. H. Bradley, nor from his brother William's Pragmatism, nor (least of all) from his father's Swedenborgian system. I have supposed he took it from the ambient air of nineteenth-century speculation, whose main current was the preoccupation with the phenomenon of self-consciousness. To this air he had been exposed from his earliest years; and the animating intellectual atmosphere of his remarkable home, created by his father and the circle of gifted friends and relations . . . made perhaps the heaviest contribution to Henry James's philosophical development.[16]

Krook is surely correct in her rejection of the idea of any wholesale appropriation by James of any system of thought. The issue seems to be the precise quality of that 'ambient air of nineteenth-century speculation' in which the novelist was suffused. Insofar as the elder James participated in that ambience and concerned himself with ideas of identity and selfhood (and despite Krook's 'least of all' warning), we can profitably look at his contribution to the creation of a family consciousness without having to transform influence of this kind into direct and seamless incorporation. Although James may have 'had a mind so fine that no idea could violate it',[17] this expresses not so much the novelist's refusal to engage in ideas but rather an insistence that his art is not tampered with by them. For James systematic thought must be relocated in the realm of experience; abstract concepts can only be tested, and thus rendered meaningful, in the chaotic world of the actual. To illustrate this with regard to *The Ambassadors* I want to quote a passage from James Senior containing an image which is later taken up by his son in the novel. In *Christianity the Logic of Creation* (1857) the elder James writes:

> My moral experience tells me that justice is good and injustice evil, that he who injures his neighbour is an evil man, and he who refrains from injuring him a good man. Now these moral judgements serve simply as a mould or body to our spiritual perceptions, and being as such mould or body the exact inversion of what is moulded or embodied in them, they have obviously no

more right to control our spiritual perceptions than an egg has to control the chicken, than the foundation of a house has to control the superstructure, than the kitchen has to control the drawing-room, than the stream has to control the fountain.[18]

Here is rejected the notion of a socially sanctioned morality (the 'mould') that seeks to determine man's actions, to contain him within a rigid form that does not allow him his spiritual freedom. James Senior's scorn at this kind of moralistic determinism had found an obvious target the previous year in Auguste Comte, whose philosophy of positivism sought to explain human behaviour by the application of scientific methods of observation and experimentation. James Senior's antipathy to what he saw as the creation of a religion of rationality with Comte as its god found expression in the strongest personal terms: 'So charmed is our new and scientific Stylites with this achievement – so intent is he upon spreading the serene and majestic tail of his extraordinary merits before the eyes of the world – that he not only with French egotism, minutely and gravely depicts the starting-point of the new cultus, in a certain erotic hallucination... but with more than French bombast also takes every occasion publicly to subscribe himself AUGUSTE COMTE, *Fondateur de la religion de l'Humanité*.'[19] In an earlier newspaper article in the *Tribune*, in which he rehearsed his thoughts on Comte, James Senior's objections are focused on his subject's ignorance of the concept of the fall. Comte sees this 'great theologic dogma' as the major impediment to 'the progress of . . . scientific understanding', yet fails to understand that the fall does not 'necessarily imply the endless deterioration of man, for the simple reason that [it], with more or less clearness, also affirm[s] a Divine deliverance from that catastrophe'.[20] As I have shown, the elder James was steeped in the Calvinist tradition that man is utterly dependent upon the graciousness of God for his salvation, so that any form of self-reliance works against man's deepest needs and ultimate destiny. He did not, however, follow his Calvinist forbears by locating and defining the transcendence of divine grace in spatial terms, somewhere unreachably above and outside the human realm. Deliverance from the consequences of the fall is possible by man's consciously overcoming his self-centredness and aligning himself with the divine reality which is the basis of his true humanity. Since God is a source and sustaining power of all human beings, man encounters redemption by opening himself to the manifold possibilities of human experience. The notion of human freedom was necessary for this process of redemption – the individual must retain the ability to refashion himself according to his encounter with the experiential world. Only through achieving this could he hope to come to a transformed relation with God and his fellow men and live in a divinely redeemed society.

In Gloriani's garden Lambert Strether is overwhelmed by the concentrated 'assault of images' (I, 196) which beset his imagination.[21] Like Hyacinth Robinson, who discovers Parisian art and culture in *The Princess Casamassima*, Strether feels that the 'windows of his mind' are opened to receive 'the sun of a clime not marked in his old geography' (I, 196–7). He persistently associates images of light with the sculptor: he is suffused with 'the light, with the romance, of glory' (I, 196); his face is a 'most special flare, unequalled, supreme, of the esthetic torch' (I, 197); and Strether feels himself to be 'dazzled' by Gloriani's presence (I, 198). This abundance of new aesthetic impressions prompts him to evaluate his own life in America and, in a famous speech to Little Bilham, he exhorts him not to make the same mistakes that he has: 'Live all you can; it's a mistake not to.' The train had waited at the station, but he had not had 'the gumption to know it was there' and it had left without him (I, 217). Strether goes on to employ one of the images used by the elder James in the passage just quoted:

> The affair – I mean the affair of life – could n't, no doubt, have been different for me; for it's at the best a tin mould, either fluted and embossed, with ornamental excrescences, or else smooth and dreadfully plain, into which, a helpless jelly, one's consciousness is poured – so that one 'takes' the form, as the great cook says, and is more or less compactly held by it: one lives in fine as one can. Still, one has the illusion of freedom; therefore don't be, like me, without the memory of that illusion. (I, 218)

Strether is suggesting here a philosophy of cultural determinism, one which seems to accept the limitations of the mould in a way that the elder James did not. While this culture provides the forms for human self-expression and understanding, Strether recognises that it also imposes limitations, for at the heart of his theory of experience is the understanding that the individual cannot truly comprehend that which is outside his or her own cultural sphere, nor can the individual develop along radically differently lines from those established by his or her own cultural models. The imagination cannot finally provide that Arnoldian bridge into the different, and by the end of Strether's speech the thrust of his 'Live-all-you-can' appeal is rather muted. He implores Bilham to maintain the 'illusion' of freedom because otherwise only despair remains.

Although several critics have remarked on the similarities between the two men, to confuse Strether with his creator here can be no more than dubious speculation. Christof Wegelin notes that Strether is 'the one among all of James's important characters one is tempted to identify with his author', and Oscar Cargill states much the same, being 'inclined to think that James identified himself with Strether in the latter's dilemma more closely than he identified with any other character in his fiction'.[22]

Yet the relevance of Strether's speech to the framework of the novel's overall investigation into the dynamics of human experience is more problematic. In incorporating the idea of cultural determinism into his narrative James was not simply willing to reject it outright as a restricting mechanism, as his father had done. Neither was he prepared to endorse Strether's view of it as the lamentable final word on the human condition. On the subject of Comtean philosophy James had been less than enthusiastic. Discussing the similarities between Balzac's *Comédie Humaine* and Comte's *Cours de philosophie positive*, he had noted that 'these great enterprises are equally characteristic of the French passion for completeness, for symmetry, for making a system as neat as an epigram – of its intolerance of the indefinite, the unformulated. The French mind likes better to squeeze things into a formula that mutilates them, if need be, than to leave them in the frigid vague' (*EWP*, 41). For a writer so committed to the ambiguous and indeterminate, one for whom vagueness was never 'frigid' but rather a sign of creative health, Balzac's schematisation of experience could only be viewed with distrust, despite James's professed admiration for the Frenchman's 'colossal completeness' (*EWP*, 44). Theodora Bosanquet, James's amanuensis, characterised his dislike of the overtly philosophical in terms useful to our discussion: 'He could let Huxley and Gladstone, the combatant champions of Darwinian and orthodox theology, enrich the pages of a single letter without any reference to their respective beliefs ... the personal impression [was] the thing sought.'[23] For Strether it is the 'personal impression' that dominates his experience of Paris, and that sense of life's limitations implied by his theorising speech is undermined during the course of the narrative, as he engages in a creative experience with Europe long before he even becomes aware of it. Jonathan Levin's analysis is useful here, for he notes that 'James is frequently drawn to scenes which exceed either a character's or even the narrator's understanding of events' as a means by which to stage the 'dynamic processes' of a mind in transition.[24]

Although in the preface James states that Strether's outburst in the garden is the 'essence' of the novel, thus lending authority to what he says, at the same time James seeks to undermine its deterministic message. Strether's speech was 'planted or "sunk", stiffly and saliently, in the centre of the current, almost perhaps to the obstruction of traffic' (*EWP*, 1304), implying that Strether's deliberate rationalisations about his own possibilities of expanded living may in fact serve as an impediment to his ability to embrace those very possibilities. Elsewhere in the preface James presents Strether's development in Paris in a positive light. Asking himself whether there can be 'reparation' for Strether, he answers: 'he now at all events *sees*; so that the business of my tale and the march of my action, not to say the precious moral of everything, is just my demonstration of this process of vision' (*EWP*, 1305). Strether's remarkable development is confirmed in no uncertain terms when James explains that his character 'had come to Paris in some state of mind which was literally undergoing, as a result of new and unexpected assaults and infusions, a change almost from hour to hour' (*EWP*, 1310). At the beginning of the novel we read that Strether had 'such a consciousness of personal freedom as he had n't known for years' (I, 4) but that the limit of this freedom 'had been transcended within thirty-six hours' (I, 13). Almost against his will it seems, Strether is embarking on the process for which he is constitutionally and temperamentally qualified and yet which he has managed to escape for many years, a process which Wegelin characterises as 'the making of an American cosmopolitan'.[25] In a review from 1900 of a volume of Robert Louis Stevenson's correspondence, James had characterised his subject's Samoan sojourn as one in which he could 'make his account with seeing and facing more things, seeing and facing everything, with the unrest of new impressions and ideas, the loss of the fond complacencies of youth'. James then goes on to quote from one of Stevenson's letters in which 'the prim obliterated polite face of life' is juxtaposed with 'the broad, bawdy and orgiastic – or mænadic – foundations' (*EAE*, 1269). James's appreciation of Stevenson's appreciation of the latter, in all its pagan sensuality, reminds us of the novel he was soon to write, where Strether sacrifices himself to 'strange gods' (II, 167), a phrase devoid of moral, Protestant judgement and resonant of seductive curiosity.

Critical responses to the novel have often centred around Strether's apparent declaration of a deterministic philosophy and, as a result, many have questioned James's claims for his character's development in the novel. F. O. Matthiessen accepted that Strether's vision is expanded but denied that this expansion has any great consequences for his future life: 'The burden of *The Ambassadors* is that Strether has awakened to a wholly new sense of life. Yet he does nothing at all to fulfil that sense. Therefore, fond as James is of him, we cannot help feeling his relative emptiness.'[26] Laurence Holland went so far as to doubt the validity of Strether's imaginative development. Strether is 'making up late for what [he] didn't have early' but 'he will and can do so only by living vicariously through the experience of younger people'.[27] More recently, Carren Kaston has elaborated on Holland's analysis, viewing Strether's experience as a perversion of the Emersonian transcendentalist vision. James, she says, 'socialised or domesticated Emerson's visionary eyeball self. Being visionary now meant floating out over other characters' consciousness, becoming a medium of reception capable of registering what it is like to be them, at the risk, as with Emerson, of making the personal self tenuous.' Thus Strether and other Jamesian characters 'accumulate experience, but lack what would be thought of as a self.'[28] Matthiessen,

Holland and Kaston accept Strether's mould theory, viewing the kind of experience in which he is engaged as a substitute for real development. Those critics who defend Strether's vision tend to draw on the Romantic concept of an autonomous imagination; both Joyce Rowe and Richard Poirier, for example, regard the construction of imaginary worlds as a valid attempt by James's characters to escape the limitations imposed on them by the 'real'. Poirier asserts that *The Ambassadors* 'offers remarkably beautiful instances of the hero's effort to transform the things he sees into visions, to detach them from time and from the demands of nature, and to give them the composition of *objets d'art*'.[29] Rowe interprets Strether's final choice to return to Woollett as an effort to restore the 'Emersonian claim that consciousness provides its own satisfaction'.[30] This polarity of readings, one which either stresses Strether's inability to transcend the confines of his environment or celebrates his skill in constructing an independent reality of the mind, inevitably calls for a response mediating between the two positions. Although Strether's reaction to Paris is culturally determined by his Woollett background – one that he has experienced as a mould – it is finally not an impediment to his imaginative and interpretative development. This development is dependent on Strether's recognition of both his own cultural embeddedness and his cultural difference. Subjectivity is neither natural nor autonomous; the self is located rather than transcendent, and Strether's final decision to return to Woollett honours this fact.

In the preface James describes the interaction between Strether's consciousness and the Parisian reality in terms of a chemical reaction. 'He had come with a view that might have been figured by a clear green liquid, say, in a neat glass phial; and the liquid, once poured into the open cup of *application*, once exposed to the action of another air, had begun to turn from green to red, or whatever, and might, for all he knew, be on its way to purple, to black, to yellow' (*EWP*, 1310). Strether's consciousness undergoes a radical change while still maintaining a certain continuity; the new does not replace the old but develops from it. For James, knowledge is a process of 'application', and a person's previous experience, the 'mould' of character and culture, is seen as the foundation and beginning of that knowledge. As already mentioned, this echoes the importance which the elder James attached to Europe for the development of America, where the mould of the Old World inheritance could provide a base for New World improvement. For the novelist, Europe suggests the possibility of attaining a more complex view of human understanding with which Strether can return to Woollett. Paris appears to him as some 'huge iridescent object, a jewel brilliant and hard, in which parts were not to be discriminated nor differences comfortably marked. It twinkled and trembled and melted together, and what seemed all surface one moment seemed all depth the next' (I, 89). The surface is seductive and yet immune to Strether's capture – he is unable to 'read' it, feeling that the Parisian world is constructed according to principles altogether different from his native America where appearances seem to be of little concern. As Richard Salmon has recently noted, such a language of symbolism and metaphor is characteristic of the difficulty inherent in decoding such a radically unfamiliar system of signs, where registers of surface and depth are constantly changing and where diverse parts lose their unique structures, coalescing into unexpected wholes.[31] Woollett, in the form of the formidable presence of the absent Mrs Newsome, is largely organised according to utilitarian and moral principles. Julie Rivkin points out that Mrs Newsome belongs (in exaggerated form) to the tradition of the narrator of realist fiction, an organising force who carefully marshals discourse to present a powerful impression of seamless reality through a deliberately constructed rhetorical strategy.[32] She is part of that genteel tradition that Santayana characterised as diluted Puritanism, softened still further by transcendentalism and centuries of New England culture; this was a tradition regarding itself as humane and urbane, yet also often mildly dogmatic and intensely conservative. In Paris realism is under threat, for appearance is of paramount importance and the aesthetic principle dominates. Strether says to Miss Barrace and Bilham: 'You've all of you here so much visual sense that you've somehow all "run" to it' (I, 206). Miss Barrace seems to confirm this impression when she answers:

> 'We're all looking at each other – and in the light of Paris one sees what things resemble. That's what the light of Paris seems always to show. It's the fault of the light of Paris – dear old light!'
> 'Dear old Paris!' little Bilham echoed.
> 'Everything, every one shows,' Miss Barrace went on.
> 'But for what they really are?' Strether asked.
> 'Oh I like your Boston "reallys"! But sometimes – yes.'
> 'Dear old Paris then!' Strether resignedly sighed while for a moment they looked at each other.   (I, 207)

Accustomed to being able to discern and judge effortlessly in Woollett, Strether is unaware of the extent to which his perception is mediated and restricted by cultural knowledge. He proceeds on the assumption that things in America are 'transparent', and that this transparency (imaged perhaps as a sheet of clear glass in comparison with the deceptively shifting surfaces of an iridescent Paris) is easily transferable, allowing the individual to grasp essences ('reallys') easily. In her playful way Miss Barrace corrects Strether's misconception, denying that the human mind can have a direct channel to the essence of things. If an object is to be understood it has to be viewed in the right 'light', in the proper perspective. That is to say, in the perspective of those who live within a culture. But even for those within that culture there is no easy leap to essence, only a detour *via* other surfaces, other resemblances: 'in the light of Paris one sees what things resemble'. One can draw a parallel here with *The Portrait of a Lady*. Strether may come to re-evaluate his own preconceptions at a much earlier stage than does Isabel Archer (his bewildered yet enthralled response to Europe is immediate, whereas Isabel maintains an Emersonian belief in her abilities until the celebrated night vigil scene of chapter 42), yet Isabel's discussion with Madame Merle on the role of clothes is centred on just this question of 'Boston "reallys"'. Whereas Isabel, like Strether, believes that the self is transparent, Madame Merle insists that it relies on cultural forms for its self-expression. Strether's particular way of thinking can be studied in his first encounter with the apparently wayward Chad in Paris. Strether has rented a stall at the opera and, together with Miss Barrace, waits for Bilham to join them. Chad enters instead of Bilham:

> The phenomenon that had suddenly sat down there with him was a phenomenon of change so complete that his imagination, which had worked so beforehand, felt itself, in the connexion, without margin or allowance. It had faced every contingency but that Chad should not *be* Chad, and this was what it now had to face with a mere strained smile and an uncomfortable flush.
> (I, 136–7)

Strether's 'bewilderment' (I, 136) is founded on the realisation that his Woollett prejudice makes no provisions for this situation. He is face to face with otherness. Unlike his friend Waymarsh who denies otherness altogether, Strether takes it in full stride. He may think that he has worked out things in advance, yet his mind is not, as he says, entirely without 'margin'. The full meaning of this term becomes apparent in a later passage in which he describes Mrs Newsome to Maria Gostrey. Mrs Newsome's difficulty is that 'she does n't admit surprises':

> She had, to her own mind, worked the whole thing out in advance, and worked it out for me as well as for herself. Whenever she has done that, you see, there's no room left; no margin, as it were, for any alteration . . . she hangs together with a perfection of her own . . . that does suggest a kind of wrong in *any* change of her composition.
> (II, 238)

Strether's image of the margin points at a solution to the problem presented in his speech in Gloriani's garden, namely, how human beings can overcome their cultural moulds. The idea of marginal thinking takes into account the fact that preconceptions must be applied for knowledge to be gained. While we cannot choose to put our preconceptions aside, we still have the choice of how to apply them to the world. It is a form of thinking that allows for the freedom of a creative response to cultural models, of the sounding of discriminating vibrations to counter the habit of relying on habitual modes of interpretation.

Strether finds that the cultivation of marginal thinking imperils his previously held convictions of an essential self. Maria Gostrey's inquiry of him, '*Will* you give yourself up?' (I, 20), questions just this notion, suggesting instead a formulation of the self as a provisional construct that can be made and unmade. She presents an option to Strether which he 'unspeakably' (I, 20) wishes to pursue. His consciousness of difference, one which feeds on irony, contingency and complications, makes the simplicity of preordained, direct action an impossibility – and makes Mrs Newsome an impossible employer of ambassadorial services. Hers is what I have earlier characterised as a Cartesian method of complacency that excludes surprises, reflecting her life of efficient managerial regulation of her family, her literary review, and of her ambassador sent to tidy up a domestic difficulty. Her regular letters to Strether, their contents teasingly unrevealed by James but their influence evidently powerful, attest to her desire for control and results. It is the encounter with surprises, with difference, which provokes Strether's liberating sense of escape. Strolling around Paris at the beginning of his mission he decides that 'what carried him hither and yon was an admirable theory that nothing he could do would n't be in some manner related to what he fundamentally had on hand, or *would* be – should he happen to have a scruple – wasted for it' (I, 76). Mrs Newsome's insistent timetable is thus contrasted with a characteristically Jamesian embrace of waste, of the conventionally scorned. The gentle irony of Strether's statement is that his immersion in Paris turns out to be the most productive thing he can do. But for himself, not for Woollett.

In his 'Project of Novel', James notes that for Strether in Europe 'everything is different. Nothing is manageable, nothing final – nothing, above all, for poor Strether, natural'.[33] This sense of unnaturalness extends to the way in which language is used. In England Strether finds himself in an environment quite other from the morally ordered one he has known in Woollett. He encounters a European use of language which intends indirection, whereas he has been accustomed to direct speech, to the assumption that the proper use of language will guarantee him understanding. Visiting the theatre in London with Maria Gostrey, Strether discovers that the world of the stage has come into the audience, transforming the world of real people into 'types' as unreal to him as those in art. It is revealed to him that this European world is composed of metaphor and not of the unmediated, prosaic apprehension of reality upon which Woollett has come to depend. Strether remarks: 'It was an evening, it was a world of types, and this was a connexion above all in which the figures and faces in the stalls were interchangeable with those on the stage' (I, 53). Rather than attempting to describe objects with precision, Strether realises that his fellow theatre-goers attest to the impossibility of such a task and even celebrate that indirection and indeterminacy. The 'great stripped handsome red-haired lady' seated next to him talks in 'stray dissyllables' composed of 'so much sound that he wondered they hadn't more sense' (I, 53). In Paris Strether confronts the full potential of indirect speech, armed with the language of Woollett which a more subtle culture exposes as inadequate. The failure of Strether's 'Woollett words' is shown in a conversation with Chad in which Strether reveals his motives in halting, unadorned prose: 'I've come, you know, to make you break with everything, neither more nor less, and take you straight home; so you'll be so good as immediately and favourably to consider it' (I, 147). Strether's words fall on culturally deaf ears, for Chad has circumvented that authority which Strether assumes they possess with the linguistic freedom of the Continent. The ambassador's dated notions of language, and its communicability, must therefore be revised: 'He had originally thought of lines and tunes as things to be taken, but these possibilities had now quite melted away. There was no computing at all what the young man before him would think or feel or say on any subject whatever' (I, 150). Like James's own circuitous style, the language of Paris refuses to render up a focused image. By participating in this alternative community Strether registers an alternative to the style of Mrs Newsome and Waymarsh, who speak in a language which borrows from established channels of authority and who assume a directness of communication. Martha Nussbaum has noted how, with her categorical if absent 'I' and her assumption of universal rules in the exercise of moral agency, Mrs Newsome represents 'a brilliantly comic rendering of some of the deepest features of Kantian morality'.[34] The problems that Kantian aesthetics pose for the literary text centre on the placing of moral principles regarded as universal into the contingent and practical world of narrative. Nussbaum cites Strether as an instance of a character who comes to reject the Kantian premise of intuitive obedience, suggesting instead that morality is acquired and enacted through the operation of imaginative vision, of the kind of attentive seeing that recognises life as 'perplexed, difficult, unsafe' (181).

The acceptance of difference, even its recognition, is emphasised throughout the novel as fundamental to Strether's development. As with *The Portrait of a Lady*, the opening words of the book are highly significant: 'Strether's first question . . .' (I, 3) indicates the degree to which the previously unencountered will impinge upon him. In his 'Project' James stresses the positive implications of this: 'Difference' is what Strether finds 'himself sinking [in] . . . up to his middle . . . difference from what he expected, difference in Chad, difference in everything'. 'Difference', James asserts, 'is what I give'.[35] The incessant curiosity of the observer, a form of behaviour later so richly analysed in James's autobiographies, unravels the simplicity of original intentions to such a degree that Strether is left feeling stranded in the quicksand of otherness. Paris confronts Strether with a 'consciousness of difference... What he wanted most was some idea that could simplify' (I, 81, 82). But before too long 'an uncontrollable, really, if one would, a depraved curiosity' assails him and never relents (I, 93). Millicent Bell observes that 'it is tempting, though not at all necessary, to give "difference"... a deconstructive sense James could not have intended, as a pun upon deferral indefinitely prolonged'.[36] This idea of unending difference has been taken up by certain critics who wish to stress James's affinities with the aesthetics of Walter Pater. The minds of James's characters are sometimes seen as ever-changing recipients of what Pater calls 'impressions unstable, flickering, inconsistent'.[37] Philip Sicker, for example, argues that 'the self for both James and Pater is merely the sum of its experiences, and, because this experience is a whirlpool of impressions, it follows that there can be no stable source of identity within the conscious mind'.[38] Although James's characters may find impressions merging, fluid and blurred, the use of the word *whirlpool* (Pater's term in his 'Conclusion') does not quite accurately capture the process of re-evaluation in James. In the preface to *The Portrait of a Lady* he describes the observer's use of a field glass to discern 'an impression distinct from every other' (*EWP*, 1075). Whereas Pater embraces flux as an end in itself (Richard Hocks characterises the end of Pater's fictions as 'like a mind which has closed down shop for the day'[39]), James uses plot and dialogue to correct first impressions; the mind is a palimpsest on to which new experience is overwritten, for impressionism is constructive and positive, rather than solipsistic.

Strether frequently interprets his experience aesthetically, though with a readiness for ethical awareness which makes him a less hedonistically intense personality than a truly Paterian figure. James achieves a 'fusion of aesthetic and social criticism' which Jonathan Freedman has described as Ruskinian, a combination of aesthetic considerations, social critique and moral drama that embraces Paterian conventions even as it undermines them.[40] Though Strether suffers an 'assault of images' in Gloriani's garden that may suggest a certain passivity and moral neutrality, even at this early stage he also discerns darker and uncharted depths which hint at James's preoccupation with the process of loss of innocence. The garden may be an Eden suffused with beauty and light, yet disquieting elements are present. Gloriani's face is described as being 'like an open letter in a foreign tongue' (I, 196), suggestive of American incomprehension of the European character; his smile, although 'charming', cannot hide 'the terrible life behind it' (I, 197); and Strether admires this 'glossy male tiger, magnificently marked' (I, 219). Echoing the tiger/lamb experience/innocence archetypes, James intimates that great art and civilisation are both connected necessarily to the play of primal energies, to forbidden knowledge. The garden of high culture is not immune from, but rather dependent upon, the 'waft from the jungle' (I, 219).

Strether's encounter with Chad and Madame de Vionnet on the river is the novel's greatest instance of purely aesthetic impressionism rudely interrupted.[41] His walk in the French countryside begins as a 'picture'. Relaxing from the strain of Parisian ambiguities, he encounters a landscape which is beautifully composed:

> The oblong gilt frame disposed its enclosing lines; the poplars and willows, the reeds and river – a river of which he did n't know, and did not want to know, the name – fell into a composition, full of felicity, within them; the sky was silver and turquoise and varnish; the village on the left was white and the church on the right was grey; it was all there, in short – it was what he wanted: it was Tremont Street, it was France, it was Lambinet.   (II, 247)

Strether imposes the frame of his memory on the landscape, the memory of a youthful aesthetic adventure when he was once on the verge of buying a Lambinet painting. Coming upon the very scene in nature that he had almost purchased in art, Strether 'freely' walks around in it: 'He really continued in the picture . . . all the rest of this rambling day . . . and had meanwhile not once overstepped the oblong gilt frame. The frame had drawn itself out for him, as much as you please; but that was just his luck' (II, 252–3). This comment serves as a counterweight to the deterministic philosophy expressed in Strether's speech to Little Bilham, for Strether has developed, not by breaking or breaking out of his 'mould' in any transcendent flight, but by extending it. The metaphor of the extending frame points to a conception of a form that can constitute experience without limiting it. The size of the margin can be increased.

The allusions to pictorial representation gradually give way to those of the scenic arts as Strether imagines himself in the midst of a 'drama' in which 'the very air of the play was in the rustle of the willows and the tone of the sky' (II, 253). For so long the bewildered observer of performances in Paris, Strether can direct, Prospero-like, on the stage of his own mind (and during the relaxed atmosphere of his wanderings) a drama in which a harmony abounds that was lacking in the real performance: 'The play and the characters had, without his knowing it till now, peopled all his space for him, and it seemed somehow quite happy that they should offer themselves, in the conditions so supplied, with a kind of inevitability. It was as if the conditions made them not only inevitable, but so much more nearly natural and right as that they were at least easier, pleasanter, to put up with' (II, 253). The appearance of Chad and Madame de Vionnet transforms the picture into a scene in which Strether's youthful recreation is shattered along with his 'virtuous attachment' theory and the insistent strain of innocence which it represents. The 'frame' of Strether's consciousness, however, not only remains whole, but is actually eager to include the new elements:

> What he saw was exactly the right thing – a boat advancing round the bend and containing a man who held the paddles and a lady, at the stern, with a pink parasol. It was suddenly as if these figures, or something like them, had been wanted in the picture, had been wanted more or less all day, and had now drifted into sight, with the slow current, on purpose to fill up the measure.
>
> (II, 256)

During this final stage of Strether's initiation, knowledge again comes through the margin. One corner of the picture had been left empty, virtually insisting on completion. 'What he saw was exactly the right thing' – the very component which completes the picture aesthetically renders it true to life as the last vestiges of Strether's disabling innocence are removed. As in other instances, Strether is not immediately aware of all the implications of what he has seen, but later, sitting in the darkness of his room, understanding is reached: 'He was at that point of vantage, in full possession, to make of it all what he could' (II, 262). Strether now sees things in the Parisian light described by Miss Barrace – he now knows what they resemble. His consciousness of difference must inevitably complicate the composed and idealised harmony of his mental journeying. Unexpectedly exposed to a 'sharp, fantastic crisis' (II, 257), Strether regards the encounter as something 'quite horrible . . . some un-provoked harsh note' that destroys the placidity of his earlier musings (II, 258). Yet his whole Parisian education has demonstrated to him that the assumption of interpretative simplicity is continually threatened and compromised by the shock of difference and the acquisition of new vo-cabulary. Having been lulled by his walk into repressing this dialectic, Strether feels the weight of his self-deception, articulated in terms of childhood innocence. He is like a 'little girl' who has 'dressed her doll' (II, 266). But if Strether's dressing up of the intimacy between Chad and Marie in a large 'quantity of make-believe' (II, 266) has contributed to his infantile state, its more important effect is to have maximised shock, thus fulfilling his deeper need to experience the disruption of otherness. The interpretative lenses of common sense and Protestant propriety are finally revealed as blinkers, because the truth that Strether was commissioned to establish resides at the fringes, out of reach of the Woollett field of vision. The final loss of innocence enables Strether to approach that kind of cosmopolitan sensitivity which James so admired in Arnold. That this entails returning to Woollett should not come as a surprise. Home may well prove for Strether to be a sunless sea to which he will float 'doubtless, duly, through those caverns of Kubla Khan' (II, 293), yet the Coleridgean allusion suggests the abandonment of his illusions of a French paradise for an acknowledgement of deeper, ancestral forces. Strether's self-criticism will attain its final clarity in Woollett; his decision not to remain in Paris with Maria Gostrey, even though he has lost the favour (and presumably the hand) of Mrs Newsome, indicates his unwillingness to succumb to the potentially perpetual pleasures of the aesthetic. The neat closure to Strether's life that this 'endless deferral' would ironically provide is rejected in favour of a return to a changing America where his cultivated consciousness of observation mixed with discrimination has resulted in the development neither of a crude American nationalism nor of an unthinking embrace of all things European. Strether is the unseduced Europhile. As James Senior suggested, he has used his encounter with Europe as the basis for his own future development – it has been the catalyst of his emergence into maturity. The fact of America's social and cultural fluidity – early on in the novel he remarks to Maria Gostrey that 'everything changes, and I hold that our situation precisely marks a date' (I, 73) – ensures that for Strether difference will never be too far away.

Conclusion

'The imminence of a transformation scene'

That James Senior's concern for and celebration of the lowly and the quotidian was made possible by a generous inheritance from his businessman father is just one of the paradoxes that emerges from a close inspection of his life and intellectual career. He writes with undisguised enthusiasm about the everyday passengers of an omnibus, that 'social institution' whose occupants, 'honest and faithful men and women' all, induce unease in the faces of the more aristocratic owners of any passing barouche. Yet the ability to offer such a paean to the democratic masses is due in large part to the freedom of not having to join those same commuting hoards because of a wealth derived from a man probably more accustomed to the barouche than the bus.[1] James Senior's intellectual dilettantism, his enjoyment of the occasional lecture series or journalistic commission, did not prevent him from tirelessly publishing lengthy works attempting to explain the philosophical system he had derived from his masters Swedenborg and Fourier. As William James noted in his introduction to his father's writings, 'Probably few authors have so devoted their entire lives to the monotonous elaboration of one single bundle of truths.'[2] The delicate balance that William attempted to maintain between admiration of his father and gentle criticism – despite their monotony, these are after all 'truths' – is similarly found in Henry James. '"Father's Ideas"' may have 'pervaded and supported his existence', yet James felt that they were probably more suited to 'the thin wilderness' of America 'than the thick' (and therefore more richly stimulating) milieu of Europe (*A*, 330, 275).

Despite being generously labelled by one newspaper in the year before his death as 'the foremost philosopher in America since the time of Jonathan Edwards', James Senior's abstruse and demanding work had, understandably perhaps, only a small if devoted readership.[3] E. L. Godkin, his occasional editor, remarked how James Senior had managed to become a sect unto himself, and William Dean Howells more famously quipped that *The Secret of Swedenborg* (the title of one of the elder James's books) had been most definitely 'kept'.[4] After his death, James Senior's ideas would continue to be circulated by a small band of disciples, most notably Julia Kellogg, who produced a digest of his writing in 1883, and Caroline Eliot Lackland (the future great-aunt of Thomas Stearns Eliot) who, in 1885, offered a thoughtful appraisal of his ideas in the *Journal of Speculative Philosophy*, America's first philosophical review. Despite the fact that James Senior's 'vernacular is confusing and thwarting' and that 'one must dig for his fine gold' which 'comes in blinding dust as well as in nuggets', Lackland praised her subject for 'descending like refreshing rain upon souls athirst for spiritual truth'.[5] But these were minority voices, and it has been James Senior's eccentricity and dubious parenting techniques that have largely undermined his reputation. If he is finally considered a minor figure in the history of American letters, my contention that he nevertheless played a significant role in the intellectual development and creative choices of his novelist son evidently requires different, less easily demonstrable, evidence. By his own admission, Henry James had read very little of his father's philosophy. Unlike William, who in many respects took up the challenge of James Senior's ideas to find in the process areas of close connection with his own thought, Henry was not interested in the elaboration of a philosophical system. Those writings of his father's which he had read, passages from *The Literary Remains* (including William's comprehensive introduction) and certain articles in the major literary magazines to which he also contributed, suggested enough to at least give him a working knowledge of his father's output. The family atmosphere itself, one in which philosophical ideas freely circulated, provided more of an education for James than his many, and often brief, school experiences ever did. It is difficult to document such a process of intellectual osmosis in any conclusive sense. There are references to an environment of almost obsessive mental stimulation in both William's letters and Henry's autobiography, but finally justification for my thesis of intellectual inheritance can only lie in exploring the ways in which Henry James was preoccupied, to varying degrees of sympathy, with many of the central issues upon which James Senior constructed his philosophy. My argument is based upon the assumption that, in the absence of any detailed commentary by Henry on his father's thought, the fact of certain levels of intellectual correspondence between the two men suggests the viability of this vague, and yet because vague more resonant and flexible, form of influence. Vagueness was a positive attribute in the James family, as I discussed in chapter 1, and William James's description of just that same indeterminate area of knowledge and experience which exists beyond the margin of one's conscious mind characterises the nature of the inheritance that I have attempted to reveal. It exists, William writes, in a place where 'our whole past store of memories floats . . . ready at a touch to come in'.[6] The preoccupation of this study has been to examine the various ways in which Henry's family inheritance was borne when it indeed did 'come in'.

James Senior's preoccupations were essentially religious ones: his abiding concerns were with the nature of evil, the process of conversion and redemption, and the final restoration of man within a Christianised universal brotherhood. Writing prior to the neurological investigations of William (whose *Varieties of Religious Experience* is an attempt to examine the same religious sensibility and vocabulary from a psychological and pragmatic position), James Senior, like Nathaniel Hawthorne, whose fiction shares many of the same preoccupations, worked with the intellectual equipment available to him, that of theology and the moral philosophy of sin. It is disappointing that, aside from a fleeting reference to *The Blithedale Romance*, there is no record of James Senior's assessment of Hawthorne's work.[7] But in a letter to Emerson he described the novelist as an 'everlasting granite', one of the few who had remained steady amidst an 'old world . . . breaking up on all hands'. Such a convulsion, he felt, the strongest would be able to withstand through their knowledge that 'what is disorder and wrath and contention on the surface is sure to be the deepest peace at the centre, working its way to a surface that shall *never* be disorderly' (*WJ*, 1, 89–90).

James Senior's belief in the possibility of a utopian future would make its appearance in the most unexpected of contexts, such was his need to reiterate his sense of living at, as his son Henry later characterised it, 'a great historic hour' (*A*, 362). In a postscript to his letter to Emerson regarding Hawthorne, he succeeds in juxtaposing the trivial with the universal, effecting a quite breathtaking but not atypical transition: 'Weren't you shocked at – –'s engagement? To think of that prim old snuffers imposing himself on that pure young flame! What a world, what a world! But once we get rid of Slavery the new heavens and new earth will swim into reality' (*WJ*, 1, 90). From gossiping about a marriage of which he disapproves, James Senior abruptly abandons the particular to consider a time of redemption in which humankind will be transformed to such an extent that slavery (including its conjugal manifestations) will have become a thing of the past. Commenting on this passage after transcribing it in *Notes of a Son and Brother*, James notes that it illustrates 'no better example of my father's remarkable and constant belief, proof against all confusion, in the imminence of a transformation-scene in human affairs' (*A*, 362). As a description of his father's belief in the self's constant readjustment and redefinition it recognises the essentially dramatic and dynamic aspects of James Senior's philosophy – elsewhere he had described it as operating solely within the 'theatre of experience'.[8] But James's words also sound echoes of those processes of transformation operating within his own work – not only those, like the supplanting of innocence by experience around which his father had based much of his own thought, but also other elements of change and differing emphasis which, in a wider sense, have implications for the ways in which James Senior's ideas are treated. One generation on from his father, James is writing for a predominantly secular and cosmopolitan readership, and his chosen form is fiction rather than the philosophical treatise. Instead of the freedom offered by the latter for the advocating of theoretical religious and moral certainties, in fiction such certainties require testing within the often unpredictable and untidy world of rendered human experience. Yet James's employment of narratives of conversion, those charting the changed state of conscious-ness of his fictional characters and of the character of 'Henry James' in the autobiographies, illustrates the extent to which the religious cast of mind, although diluted through secularisation, retained a potent residual force. James does not imply that moral experience is necessarily spiritual; he is obviously not offering a theological blueprint. But his method dis-plays the conviction that there are subtleties of feeling for which there is no language but that of spiritual crisis and growth. Giles Gunn writes that James Senior's children 'took to heart their father's view of the uni-verse as unfinished. Creation was to them as to him an ongoing process' in which the tropes of progress and transition, of identity constructed through narrative, could take on a spiritual hue.[9]

Such is evident for example in the title of his autobiographical frag-ment, 'The Turning Point of My Life' (1909). Originally commissioned (like 'Is There a Life After Death?') by *Harper's Bazar* as a subject for the consideration of a selection of writers, from the start James seems to have been unsure of his ability to complete his piece. In a letter to Elizabeth Jordan, and with the contribution of another on the same theme in front of him, he writes: 'I will with pleasure do my best with Howells's good example before me to become conscious, first of what the Turning Point of my Life may have been – if it – my Life – ever had any; & then to give you as vivid account of it as possible.'[10] All that James finally produced was a brief sketch, but one which, although describing a moment of artistic rather than spiritual decisiveness, centres around a moment of Damascus-like significance. Attributing to an old unnamed friend (probably Howells) the notion that 'every man's life had its "turning point"', James goes on to relate 'one of these momentous junctures in question'. Enrolled at Harvard Law School in 1862, he had 'stood at the parting of my ways' and consciously committed himself to a career as a writer. Employing the language of parable, he remarks that his stories, al-though 'small sickly seed enough', were 'to be sown and to sprout up into such flowers as they might'. We see James here self-consciously defining the moment at which his artistic life commenced.[11] Indeed the James family autobiographies offer the clearest examples of a shared concern with the experience of conversion, as a narrative strategy and as a *modus vivendi*. James Senior's various autobiographical fragments, including the accounts of his vastation experience of 1844, are deliberately aestheticised. They are made 'scenic' in the sense that their significance is as representative exemplars of certain fundamentals which their author holds dear. Rather than merely telling the life of a single individual, they distort the reality of their factual inspiration to become brushed over with the lustre of archetypal significance. The question of truthfulness and accuracy becomes redundant, as it does with James's account of his experience of the Civil War and his 'obscure hurt'. Conversion narratives, whether their goal is the justification of certain religious or aesthetic choices, are not concerned necessarily with the verifiable. In a letter to Charles W. Eliot in 1902, William James summarises this point in a manner which makes his insertion of explanatory 'factual' footnotes into his father's Stephen Dewhurst fragment the more curious. In such narratives, William argues, '*no man's* account can be accepted as literally true ... Everyone aims at reproducing an ideal type which he thinks most significant and edifying. But ... I think these inaccuracies of detail no great moment, for ideals all are *pointed to* by experience' (*WJ*, II, 337–8).

For both Henry Jameses the testimony of any past experience becomes productive in that the necessary and inevitable substitution of memory serves to function as a *new* experience, creating its own consequences and effects, often more imaginary than actual. James's acute awareness of the possibility of working up the 'scene' of a life in this manner is frequently expressed. Thus James Senior's vastation experience is alluded to in *Notes of a Son and Brother* so as to enable his son to cite those elements of it which he, the elderly autobiographer, would have chosen to emphasise: 'the *real* right thing' for James would have been to focus on 'the hurrying drama of the original rush'. Where James Senior's care in telling his story is to ensure that the emphasis rests firmly on the relief provided by Swedenborg's ideas, his son is attracted to the striking incidental image, the peripheral figure. The enigmatic Mrs Chichester, nominated by James Senior as his first teacher of Swedenborg, becomes 'the sweet legend' of the story. The Swedish seer's volumes lined up in his father's library shine for James as 'tokens of light' which formed 'the purplest rim' on the shelf (*A*, 340–1). In *A Small Boy and Others*, the autobiographer offers an account of the genesis of this sense of aesthetic potential, of the possibility of a creative manipulation or enhancement of the barest facts. A visit to the home of his uncle Augustus, during which a misbehaving daughter had been warned not to make a 'scene', prompted

the young Henry to consider the imaginative playing out of such pro-
hibited behaviour, the creation of his own 'scene' evoking for him a new
sense of pleasure at the 'rich accession of possibilities' which might ensue
(*A*, 107). Roland Barthes's description of the initiatory impact of such a
scene on Goethe's Young Werther echoes this sense of the importance
of the scenic for James. Werther sees Charlotte for the first time within a
carefully circumscribed border (she is framed by a door, buttering bread
for some children). Such a composition, Barthes suggests, is central both
to the possibility of provoking Werther's emotions and to the effectiveness of Goethe's writing: 'of all the arrangements of the objects, it is the
scene which seems to be seen best for the first time: a curtain parts: what
had not yet ever been seen is discovered in its entirety, and then devoured
by the eyes; what is immediate stands for what it fulfilled'.[12] For James
the power of the scenic, the early recognition of which we can thank his
misbehaving relative for, allowed for the possibility of revelation, nuanced
perhaps but still strongly felt.

But in addition to James's own account of the birth of his imaginative
life, I have suggested that his creative suppleness was fostered (although not
unproblematically) by James Senior's rejection of the twin orthodoxies
of a fast-growing business culture and strident individualism. His general suspicion of conventional and moralising strictures, those voiced
by a democratic society in which majority opinion often meant that
more thoughtful minority voices were ignored, encouraged a disposition
in his future novelist son to withhold commitment, to be unwilling to
compromise a deliciously situated vantage point reserved for the acutely
intelligent observer. The importance which James Senior attached to
the acquisition of experience and to spontaneous encounters with the
unfamiliar, elements which he considered central to the realisation of a
redeemed society, is upheld by James, but reformulated by him to as-
sist in the cultivation of his own artistic sensibility. Such continuing but
transformed inheritances suggest the persistence of certain sentiments in
a culture long after the ideas in which they were first embodied have
lost their expressive power. James Senior clearly perceived this, for writing to Emerson he remarked that 'a vital truth can never be transferred
from one mind to another. The most one can do for another is to plant
the rude formula of such truth in his memory, leaving his own spiritual
chemistry to set free the germs whenever the demands of his life exact
it' (*WJ*, 1, 71). It is these truths, 'the germs' (a characteristically Jamesian
choice of word), and not necessarily the ideas in which they were first
embodied, which survive the disintegration of theological doctrine or
denominational codes. For James, they are now less a system of creeds,
but constitute instead a manner of experience, a means of living, and an
imaginative account of belief and growth.

In considering the nature of this reformulated but still potent legacy I have sought to locate James Senior in relation to American transcendentalism, both to illustrate the degree to which his ideas differ from many of the more ahistorical and Edenic strains of that protean movement and to suggest the nature and manner of his son's own response to Emerson in particular and to transcendentalism more generally. James Senior's relationship with Emerson is a fascinating example of misplaced admiration, of early lionisation soon giving way to frustration and, at times, public criticism. James Senior's Emerson, much to his regret, was the writer of the First Series of *Essays* (1841), the romantic optimist with an apparent obliviousness to evil, the individualist who cared little for projects of actual reform. The elder James's opinion of Thoreau, recorded late in life, was only a more aggressively polemical version of many of the characteristics he had lamented in Emerson. Thoreau, he was reported as saying, 'was literally the most childlike, unconscious and unblushing egotist it has ever been my fortune to encounter in the ranks of manhood'. As a result of this judgement, Thoreau's works went unread by James Senior: the 'prejudice derived from PERSONAL CONTACT WITH HIM' was apparently enough to prevent the reading of *Walden* or *Civil Disobedience*.[13] Emerson's response to both the otherness of Europe and the historiography of America tended to stress the irrelevance and inferiority of the one compared with a pattern of seamlessly providential destiny marked out by the other. Thoroughly enmeshed in an endeavour to escape the significance of the Genesis story, Emerson's America is a bright, young nation; Europe represents the fall and its decaying results. James Senior's understanding of the polarities of Europe and America is not so easily determined; for him the fall is indeed a fortunate occurrence, effecting a complete transformation of the human condition. The America of recaptured primal innocence represents a false dawn.

Yet the second Emerson, the stoical author of 'Experience' and 'Illusions', failed to make much of an impact upon either Henry James. James Senior misunderstood the diffuse complexity of the Concord writer's concept of evil, and his belief in Emerson's serene aloofness from the unpleasant brought along with it the charge of spiritual immaturity. Where for James Senior Emerson's blindness had been religious, Henry James's 1887 charge of moral simplicity takes account of his position within a more secular society. Emerson now represents the cultural naïvety and provinciality of antebellum America which so compromised and undermined its writers. Yet although Emerson's innocence is read as a lack of sophistication rather than theological childishness, elsewhere the resonance of the Genesis narrative is strong enough to be employed as a metaphor to describe the painful and rapid transition in American consciousness after the Civil War: 'The good American, in days to come, will be a more critical person than his complacent and confident grandfather. He has eaten of the tree of knowledge' (*EAE*, 427–8). The collective fall brought about by the 'great convulsion' shatters the comfort felt by Emerson's generation, yet such a transformation will be beneficial to the American citizen, whose new mental state explicitly receives Henry's approval through his choice of the adjective 'good'. Emerson's apparent self-centredness and individualism resonated as part of a dialectic which saw it pitted against notions of integration and religious covenant, ideas which had informed the American mission from its puritan beginnings. John Winthrop had urged the importance of being 'knit together in this work as one man', such that 'we . . . make other's conditions our own, rejoice together, mourn together, labor and suffer together'.[14] Yet a community founded upon the effects of religious schism, formed by individual and minority rebellion against the dominant and dominating tradition, had already designed for itself a paradigm for future dissent and rupture. American transcendentalism, in its most individualistic strain, sought to refute the validity of Winthrop's sentiments, preferring instead to elevate and privilege the autonomous self over the commonweal. Thus Bronson Alcott: 'Church and state are responsible to *me*, not I to them . . . Why should I employ a church to write my creed or a state to govern me? Why should I not write my own creed? Why not govern myself?'[15] There were voices searching for a middle path between individualism and community: Alcott himself would elevate the status of the family as the ideal social grouping in his utopian community, Fruitlands; the marginal transcendentalist Orestes Brownson, writing in 1842 before his conversion to Catholicism and the social conservatism to be found in *The Spirit-Rapper*, aspired to 'communalism and individuality harmonized, or as we may say, *atoned*'; and the 'detached' soul of Whitman's 'A Noiseless Patient Spider' ceaselessly flings out its filaments to others, 'Till the bridge you will need be form'd, till the ductile anchor hold'.[16] Despite these efforts at accommodations, for a highly eloquent strain of American Romanticism the powerful poles of 'self' and 'other' remained largely distinct and at odds. For James Senior, the self at its worst represented ignorant egotism and solipsistic excess, divorced from the redemptive power of community; for Emerson and his disciples, the self was the sole refuge against social tyranny. Henry James's *The Bostonians*, his most explicit treatment of the social and intellectual milieu of his father, represents a complex (and, I have suggested, not altogether successful) exploration of these two positions: the 'self' of Basil Ransom, part James Senior, part Thomas Carlyle, encounters the strangeness of faded New England reformers and social activists in a narrative of inconsistent satirical and ideological focus. The unsureness of the book in part betrays the difficulties which the novelist faced in attempting to incorporate some of his father's ideas, in a more transparent manner than elsewhere, into his own art.

Instead of using the particularities of James Senior's background for an examination of these ideas of self and society, more profitable by far for James was his father's appropriation of the dynamic of the fortunate fall. This provided a narrative framework which, although removed from its religious roots, allowed the novelist to submit his characters to refreshing states of uncertainty and disillusion brought about by encounters with unfamiliar cultures. To use Matthew Arnold's distinctions, antebellum New Englanders seemed Hebraic rather than Hellenic, exhibiting a 'strictness of conscience' rather than that 'spontaneity of consciousness' of Europe which might foster moral and aesthetic sophistication.[17] James's tale 'Benvolio' (1875) dramatises this dilemma for an American artist: rejecting the European Countess for the more virtuous yet prosaic charms of the New England Scholastica, Benvolio's poetry, we are told, becomes 'dismally dull'.[18] More ambivalent in their response to Europe are Isabel Archer and Lambert Strether, for whom the customary and safe American harbours of, respectively, a strong sense of self-reliance and the New England mentality of Woollett are undermined by encounters with an at times shockingly unfamiliar otherness. For both characters, the cosmopolitan yet dangerous mentality of Europe forces an unsettling of assumptions, about one's self and about others. The novels effectively play out a succession of 'transformation-scenes' in which the arc of the fall (with its beneficial aftermath) is examined from a distinctly secular and psychological perspective. James Senior's utopian aspirations of man divinely redeemed and universally socialised are no longer relevant to a later generation and a fictional world of realistic accommodation and compromise. There is no getting beyond tragedy for James's characters, but the necessity of experiencing it, something repetitively asserted by his father, is essential for their moral development.

In the winter of 1860, whilst in Geneva and experimenting with Continental education for his children, James Senior wrote to Caroline Tappan, a mutual friend of Whitman's and Emerson's. The letter shows him at his most direct and eloquent. Beneath its language of absolutes and future millenarian certainties, it describes a narrative of transformation and growing maturity dependent upon a historical awareness, a narrative which is found diffused through the writings of his novelist son:

> You transcendentalists make the fatal mistake of denying education, of sundering present from past and future from present. These things are indissolubly one, the present deriving its consciousness only from the past, and the future drawing all its distinctive wisdom from our present experience. The law is the same with the individual as it is with the race: none of us can dodge the necessity of

regeneration, of disavowing our natural ancestry in order to come forth in our own divinely-redeemed proportions . . . [The Deity] is a perfect man, incapable of the slightest quackery, capable only of every honest and modest and helpful purpose, and these are perfections to which manifestly no one is born, but only *re*-born. We come to such states not by learning, only by *unlearning*. (*A*, 376)

The 'natural ancestry' to be relinquished is that which inhibits and blinkers, whether that ancestry is founded on Puritan rigidity, Emersonian innocence, or the kind of Americanisation imagined by Theodore Roosevelt. 'Unlearning' perfectly describes the flexibility of response to which the Jamesian self aspires: it embodies the radical scepticism of Charles Peirce's paradoxical assertion that 'our knowledge is never absolute but always swims, as it were, in a continuum of uncertainty and of indeterminacy'.[19] With Henry James's fictional and autobiographical creations, evidence of unlearning betrays a lesson well taught.

Notes

INTRODUCTION: THE NATURE OF INHERITANCE

1 'Are we to Lose Henry James?', *New York Times*, 18 July 1915, p. 14.

2 'Mr James a British Citizen', *New York Times*, 29 July 1915, p. 8.

3 'Mr Roosevelt's Creed', *New York Times*, 19 October 1884, p. 2.

4 Letter to Grace Norton, 14 November [1884], bMS Am 1094 (961), *James*.

5 Theodore Roosevelt, *American Ideals: And Other Essays Social and Political* (New York: G. P. Putnam's Sons, 1897), p. 26. Further references are cited in the text.

6 J. R. Pole, *The Pursuit of Equality in American History* (Berkeley: University of California Press, 1993), p. 287.

7 Martha Banta, 'Men, Women, and the American Way', in *The Cambridge Companion to Henry James*, ed. Jonathan Freedman (Cambridge: Cambridge University Press, 1998), pp. 21–39 (26).

8 Amos Pinchot, 'The Courage of the Cripple' (1917), in William L. O'Neill (ed.), *Echoes of Revolt: The Masses 1911–1917* (Chicago: Quadrangle Books, 1966), p. 277.

9 Theodore Roosevelt, *The Strenuous Life: Essays and Addresses* (London: Duckworth & Co., 1910), p. 1. Further references are cited in the text.

10 Lyall H. Powers (ed.), *Henry James and Edith Wharton: Letters 1900–1915* (London: Weidenfeld and Nicolson, 1990), pp. 44–5.

11 The two instances occur in an essay on Lowell for the *Atlantic Monthly* in 1892, and in the introduction which James wrote for Lowell's appearance in the *Library of the World's Best Literature Ancient and Modern* series (1896).

12 Daniel Walker Howe, *Making the American Self: Jonathan Edwards to Abraham Lincoln* (Cambridge, MA: Harvard University Press, 1997), p. 9.

13 Seymour Martin Lipset, *American Exceptionalism: A Double-Edged Sword* (New York: W. W. Norton, 1997), p. 54.

14 Stephen Pearl Andrews (ed.), *Love, Marriage, and Divorce, and the Sovereignty of the Individual: A Discussion by Henry James, Horace Greeley, and Stephen Pearl Andrews, including the Final Replies of Mr Andrews rejected by the Tribune* (New York: Stringer & Townsend, 1853), p. 33. Further references are cited in the text.

15 Carl J. Guarneri, *The Utopian Alternative: Fourierism in Nineteenth-Century America* (Ithaca: Cornell University Press, 1991), p. 366.

16 See V. F. Calverton, *The Liberation of American Literature* (New York: Scribners, 1932) and Granville Hicks, *The Great Tradition: An Interpretation of American Literature Since the Civil War* (New York: Macmillan Company, 1935).

17 Henry James Senior, *Society, The Redeemed Form of Man* (Boston: Houghton Osgood, 1879), p. 183; my emphasis.

18 John Jay Chapman, *Emerson and Other Essays* (New York: Charles Scribners, 1898), p. 43.

19 Richard Poirier, *The Renewal of Literature: Emersonian Reflections* (New York: Random House, 1987), p. 70. Of course, Poirier's reading has been countered by other critics who locate Emerson centrally within a social and political framework. See, for example, Len Gougeon, *Virtue's Hero: Emerson, Anti-Slavery and Reform* (Athens: University of Georgia Press, 1990) and T. Gregory Garvey (ed.), *The Emerson Dilemma: Essays on Emerson and Social Reform* (Athens: University of Georgia Press, 2001). I cite Poirier here as a reading of Emerson heavily inflected by James's own estimation.

20 *The Collected Papers of Charles Sanders Peirce*, ed. Charles Hartshorne and Paul Weiss, 8 vols. (Cambridge, MA: Harvard University Press, 1931–58), I, 3–4.

21 Charles Sanders Peirce, 'The Law of Mind', *The Monist* 2 (July 1892), pp. 533–4.

22 *Collected Papers of Charles Sanders Peirce*, I, 58.

23 *Ibid.*, v, 5.

24 For a discussion of the philosophical similarities between Peirce and James Senior, see Richard Louis Trammell, 'Charles Sanders Peirce and Henry James the Elder', *Transactions of the Charles S. Peirce Society* 9 (fall 1973), pp. 202–17. Beverly Haviland has an excellent account of Peirce's semiotics and their relevance to many of Henry James's epistemological concerns (*Henry James's Last Romance: Making Sense of the Past and the American Scene* (Cambridge: Cambridge University Press, 1997), pp. 59–73).

25 Quentin Anderson, *The Imperial Self: An Essay in American Literary and Cultural History* (New York: Alfred A. Knopf, 1971), p. viii. Further references are cited in the text.

26 Quentin Anderson, *The American Henry James* (New Brunswick: Rutgers University Press, 1957), p. 42. Further references are cited in the text.

27 Richard A. Hocks, *Henry James and Pragmatist Thought: A Study in the Relationship Between the Philosophy of William James and the Literary Art of Henry James* (Chapel Hill: University of North Carolina Press, 1974), p. 4. Further references are cited in the text.

28 Paul B. Armstrong, *The Phenomenology of Henry James* (Chapel Hill: University of North Carolina Press, 1983), pp. 99–135.

29 Merle Williams, *Henry James and the Philosophical Novel: Being and Seeing* (Cambridge: Cambridge University Press, 1993), pp. 12, 17. In addition, and following the work of Martha Nussbaum, is Robert Pippin's excellent recent reading of James as a moral philosopher. See *Henry James and Modern Moral Life* (Cambridge: Cambridge University Press, 2000).

30 C. Hartley Grattan, *The Three Jameses: A Family of Minds* (1932) (New York: New York University Press, 1962), p. 359.

31 Alfred Habegger, *Gender, Fantasy, and Realism in American Literature* (New York: Columbia University Press, 1982), p. 225. Further references are cited in the text.

32 Poirier, *Renewal of Literature*, p. 11. Further references are cited in the text.

33 Habegger, *Gender, Fantasy, and Realism*, p. 294.

34 Dominick LaCapra, *Rethinking Intellectual History: Texts, Contexts, Language* (Ithaca: Cornell University Press, 1983), p. 35.

35 Paul Giles, 'Reconstructing American Studies: Transnational Paradoxes, Comparative Perspectives', *Journal of American Studies* 28 (1994), pp. 335–58 (348).

36 Adeline Tintner, *Henry James's Legacy: The Afterlife of his Figure and Fiction* (Baton Rouge: Louisiana State University Press, 1998), p. 438.

37 Clifford Geertz, *The Interpretation of Cultures* (New York: Basic Books, 1973), pp. 123, 89.

38 Susan L. Mizruchi, *The Science of Sacrifice: American Literature and Modern Social Theory* (Princeton: Princeton University Press, 1998), p. 198. Further references are cited in the text.

39 *Collected Papers of Charles Sanders Peirce*, VI, 494.

40 William James, *Writings 1878–1899* (New York: Library of America, 1992), p. 458. Further references are cited in the text.

41 Charles Eliot Norton to Henry James, 13 March 1873, bMS Am 1094 (377), *James.*

42 Henry James, *The Ambassadors*, 2 vols. (New York: Charles Scribner's Sons, 1909), II, 167–8. Further references are cited in the text.

43 Henry James Senior, *The Literary Remains of the Late Henry James* (Boston: James R. Osgood & Co., 1885), p. 127.

44 For a recent account of the genesis and development of American Swedenborgianism, see Eugene Taylor, *Shadow Culture: Psychology and Spirituality in America* (Washington, DC: Counterpoint, 1999), pp. 61–98.

45 Henry James Senior to Edmund Tweedy, 5 September [1852], bMS Am 1092.9 (4281), *James.*

46 Unpublished letter, Henry James to Henry James III, 23–24 September 1912. Quoted in Carol Holly, *Intensely Family: The Inheritance of Family Shame and the Autobiographies of Henry James* (Madison: University of Wisconsin Press, 1995), p. 3.

I AUTOBIOGRAPHY AND THE WRITING OF SIGNIFICANCE

1 *The Tales of Henry James*, ed. Maqbool Aziz, 3 vols. (Oxford: Clarendon Press, 1973–84), III, 334. Further references are cited in the text.

2 Wolfgang Iser, *Laurence Sterne: Tristram Shandy* (Cambridge: Cambridge University Press, 1988), p. 27.

3 The status of autobiography as a legitimate literary genre has been much disputed. Paul de Man's pronouncement on the 'disreputability' of the autobiographical project, its 'incompatibility with the monumental dignity of aesthetic values', stresses the fundamental instability of the categories associated with writing about the self ('Autobiography as De-Facement', *The Rhetoric of Romanticism* (New York: Columbia University Press, 1984), p. 67). Although de Man's argument is pertinent in reminding us of the dangers of assuming a quality of transparency for language which it does not inherently possess, his equating of language's opacity with the inability of the autobiographer to communicate self-knowledge is, for my purposes, ultimately unhelpful. It is just this deliberate abandonment of the verifiable, of transparent language (in de Man's terms), which defines the Jamesian autobiographical project.

4 Henry Ward Beecher, 'A Rough Picture of Life', *Star Papers, or, Experiences of Art and Nature* (New York: J. C. Derby, 1855), p. 199.

5 Ross Posnock, *The Trial of Curiosity: Henry James, William James, and the Challenge of Modernity* (New York and Oxford: Oxford University Press, 1990), pp. 166–7.

6 Henry James Senior, *Moralism and Christianity* (New York: J. S. Redfield, 1850), p. 61.

7 Alexis de Tocqueville, *Democracy in America*, ed. Richard D. Heffner (New York: Mentor Press, 1956), pp. 143–4. Further references are cited in the text.

8 Quoted in Ian Watt, *Myths of Modern Individualism: Faust, Don Quixote, Don Juan, Robinson Crusoe* (Cambridge: Cambridge University Press, 1996), p. 240.

9 Jacques Lacan, 'The Insistence of the Letter in the Unconscious', *Yale French Review* 36–7 (1966), pp. 112–47 (135).

10 See Stanley Cavell, 'Being Odd, Getting Even: Threats to Individuality', *Salmagundi* 67 (summer 1985), pp. 97–128 for a discussion of Emerson's interpretation of the performative aspects of the Descartian self. 'Self-Reliance', he suggests, represents 'the moment (private and public) at which the theatricalization of the self becomes the sole proof of its freedom and its existence' (128).

11 James Senior, *Moralism and Christianity*, p. 100.

12 Henry James Senior, *The Secret of Swedenborg* (Boston: Fields, Osgood & Co., 1869), p. 186.

13 James Senior, *Society, Redeemed Form of Man*, p. 9.

14 Francis J. Grund, *The Americans, in Their Moral, Social, and Political Relations*, 2 vols. (London: Longman, Rees, Orme, Brown, Green, & Longman, 1837), I, 263–4.

15 Henry James Senior, *Tracts for the New Times: No 1. Letter to a Swedenborgian* (New York: John Allen, 1847), p. 20.

16 Posnock, *Trial of Curiosity*, p. 30. Further references are cited in the text.

17 William James, *Writings 1878–1899*, pp. 620, 621, 626.

18 Joseph M. Thomas, 'Figures of Habit in William James', *New England Quarterly* 66: 1 (March 1993), pp. 3–26 (6, 15).

19 William James, *Writings 1902–1910* (New York: Library of America, 1987), p. 598.

20 William James, '*The Emotions and the Will*, by Alexander Bain and *Essais de critique générale* by Charles Renouvier', in *Essays, Comments and Reviews* (Cambridge, MA: Harvard University Press, 1987), pp. 325, 326.

21 William James, *Writings 1902–1910*, p. 505.

22 Howard M. Feinstein, *Becoming William James* (Ithaca: Cornell University Press, 1985), p. 138.

23 *Collected Papers of Charles Sanders Peirce*, V, 505.

24 Henry James Senior, 'Some Personal Recollections of Carlyle', *Atlantic Monthly* 47 (May 1881), pp. 593–609 (607).

25 Leon Edel and Lyall H. Powers (eds.), 'Henry James and the *Bazar* Letters', in *Howells and James: A Double Billing* (New York: New York Public Library, 1958), pp. 27–55 (54).

26 Henry James, 'Is There a Life After Death?', in *In After Days: Thoughts on the Future Life* (New York: Harper & Bros, 1910), pp. 193–233 (203–4). Further references are cited in the text.

27 Haviland, *Henry James's Last Romance*, p. 104.

28 Henry Adams, *The Letters of Henry Adams (1892–1918)*, ed. Worthington Chauncey Ford (Boston: Houghton Mifflin, 1938), p. 163.

29 Posnock, *Trial of Curiosity*, p. 180.

30 Wendy Graham, *Henry James's Thwarted Love* (Stanford: Stanford University Press, 1999), p. 131.

31 Quoted in Giles Gunn (ed.), *Henry James, Senior: A Selection of his Writings* (Chicago: American Library Association, 1974), pp. 144–5.

32 Henry James Senior, 'The Divine Life in Man', *Harbinger* 7:9 (1 July 1848), p. 69.

33 That William as editor included clarifying footnotes to his father's narrative heightens the discrepancy between the actual family history and the imaginative conversion of it. William writes: 'The few items of personal and geographic fact he gives have been rectified in foot-notes, so as to be true of Mr James rather than of his imaginary mouthpiece' (James Senior, *Literary Remains*, pp. 7–8).

34 Henry James Senior, 'Essay on Seminary Days; on the Church; the State; Civilization', bMS Am 1094.8 (5), *James*. From internal evidence Alfred Habegger dates this

manuscript from 1865–6 (see 'Henry James, Sr, in the Late 1830s', *New England Quarterly* 64 (1991), pp. 46–81 (50, n. 10)), although reference to a still living Abraham Lincoln indicates that sections of it were written earlier.

35 *The Letters of William James*, ed. Henry James III (Boston: Atlantic Monthly Press, 1920), pp. 241–2.

36 James Senior, *Literary Remains*, pp. 145–6.

37 *Ibid.*, pp. 124, 125.

38 Henry James Senior, 'Theological Differences in Association', *Harbinger* 6:26 (29 April 1848), pp. 203–4 (203).

39 James Senior, *Society, The Redeemed Form of Man*, p. 45. Further references are cited in the text.

40 Feinstein, *Becoming William James*, pp. 68–70.

41 Merle Williams usefully links Kierkegaard with both Henry Jameses in her phenomenological discussion of the novelist (*Henry James and the Philosophical Novel*, especially pp. 17, 23).

42 Feinstein, *Becoming William James*, p. 69. An earlier (and shorter) version of the vastation story was published in *Substance and Shadow* (Boston: Ticknor and Fields, 1863).

43 James Senior, *Society, The Redeemed Form of Man*, p. 50.

44 *Ibid.*, p. 53

45 Wilkinson to James Senior, no. 1 (1 February 1844), James Garth Wilkinson Papers, Swedenborg Library, London.

46 *The Papers of Joseph Henry*, ed. Nathan Reingold, 8 vols. (to date) (Washington: Smithsonian Institute Press, 1972–), v, 368. Further references are cited in the text.

47 James Garth Wilkinson, *Emanuel Swedenborg: A Biography* (London: William Newbery, 1849), pp. 75–7.

48 Henry James, *Italian Hours*, ed. John Auchard (Pennsylvania: Pennsylvania State University Press, 1992), p. 61.

49 Percy Lubbock, in his 1920 edition of James's letters, decided to omit those passages of the November 1913 letter to Henry III which indicate James's dislike of the 'straight', merely historical, autobiographical form. The irony of this editorial decision, given the subject being discussed by James, seems to have been lost on Lubbock. Michael Anesko describes the editorial strategies evident in Lubbock's edition in ' "God Knows They *Are* Impossible": James's Letters and Their Editors', *Henry James Review* 18:2 (spring 1997), pp. 140–8.

50 Henry James, *The American Scene* (1907) (Harmondsworth: Penguin, 1994), pp. 136–7.

51 James Senior, 'Divine Life in Man', p. 69.

52 James Senior, *Moralism and Christianity*, pp. 57–8.

53 Henry James Senior, *Lectures and Miscellanies* (New York: J. S. Redfield, 1852), pp. 102, 113.

54 James Senior, *Literary Remains*, p. 139. Further references are cited in the text.

55 Richard Poirier has commented on the impossibility of confidently fixing Emerson within a set of philosophical principles. He writes that 'the [Emerson] boom does not mean that a simple or even consistent image of Emerson will emerge ... It is no longer permissible to go to him as to some department store that might or might not supply your list of household needs' ('Human, All Too Human', *New Republic*, 2 February 1987, pp. 29–36 (30)). As I suggest in the following chapter, both Henry Jameses record critiques of Emerson which share a dependence upon an illusive and illusory consistency.

56 W. Robertson Nicoll, 'Ralph Waldo Emerson', *North American Review* 176 (May 1903), pp. 675–87 (684).

57 Sacvan Bercovitch, *The Rites of Assent: Transformations in the Symbolic Construction of America* (New York: Routledge, 1993), p. 333.

58 *Ibid.*, p. 334. For a specific critique of Bercovitch's reading, see John Carlos Rowe, '"Hamlet's Task": Emerson's Political Writings', *At Emerson's Tomb: The Politics of Classic American Literature* (New York: Columbia University Press, 1997), pp. 17–41.

59 Philip Schaff, *America: A Sketch of the Political, Social, and Religious Character of the United States of America* (1855), ed. Perry Miller (Cambridge, MA: Harvard University Press, 1961), pp. 211–12. On liberal New England, Schaff writes 'of the extravagancies of Garrisonian abolitionism and female emancipation ... which have been promulgated in writings, public assemblies, and sometimes even from the pulpit, by such men as Theodore Parker and Ralph Emerson, to the great sorrow not only of the orthodox Puritans, but even of all earnest and sober-minded Unitarians' (117–18).

60 Daniel Aaron, 'Emerson and the Progressive Tradition' (1951), rpt. in Milton R. Konvitz and Stephen E. Whicher (eds.), *Emerson: A Collection of Critical Essays* (Englewood Cliffs, NJ: Prentice Hall, 1962), pp. 85–99 (94). Perry Miller, *The Responsibility of Mind in a Civilization of Machines*, ed. John Crowell and Stanford J. Searl, Jr. (Amherst: University of Massachusetts Press, 1979), p. 205.

61 See, for example, Perry Miller, 'Emersonian Genius and American Democracy', *Nature's Nation* (Cambridge, MA: Harvard University Press, 1967), pp. 163–74.

62 Daniel T. Rodgers, *The Work Ethic in Industrial America 1850–1920* (Chicago: University of Chicago Press, 1974), pp. 7, 14.

63 Augustus Woodbury, *Plain Words to Young Men* (Concord, NH: Edson C. Eastman, 1858), pp. 104–5.

64 Habegger, *Gender, Fantasy, and Realism*, p. 57. Further references are cited in the text.

65 George Santayana, 'The Genteel Tradition in American Philosophy', *Selected Critical Writings of George Santayana*, ed. Norman Henfrey, 2 vols. (Cambridge: Cambridge University Press, 1968), II, 86.

66 Dorothy C. Broaddus, in her study of the rhetorical structures of the cultural elite of nineteenth-century Boston, describes her subjects as men whose 'words are the product of a way of thinking of which they were not original producers. Yet often these writers try to effect change, to become themselves primary producers' (*Genteel Rhetoric: Writing High Culture in Nineteenth-Century Boston* (Columbia: University of South Carolina Press, 1999), p. 13).

67 Oliver Wendell Holmes, Jr, 'The Soldier's Faith', reprinted in Max Lerner (ed.), *The Mind and Faith of Justice Holmes: His Speeches, Essays, Letters and Judicial Opinions* (Boston: Little, Brown & Co., 1943), pp. 24, 19, 23, 20, 23.

68 Edel, *Life of Henry James*, I, 149, 148. Further references are cited in the text.

69 Quoted in Alfred Habegger, *The Father: A Life of Henry James, Sr* (New York: Farrar, Straus and Giroux, 1994), p. 430.

70 Quoted in Gunn, *Henry James Senior*, p. 116. Further references are cited in the text. In an undated fragmentary MS essay James Senior's recasts the Civil War in purely symbolic terms. The dehistoricising is explicit: 'In this great consummation the South represents the perishing interest, and the North the nascent one: and yet neither South nor North has the least adequate consciousness of its strictly *representative* significance. They both suppose that they are the sole real forces in antagonism; whereas they are all simply the helpless ultimate forms, the obedient but indispensable chessmen, by which the unseen universal powers announce themselves, and contend for relative supremacy' ('Prognostics. Apropos of page 341, volume VI of Carlyle's Frederic, and sundry similar petulancies', bMS 1094.8 (40), *James*).

71 See James M. Cox, *Recovering Literature's Lost Ground – Essays in American Autobiography* (Baton Rouge: Louisiana State University Press, 1990), pp. 168–90.

72 Paul John Eakin, 'Henry James and the Autobiographical Act', *Prospects* 8 (1983), pp. 211–60 (247).

73 James Olney, *Autobiography: Essays Theoretical and Critical* (Princeton: Princeton University Press, 1980), p. 21.

2 READING THE 'MAN WITHOUT A HANDLE': EMERSON AND THE CONSTRUCTION OF A PARTIAL PORTRAIT

1 'Some Staccato Thoughts Suggested by the American Fiction of our Present Day', *New York Herald*, 31 December 1904, p. 12.

2 George Willis Cooke, 'Emerson's View of Nationality', *The Genius and Character of Emerson: Lectures at the Concord School of Philosophy*, ed. F. B. Sanborn (Boston: James R. Osgood & Co., 1885), pp. 310–38 (338). Further references are cited in the text.

3 F. O. Matthiessen, *The James Family* (New York: Alfred A. Knopf, 1961), p. 428.

4 Hansel Baugh, 'Emerson and the Elder James', *Bookman* 68 (November 1928), pp. 320–2; William Stafford, 'Emerson and the James Family', *American Literature* 24 (1952–3), pp. 433–61. More recently Giles Gunn has explored the relationship between Emerson and James Senior in terms of both men's anticipation of pragmatist philosophy (*Thinking Across the American Grain: Ideology, Intellect, and the New Pragmatism* (Chicago: University of Chicago Press, 1992), pp. 40–69).

5 The final communication prior to James Senior's European trip was a letter from Emerson dated 11 and 15 October 1843 (*WJ*, I, 52). The 1847 letter is mentioned in a letter from Emerson to his brother (*LE*, III, 387).

6 Clifford E. Clark, Jr refers to this group (which also included George Ripley, Horace Bushnell and Frederick Law Olmsted) in his *Henry Ward Beecher: Spokesman for a Middle-Class America* (Urbana: University of Illinois Press, 1978), p. 122.

7 Henry James Senior to Emerson, 31 October [1874], bMS Am 1280 (1687), *James* (underlining in original). James Senior's pamphlet was never published, although a MS fragment of his writing on the subject is extant (bMS Am 1094.8 (77) (29), *James*). The broader historical significance of the episode is discussed by Richard Wightman Fox, *Trials of Intimacy: Love and Loss in the Beecher–Tilton Scandal* (Chicago: University of Chicago Press, 1999).

8 Caroline Wells Healey Dall, diary entry, 10 February 1851. Caroline Wells Healey Dall Papers, Massachusetts Historical Society.

9 William G. McLoughlin, *Revivals, Awakenings and Reform* (Chicago: University of Chicago Press 1978) p. 20.

10 Henry James Senior, *The Nature of Evil* (New York: D. Appleton & Co., 1855), p. 11.

11 Quoted in Habegger, *The Father*, p. 121.

12 James Senior, *Lectures and Miscellanies*, p. 378.

13 James Senior, 'Essay on Seminary Days', fos. 20–1.

14 In a newspaper interview forty-four years later James Senior would describe how, during his stay in London, he had bought several books which 'went to the roots of the questions' which were exercising his mind ('Henry James, Sr. The Foremost Metaphysician and Philosopher in America. Successive Steps in his Development of Opinions', *Boston Herald*, 17 April 1881, p. 3).

15 Robert Sandeman, *Letters on Theron and Aspasio*, ed. Henry James Senior (New York: Taylor, 1838), pp. 73, 76.

16 Gunn, *Thinking Across the American Grain*, p. 56.

17 Inge Jonnson describes this fragment as consisting of 'twenty-one examples, in which propositions from three areas are compared and discussed. The domains are the natural, the spiritual-intellectual, and the divine; and the author tries to demonstrate that, by

exchanging the central terms, the validity of these propositions can be transferred to their correspondences' (*Emanuel Swedenborg* (New York: Twayne, 1975), p. 105).

18 Reed quoted in John T. Irwin, *American Hieroglyphics: The Symbol of the Egyptian Hieroglyphics in the American Renaissance* (New Haven: Yale University Press, 1980), p. 9.

19 In *Representative Men* (1850), Emerson would characterise Swedenborg as one for whom the world is 'a grammar of hieroglyphs' (*CWE*, IV, 121).

20 Gunn, *Thinking Across the American Grain*, p. 46.

21 Henry James Senior, *The Church of Christ not an Ecclesiasticism*, 2nd edn (London: William White, 1856), p. 96.

22 Henry James Senior to Caroline Tappan, 28 October 1868, bMS Am 1092.9 (4276), James.

23 *Boston Commonwealth* reference in Robert E. Burkholder and Joel Myerson, *Emerson: An Annotated Secondary Bibliography* (Pittsburgh: University of Pittsburgh Press, 1985), p. 150. 'Emerson, Fourier and "Warrington"', *Springfield Daily Republican*, 2 December 1868, p. 2, col. 5.

24 The only other occasion I have been able to find where James Senior allowed a sustained criticism of Emerson to circulate publicly was two years earlier, in 1866. Writing in *The Radical* he complained that in Emerson's 'balsamic and fragrant' speech is 'no conception that the greatest and most powerful of beings, is also the least ostentatious or demonstrative'. Emerson, he continued, misunderstands that the deity 'is the grimiest, sootiest, sweatiest, most unpresentable, patient, and unrewarded Vulcan that ever toiled in a smithy'. Emerson's language is 'poetic', 'having no relation to the common mental habit of men' ('The Radical Dogmatics', *The Radical* 2 (October 1866), pp. 84–94 (87)). James Senior had initially tried to get this piece published in the more widely read *North American Review*. Charles Eliot Norton, the editor, rejected it, and in a letter to him the elder James worries about the effect his words may have on Emerson: e.g. 'Does it strike you that there is a word in my paper about the Radicals, which may be colorably interpreted into personal unfriendliness on my part towards Mr Emerson? . . . If you will frankly give me your opinion thereupon, you will confer an essential favour upon me. I will then – in case you think any objection lies to my phraseology, modify it' (6 June [1866], bMS Am 1088. (3836), James).

25 Henry James Senior, 'Emerson', *Atlantic Monthly* 94 (1904), pp. 740–5 (742).

26 See *LE*, VI, 221, 256, 266.

27 James Senior, *Literary Remains*, p. 293. Further references are cited in the text.

28 Susan L. Roberson, ' "Degenerate Effeminacy" and the Making of a Masculine Spirituality in the Sermons of Ralph Waldo Emerson', in *Muscular Christianity: Embodying the Victorian Age*, ed. Donald E. Hall (Cambridge: Cambridge University Press, 1994), pp. 150–74.

29 Ralph Waldo Emerson, *The Complete Sermons of Ralph Waldo Emerson*, ed. Albert J. von Frank *et al.*, 4 vols. (Columbia, OH: University of Missouri Press, 1989–92), I, 261; I, 200.

30 Henry Adams, *The Education of Henry Adams*, 1918 text, ed. Jean Gooder (Harmondsworth: Penguin, 1995), pp. 38, 37.

31 John Dunmore Lang, *Religion and Education in America: With Notices of the State and Prospects of American Unitarianism, Popery, and African Colonization* (London: Thomas Ward & Co., 1840), p. 391; James Senior quoted in F. W. Dupee, *Henry James: His Life and Writings* (New York: Doubleday, 1956), p. 11.

32 James Senior, 'Emerson', p. 740. William first described this distinction two years earlier (1902) in *The Varieties of Religious Experience* (*Writings, 1902–1910*, p. 79). Newman's

terms are from his *The Soul: Its Sorrows and Its Aspirations: An Essay Towards the Natural History of the Soul as the True Basis of Theology* (1849).

33 James Senior, *Society, The Redeemed Form of Man*, p. 43.

34 The New York *Evening Post* gave extensive coverage to these early lectures. Quotation from 31 January 1843, in Habegger, *The Father*, pp. 197–8.

35 James Eliot Cabot, *A Memoir of Ralph Waldo Emerson*, 2 vols. (Boston: Houghton Mifflin, 1887), I, 358.

36 Edith E. W. Gregg (ed.), *The Letters of Edith Tucker Emerson*, 2 vols. (Kent, OH: Kent State University Press, 1982), II, 654. 'Amita' was first published after Emerson's death as 'Mary Moody Emerson' in the *Atlantic Monthly* 52 (1883), pp. 733–45.

37 Andrew Jackson Davis, *The Magic Staff: An Autobiography of Andrew Jackson Davis* (New York: J. S. Brown & Co., 1857), p. 305.

38 *Ibid.*, pp. 316–17.

39 Andrew Jackson Davis, *The Principles of Nature, her Divine Revelations, and a Voice to Mankind* (London: John Chapman, 1847), p. 591.

40 George Bush and Benjamin Barrett, *'Davis' Revelations' Revealed; Being A Critical Examination of the Character and Claims of that Work in its Relations to the Teachings of Swedenborg* (New York: John Allen, 1847), pp. 23–4.

41 Henry James Senior, untitled review, *Harbinger* 6: 2 (13 November 1847), p. 15.

42 Edward Beecher, *The Conflict of Ages: Or, The Great Debate on the Moral Relations of God and Man* (Boston: Phillips, Sampson & Co., 1853), pp. 14–15. Further references are cited in the text.

43 Henry James Senior, 'Carlyle', *The Nation* 1 (1865), pp. 20–1 (21).

44 James Senior, *The Nature of Evil*, p. 258. Further references are cited in the text.

45 James Freeman Clarke, 'Review of Henry James's *The Nature of Evil*', *Christian Examiner* 59 (1855), pp. 116–36 (118).

46 John Albee, 'Review of William James's Literary Remains of Henry James', *Journal of Speculative Philosophy* 19 (1885), pp. 435–7 (437).

47 Caroline Dall, *Margaret and Her Friends, Or Ten Conversations With Margaret Fuller Upon the Mythology of the Greeks and its Expression in Art* (1895) (New York: Arno Press, 1972), pp. 112, 113. Further references are cited in the text.

48 F. I. Carpenter, *The Emerson Handbook* (New York: Hendricks House, 1953), pp. 122–3.

49 Arthur Christy, *The Orient in Transcendentalism* (New York: Columbia University Press, 1932), p. 121.

3 'UNDER CERTAIN CIRCUMSTANCES': JAMESIAN
REFLECTIONS ON THE FALL

1 Kenneth Graham, *Henry James: A Literary Life* (Basingstoke: Macmillan, 1995), p. 2.

2 See, for example, Richard Poirier, *The Comic Sense of Henry James* (London: Chatto and Windus, 1960), pp. 183–246, and Tony Tanner, *The Reign of Wonder: Naivety and Reality in American Literature* (Cambridge: Cambridge University Press, 1965), pp. 261–335.

3 Henry James, *The Portrait of a Lady* (1908 New York edn) (Oxford: Oxford University Press, 1987), p. 31. Further references are cited in the text.

4 G. N. Barbour, 'An Appeal to Time', *Godey's Lady's Book* 45 (1852), p. 151.

5 Jonathan Edwards, *Original Sin*, ed. Clyde A. Holbrook (New Haven: Yale University Press, 1970), p. 109. Further references are cited in the text.

6 Quoted in Benjamin T. Spencer, *The Quest for Nationality: An American Literary Campaign* (Syracuse: Syracuse University Press, 1957), p. 86.

7 James Fenimore Cooper, *Home as Found* (New York: Capricorn Press, 1961), p. xviii.

8 William Cullen Bryant, 'Sensitiveness to Foreign Opinion', *The Prose Writings of William Cullen Bryant*, ed. Parke Godwin, 2 vols. (New York: Russell and Russell, 1964), II, 389.

9 William Ellery Channing, *The Complete Works of William Ellery Channing D.D.* (London: Routledge & Sons, 1884), p. 338. Further references are cited in the text.

10 George B. Forgie, *Patricide in the House Divided: A Psychological Interpretation of Lincoln and his Age* (New York: W. W. Norton, 1979), p. 7.

11 'Henry Clay as an Orator', *Putnam's Monthly* 3 (1854), pp. 493–502 (495).

12 For an excellent history of the 'Young America' movement, see Edward L. Widmer, *Young America: The Flowering of Democracy in New York City* (New York and Oxford: Oxford University Press, 2000).

13 'Lucian and his Age', *United States Magazine and Democratic Review* 11 (1842), pp. 225–6 (225).

14 Sacvan Bercovitch, *The American Jeremiad* (Wisconsin: University of Wisconsin Press, 1978), pp. 94, 71.

15 George Bancroft, 'On the Progress of Civilization, or Reasons Why the Natural Association of Men of Letters is with the Democracy', *Boston Quarterly Review* 1 (October 1838), pp. 406–7 (407). Orestes Brownson, 'Remarks on Universal History', *United States Magazine and Democratic Review* 12 (May 1843), pp. 455–61 (458).

16 Oliver Wendell Holmes, *Ralph Waldo Emerson* (Boston: Houghton Mifflin & Co., 1885), pp. 101, 102.

17 John Milton, *The Complete Poems* (London: J. M. Dent, 1980), pp. 363–4, 368, 374.

18 Joel Porte, *Representative Man: Ralph Waldo Emerson in his Time* (New York: Columbia University Press, 1988), pp. 89–90.

19 Theodore Parker, 'The Transient and Permanent in Christianity', *Theodore Parker: An Anthology*, ed. Henry Steele Commager (Boston: Beacon Press, 1960), pp. 44, 49.

20 Cyrus A. Bartol, *Radical Problems* (Boston: Roberts Bros., 1872), p. 112.

21 Channing, *Complete Works*, p. 395.

22 Ralph Waldo Emerson, *The Early Lectures of Ralph Waldo Emerson*, 3 vols., ed. Stephen E. Whicher, Robert E. Spiller and Wallace E. Williams (Cambridge, MA: Harvard University Press, 1959–72), I, 145. Further references are cited in the text.

23 Jerome Loving, *Emerson, Whitman, and the American Muse* (Chapel Hill: University of North Carolina Press, 1982), p. 45. For a discussion of America's appropriation of *Paradise Lost*, see William C. Spengemann, *A New World of Words: Redefining Early American Literature* (New Haven: Yale University Press, 1994), pp. 94–117.

24 Porte, *Representative Man*, p. 178.

25 Phyllis Cole, *Mary Moody Emerson and the Origins of Transcendentalism: A Family History* (New York and Oxford: Oxford University Press, 1998), p. 180.

26 Porte, *Representative Man*, p. 182. Emerson's debt to the Puritan tradition has been most recently explored in Michael J. Colacurcio's *Doctrine and Difference: Essays in the Literature of New England* (New York: Routledge, 1997).

27 B. L. Packer, *Emerson's Fall: A New Interpretation of the Major Essays* (New York: Continuum, 1982), p. 67.

28 Dall, *Margaret and her Friends*, p. 118.

29 Virginia Woolf, 'Emerson's Journals', *Books and Portraits*, ed. Mary Lyon (London: Hogarth Press, 1977), pp. 67–71 (69).

30 Nathaniel Hawthorne, 'The Old Manse: Preface to Mosses from an Old Manse', *Tales and Sketches* (New York: Library of America, 1982), pp. 1145–6.

31 Ralph Waldo Emerson, *The Heart of Emerson's Journals*, ed. Bliss Perry (Boston: Houghton Mifflin, 1926), p. 182.

32 Hawthorne, *Tales and Sketches*, p. 746. Further references are cited in the text.

33 Nathaniel Hawthorne, *The Marble Faun: Or, the Romance of Monte Beni* (1859) (Harmondsworth: Penguin, 1990), p. 3.

34 Quoted in Matthiessen, *James Family*, p. 61.

35 Henry James Senior, 'The European and the American Conception of Manhood', bMS Am 1094.8 (17), *James*.

36 James Senior, *Lectures and Miscellanies*, p. 3. Further references are given in the text.

37 Walt Whitman, *Complete Poetry and Collected Prose* (New York: Library of America, 1982), p. 264.

38 bMS Am 1094.8 (77) (35), *James*.

39 Quoted in Matthiessen, *James Family*, p. 488.

40 James Senior, *Substance and Shadow*, p. 75.

41 Horace Traubel, *With Walt Whitman in Camden*, vol. 2 (New York: Rowman and Littlefield, 1961), p. 233. Further references are cited in the text.

42 Susan Sontag, *Illness as Metaphor* (New York: Vintage, 1979), p. 25; Jean Strouse, *Alice James* (London: Jonathan Cape, 1981), pp. 97–116.

43 William James, *Writings 1902–1910*, p. 82. Further references are cited in the text.

44 Milton, *Complete Poems*, p. 385.

45 A. O. Lovejoy, 'Milton and the Paradox of the Fortunate Fall', *Essays in the History of Ideas* (Baltimore: Johns Hopkins University Press, 1948), pp. 277–95 (278).

46 James Senior, *Society, The Redeemed Form of Man*, p. 165.

47 James Senior, *Christianity the Logic of Creation*, p. 120. Further references are cited in the text.

48 James Senior, *Society, The Redeemed Form of Man*, pp. 367–8. In *The Divine Love and Wisdom* (1763), Swedenborg writes that 'Love in itself is not to love self, but to love others and to be conjoined with them by love . . . Conjunction of love is by reciprocity and there is no reciprocity in self alone' ((London: Swedenborg Society, 1969), pp. 18–19).

49 Henry James Senior, 'Spiritualism New and Old', *Atlantic Monthly* 29 (1872), pp. 358–62 (362).

50 Myra Jehlen, *American Incarnation: The Individual, the Nation, and the Continent* (Cambridge, MA: Harvard University Press, 1986), pp. 90, 9.

51 Carolyn Porter, *Seeing and Being: The Plight of the Participant Observer in Emerson, James, Adams, and Faulkner* (Middletown, CN: Wesleyan University Press, 1981), p. 5.

52 Michael Kammen, *People of Paradox: An Inquiry Concerning the Origins of American Civilization* (New York: Alfred A. Knopf, 1972), p. 51.

53 Despite his admiration for those writers like Hawthorne and Melville whose stance towards the myth was a questioning one, Lewis curiously cites his preference in modern literature for those writers who show 'traces of the hopeful or Adamic condition', hoping that they 'may help release us a little from our current rigidity' (*The American Adam* (Chicago: University of Chicago Press, 1955), p. 198).

54 Theodore Roosevelt, *Hunting Trips of a Ranchman* (1885), *The Works of Theodore Roosevelt*, 28 vols. (New York: Charles Scribner's Sons, 1902–16), III, 7; *Ranch Life and the Hunting Trail* (1888), VII, 86.

55 James, *Tales of Henry James*, II, 252.

56 Henry James, 'An International Episode', *The New York Edition of Henry James* 14 (New York: Scribners, 1963), p. 320.

57 Robert Weisbuch, *Atlantic Double-Cross: American Literature and British Influence in the Age of Emerson* (Chicago: University of Chicago Press, 1986), p. 286.

58 Millicent Bell, *Meaning in Henry James* (Cambridge, MA: Harvard University Press, 1991), p. 21

59 See, for example, René Wellek, 'On Emerson and German Philosophy', *Confronta-tions: Studies in the Intellectual and Literary Relations Between Germany, England and the United States During the Nineteenth Century*, ed. René Wellek (Princeton: Princeton University Press, 1965), pp. 411–27. More recently, Pamela J. Schirmeister addresses Emerson's engagement with Kantian thought in *Less Legible Meanings: Between Poetry and Philosophy in the Work of Emerson* (Stanford: Stanford University Press, 1999).

60 F. H. Hedge, 'Coleridge's Literary Character', *Christian Examiner* 15 (1833), pp. 108–29 (124, 125). In a letter to his brother Edward, Emerson valued Hedge's essay as a 'living, leaping, logos' (*LE*, 1, 412).

61 James Senior, *Substance and Shadow*, p. 300. Further references are cited in the text.

62 James, *William Wetmore Story and his Friends*, 2 vols. (New York: Da Capo, 1969), I, 28.

63 Robert Weisbuch, 'Henry James and the Idea of Evil', *The Cambridge Companion to Henry James*, ed. Jonathan Freedman (Cambridge: Cambridge University Press, 1998), pp. 102–19 (104).

64 Arnold Kettle, *An Introduction to the English Novel*, 2 vols. (London: Hutchinson's University Library, 1953), II, 19.

65 Weisbuch, *Atlantic Double-Cross*, p. 293.

66 Isabel's transcendentalist credentials are further reinforced by her echoing Thoreau here. In *Walden* he asserts that 'We need the tonic of wildness' ((Harmondsworth: Penguin, 1987), p. 365).

67 David Minter, *A Cultural History of the American Novel: Henry James to William Faulkner* (Cambridge: Cambridge University Press, 1994), p. 9.

68 Henry James Senior, *Love, Marriage, and Divorce* (1889), ed. C. S. Weston (Weston, MA: M&S Publishing, 1975), p. 103.

69 Posnock, *Trial of Curiosity*, p. 92.

70 James, *American Scene*, pp. 81, 82.

71 Milton, *Complete Poems*, p. 388.

72 Jonathan Levin, *The Poetics of Transition: Emerson, Pragmatism and American Literary Modernism* (Durham: Duke University Press, 1999), pp. 122, 133.

73 Juliet McMaster, 'The Portrait of Isabel Archer', *American Literature* 45 (1973–4), pp. 50–66; Mary S. Schriber, 'Isabel Archer and Victorian Manners', *Studies in the Novel* 8 (1976), pp. 441–57.

74 Kettle: '[W]hat Isabel finally chooses is something represented by a high cold word like duty or resignation, the duty of an empty vow, the resignation of the defeated, and that in making her choice she is paying a final sacrificial tribute to her own ruined conception of freedom' (*Introduction*, II, 31). Habegger: 'In the end [James] produced a diminished picture of human freedom: Isabel's treacherous servility leads to a very conservative sort of responsibility, which finds freedom only in the acceptance of traditional forms' (*Henry James and the 'Woman Business'* (Cambridge: Cambridge University Press, 1989), p. 159).

75 Roslyn Jolly, *Henry James: History, Narrative, Fiction* (Oxford: Clarendon Press, 1993), p. 37.

4 DOING 'PUBLIC JUSTICE': NEW ENGLAND REFORM AND THE BOSTONIANS

1 *The Correspondence of William James*, vol. 1, *William and Henry, 1861–1884*, ed. Ignas K. Skrupskelis and Elizabeth M. Berkeley (Charlottesville: University Press of Virginia, 1992), p. 338. Further references are cited in the text.

2 Quoted in Jane Mahar, *Biography of Broken Fortunes: Wilkie and Bob, Brothers of William, Henry and Alice James* (Hamden, CN: Archon, 1986), pp. 149–50.

3 Richard Adams, 'Heir of Property: Inheritance: "The Impression of a Cousin", and the Proprietary Vision of Henry James', *American Literature* 71.3 (September 1999), pp. 463–91 (471).

4 'Lectures and Lecturing', *New York Tribune*, 24 November 1852, p. 5.

5 See Guarneri, *Utopian Alternative*, pp. 348–67.

6 Henry James Senior, 'Physical and Moral Maladies', *The Liberator* 29, 22 July 1859, p. 116.

7 James Senior, *Substance and Shadow*, p. 536; my emphasis.

8 Henry James Senior, 'The Meaning of the Present Crisis', bMS Am 1094.8 (33), pp. 7–8, *James*.

9 Henry James Senior to Samuel and Anna Gray Ward, 1 August [1863], bMS Am 1465 (729), *James*.

10 James, *William Wetmore Story*, II, 63.

11 Matthiessen, *James Family*, p. 137.

12 Henry James, *The Complete Notebooks of Henry James*, ed. Leon Edel and Lyall H. Powers (New York and Oxford: Oxford University Press, 1987), p. 18.

13 *New York Tribune*, 20 December 1850, p. 4.

14 James Senior, *Lectures and Miscellanies*, p. 407. Further references are cited in the text.

15 Henry James Senior, 'Modern Spiritualism', *Putnam's Monthly* 1 (January–June 1853), pp. 59–64 (59).

16 William Deal Howells, *Years of My Youth* (New York: Harper & Bros., 1916), p. 106.

17 William Dean Howells, *Impressions and Experiences* (New York: Harper & Bros., 1896), p. 21.

18 Redelia Brisbane, *Albert Brisbane: A Mental Biography; With a Character Study by his Wife Redelia Brisbane* (Boston: Arena, 1893), p. 339; George Ripley, 'Review of *The Principles of Nature*', *Harbinger* 5 (28 August 1847), pp. 177–84.

19 Quoted in Spencer, *Quest for Nationality*, p. 124.

20 Octavius Brooks Frothingham, *Transcendentalism in New England* (1876) (New York: Harper & Bros., 1959), p. 129.

21 Orestes Brownson, *The Spirit-Rapper: An Autobiography* (1854) (Detroit: T. Nourse, 1884), pp. 1, 29. Further references are cited in the text.

22 Fred Folio (pseud.), *Lucy Boston* (New York: J. C. Derby, 1855; New Haven: Research Publications, 1975), p. 13. Further references are cited in the text.

23 I am omitting from this grouping *The Blithedale Romance* (1852): it has been much discussed elsewhere for its influence on *The Bostonians*, most extensively perhaps by Marius Bewley in *The Complex Fate: Hawthorne, Henry James and Some Other American Writers* (London: Chatto and Windus, 1952), pp. 13–28.

24 Bayard Taylor, *Hannah Thurston: A Story of American Life*, 3 vols. (London: Sampson Low, Son, & Co., 1863), I, 111. Further references are cited in the text.

25 The review is only partially extant, four manuscript pages being missing. The MS copy (bMS Am 539.5 (47), *James*) is heavily marked with blue pencil; critical or derogatory remarks are excised.

26 Henry James, *Literary Reviews and Essays* (New York: Grove Press, 1957), pp. 230–6.

27 Johannes Wolfgang von Goethe, *Faust: A Tragedy, First Part*, tr. Bayard Taylor (London: Strahan & Co., 1871), p. 75. Goethe's lines are: 'Wass kann die Welt mir wohl gewähren? / Entbehren sollst du! sollst entbehren! / Das ist der ewige Gesang, / Der jeden an die Ohren klingt' (*Goethes Werke* 3, ed. Erich Trunz (Hamburg: Christian Wegner Verlag, 1963), I, lines 1,548–51).

28 'Passional attraction' was a law discovered by Fourier which, he claimed, would 'guide the human race to opulence, sensual pleasures, to the unity of the globe.' Translated by Guarneri in *Utopian Alternative*, p. 16.

29 Henry James Senior, 'The *Observer* and Hennequin', *Harbinger* 7.25 (21 October 1848), pp. 197–8 (198).

30 Victor Hennequin, *Les Amours au Phalanstère* (1847) (Paris: La Librairie Phalanstérienne, 1849), p. 10. Further references are cited in the text.

31 Victor Hennequin, *Love in the Phalanstery*, tr. Henry James Senior (New York: Dewitt & Davenport, 1848), p. ix.

32 Henry James Senior, 'Free love – marriage', bMS 1094.8 (11), *James*.

33 Henry James Senior, 'Remarks', *Harbinger* 8.5 (2 December 1848), pp. 36–7 (37); 'Further Remarks on A. E. F.'s Letter', *Harbinger* 8.7 (16 December 1848), pp. 53–4 (53).

34 For an excellent analysis of this exchange see Sidney Ditzion, *Marriage, Morals, and Sex in America: A History of Ideas* (New York: W. W. Norton, 1978), pp. 147–51.

35 Marx Edgeworth Lazarus, *Love vs. Marriage: Part I* (New York: Fowlers & Wells, 1852), p. 250.

36 Quoted in Habegger, *The Father*, p. 284.

37 Henry James Senior, 'The N.Y. Observer and Mr James', *New York Daily Tribune*, 16 November 1852, p. 5.

38 John Humphrey Noyes, *History of American Socialisms* (1870) (New York: Dover, 1966), p. 546.

39 Henry James Senior, 'Woman and the "Woman's Movement"', *Putnam's Monthly* 1 (March 1853), pp. 279–88 (280). Further references are cited in the text.

40 Quoted in Ann Douglas, *The Feminization of American Culture* (New York: Alfred A. Knopf, 1977), p. 46.

41 Henry James Senior, 'The Woman Thou Gavest With Me', *Atlantic Monthly* 25 (January 1870), pp. 66–72 (68). Further references are cited in the text. Two months later he reiterated his position: woman represents 'a diviner self than [man's] own; a more private, a more sacred and intimate self than that wherewith nature endows him' ('Is Marriage Holy?', originally published in the *Atlantic Monthly* 25 (March 1870), pp. 360–8; edition cited here is London: F. Pitman, 1870, p. 11).

42 William James, *Correspondence of William James*, p. 89. William's review appeared in the *North American Review* 109 (October 1869), pp. 556–65.

43 Habegger, *Henry James and the 'Woman Business'*, p. 209. Further references are cited in the text.

44 John Fraser, *America and the Patterns of Chivalry* (Cambridge: Cambridge University Press, 1982), p. 7.

45 Mark Twain, *Mississippi Writings* (New York: Library of America, 1982), p. 500. Further references are cited in the text.

46 Sandra M. Gilbert and Susan Gubar, *No Man's Land*, vol. 1, *The War of the Words* (New Haven: Yale University Press, 1988), p. 26.

47 Henry James, 'The Speech of American Women', *Henry James on Culture: Collected Essays on Politics and the American Social Scene*, ed. Pierre A. Walker (Lincoln: University of Nebraska Press, 1999), pp. 58–81 (76, 78).

48 Caroline Field Levander, *Voices of the Nation: Women and Public Speech in Nineteenth-Century American Literature and Culture* (Cambridge: Cambridge University Press, 1998), p. 19.

49 Philip Rahv, introduction to *The Bostonians* (New York: Dial Press, 1945), pp. v–ix; Lionel Trilling, *The Opposing Self* (New York: Viking, 1955), pp. 104–17; Charles R. Anderson, 'James's Portrait of a Southerner', *American Literature* 27 (1955), pp. 309–31; Kenneth Graham, *Indirections of the Novel: James, Conrad and Forster* (Cambridge: Cambridge University Press, 1988), p. 37; Elsa Nettels, *Language and*

Gender in American Fiction: Howells, James, Wharton and Cather (Basingstoke: Macmillan, 1997), pp. 77–8.

50 Ian F. A. Bell, *Henry James and the Past* (Basingstoke: Macmillan, 1991), pp. 99–101.

51 Habegger, *Henry James and the 'Woman Business'*, p. 188.

52 Thomas Carlyle, *On Heroes, Hero-Worship and the Heroic in History* (London: Chapman and Hall, 1840), pp. 147, 148.

53 Bell, *Henry James and the Past*, p. 116.

54 Habegger, *Henry James and the 'Woman Business'*, p. 195.

55 Algernon Charles Swinburne, *Note of an English Republican on the Muscovite Crusade* (London: Chatto and Windus, 1876), p. 10.

56 For a discussion of the rise of the working woman in nineteenth- century America, see Rodgers, *The Work Ethic in Industrial America*, pp. 182–209.

57 Habegger, *Henry James and the 'Woman Business'*, p. 196.

58 Henry James Senior to Charles Eliot Norton, 19 July [1865?], bMS Am 1088 (3834), Charles Eliot Norton Papers, Houghton Library, Harvard University. At the beginning of his lecture James Senior made his wishes on this matter explicit. Attached to the MS is the following instruction:

> I beg to say that the Essay I am about to read was not written for present publication: it is merely a memorial of Carlyle, harvested from an abundant observation, and to be utilized possibly by his future biographers. The personal facts and anecdotes which are embodied in it, tho' they adapt it very well to drawing-room discourse, obviously preclude it from publication during Carlyle's life, and I have never failed accordingly to request that no notes should be taken of it, and no report of it attempted.
>
> (['Recollections of Carlyle'], bMS Am 1094.8 (41), *James*)

59 William James, *Correspondence of William James*, p. 184.

60 Thomas Carlyle, *Oliver Cromwell's Letters and Speeches: With Elucidations* (1843), *The Centenary Edition of the Works of Thomas Carlyle*, ed. H. D. Traill, vols. VI–IX (London: Chapman and Hall, 1896–8), VI, 1.

61 See Andrew Hook, 'Carlyle and America', *From Goosecreek to Gandercleugh: Studies in Scottish–American Literary and Cultural History* (East Linton: Tuckwell Press, 1999), pp. 135–59.

62 Quoted in Jules Paul Seigel (ed.), *Thomas Carlyle: The Critical Heritage* (London: Routledge and Kegan Paul, 1971), p. 312. Further references are cited in the text.

63 David A. Wasson, 'A Letter to Thomas Carlyle', *Atlantic Monthly* 12 (October 1863), pp. 497–504 (501).

64 George Fitzhugh, *Cannibals All! or, Slaves Without Masters* (1857) (Cambridge, MA: Belknap Press, 1982), p. 10. Further references are cited in the text.

65 Whitman, 'Democratic Vistas', *Complete Poetry and Collected Prose*, pp. 929–94 (943).

66 James Senior, 'Some Personal Recollections of Carlyle', p. 596. Further references are cited in the text.

67 Quoted in Habegger, *Henry James and the 'Woman Business'*, p. 197.

68 James Freeman Clarke, *Nineteenth-Century Questions* (1897) (New York: Books for Libraries Press, 1972), p. 193.

5 BREAKING THE MOULD

1 Henry James, *Portraits of Places* (London: Macmillan, 1883), pp. 75–6.

2 Porter, *Seeing and Being*, p. 35.

3 Henry James, *The Sacred Fount* (Harmondsworth: Penguin, 1994), p. 93. Further references are cited in the text.

4 Robert E. Collins (ed.), *Theodore Parker: American Transcendentalist* (Metuchen, NJ: Scarecrow Press, 1973), pp. 65, 69. Further references are cited in the text.

5 Robert Weisbuch has argued persuasively that Emerson's obliviousness to the treasures of European art was a deliberate strategy on his part of post-colonial resistance, rather than James's image of provinciality ('Post-Colonial Emerson and the Erasure of Europe', *The Cambridge Companion to Ralph Waldo Emerson*, ed. Joel Porte and Saundra Morris (Cambridge: Cambridge University Press, 1999), pp. 192–217).

6 Ford Madox Hueffer, *Henry James: A Critical Study* (London: Martin Secker, 1913), pp. 100–1.

7 Quoted in Sidney Coulling, *Matthew Arnold and his Critics* (Athens: University of Ohio Press, 1974), p. 287. The lecture was delivered in America eighteen times in all.

8 *Letters of Charles Eliot Norton*, II, 167.

9 Matthew Arnold, *Discourses in America* (London: Macmillan & Co., 1896), pp. 179, 203. Further references are cited in the text.

10 James Senior, 'Meaning of the Present Crisis', pp. 51–2.

11 *Complete Notebooks of Henry James*, p. 550.

12 Nathaniel Hawthorne, 'The Ancestral Footstep', *The American Claimant Manuscripts*, ed. Edward H. Davidson *et al.* (Ohio: Ohio State University Press, 1977), p. 72. Further references are cited in the text.

13 Tony Tanner, introduction to William Dean Howells, *Indian Summer* (Oxford: Oxford University Press, 1988), p. xiii.

14 Howells, *Indian Summer*, pp. 64–5.

15 Robert Dawidoff, *The Genteel Tradition and the Sacred Rage* (Chapel Hill: University of North Carolina Press, 1992), pp. 93–4.

16 Dorothea Krook, *The Ordeal of Consciousness in Henry James* (Cambridge: Cambridge University Press, 1967), pp. 410–11.

17 T. S. Eliot, *Selected Prose of T. S. Eliot*, ed. Frank Kermode (London: Faber & Faber, 1975), p. 151.

18 James Senior, *Christianity the Logic of Creation*, pp. 221–2.

19 James Senior, *The Church of Christ Not an Ecclesiasticism*, p. 105.

20 Henry James Senior, 'An American in Europe . . . IV', *New-York Daily Tribune*, 9 October 1855, p. 6.

21 James, *The Ambassadors*, I, 196. Further references are cited in the text.

22 Christof Wegelin, *The Image of Europe in Henry James* (Dallas: Southern Methodist University Press, 1958), p. 88; Oscar Cargill, *The Novels of Henry James* (London and New York: Macmillan, 1961), p. 335n.

23 Theodora Bosanquet, *Henry James at Work* (London: Hogarth Press, 1924), p. 27.

24 Levin, *Poetics of Transition*, p. 118.

25 Wegelin, *Image of Europe*, p. 88.

26 F. O. Matthiessen, *Henry James: The Major Phase* (Oxford: Oxford University Press, 1944), p. 39.

27 Laurence Holland, *The Expense of Vision: Essays on the Craft of Henry James* (Baltimore: Johns Hopkins University Press, 1982), p. 251.

28 Carren Kaston, *Imagination and Desire in the Novels of Henry James* (New Brunswick, NJ: Rutgers University Press, 1984), p. 69.

29 Richard Poirier, *A World Elsewhere: The Place of Style in American Literature* (Oxford: Oxford University Press, 1966), p. 124.

30 Joyce Rowe, *Equivocal Endings in Classic American Novels* (Cambridge: Cambridge University Press, 1989), p. 99.

31 Richard Salmon, *Henry James and the Culture of Publicity* (Cambridge: Cambridge University Press, 1997), pp. 159–62.
32 See Julie Rivkin, 'The Logic of Delegation in *The Ambassadors*', *PMLA* 101.5 (1986), pp. 819–31.
33 *Complete Notebooks of Henry James*, p. 561.
34 Martha C. Nussbaum, *Love's Knowledge: Essays on Philosophy and Literature* (New York and Oxford: Oxford University Press, 1990), p. 179. Further references are cited in the text.
35 *Complete Notebooks of Henry James*, p. 562.
36 Bell, *Meaning in Henry James*, p. 327.
37 Walter Pater, *Essays on Literature and Art* (London: J. M. Dent, 1990), p. 45.
38 Philip Sicker, *Love and the Quest for Identity in the Fiction of Henry James* (Princeton: Princeton University Press, 1980), p. 23.
39 Hocks, *Henry James and Pragmatist Thought*, p. 67.
40 Jonathan Freedman, *Professions of Taste: Henry James, British Aestheticism, and Commodity Culture* (Stanford: Stanford University Press, 1990), p. 100.
41 See Posnock, *Trial of Curiosity*, pp. 221–49 for an excellent discussion of this scene and its rhetoric of violence.

CONCLUSION: 'THE IMMINENCE OF
A TRANSFORMATION SCENE'

1 Henry James Senior, 'The Omnibus, and its Morality', bMS Am 1094.8 (77), *James*.
2 James Senior, *Literary Remains* , p. 9.
3 'Henry James, Sr. The Foremost Metaphysician and Philosopher in America', p. 3.
4 Rollo Ogden (ed.), *Life and Letters of Edwin Lawrence Godkin*, 2 vols. (London: Macmillan Co., 1907), II, 117–18; Howells quoted by Charles Eliot Norton, *Letters of Charles Eliot Norton*, II, 379.
5 Caroline Eliot Lackland, 'Henry James, the Seer', *Journal of Speculative Philosophy* 19 (1885), pp. 53–60 (60, 54).
6 William James, *Writings, 1902–1910*, pp. 214–15.
7 In a letter to Edmund Tweedy, James Senior describes meeting an acquaintance who, on reading Hawthorne's novel, wonders if 'concubinage' was indulged at Brook Farm. James replies: 'I of course willingly protested against such an insinuation ... but the Herald and Express have so bedevilled the idea of Socialism in the minds of our spoon-fed people, that it conveys no thought to them but that of licence' (5 September 1852, bMS Am 1092.9 (4282), *James*).
8 James Senior, *Christianity the Logic of Creation*, p. 24.
9 Gunn, *Thinking Across the American Grain*, p. 68.
10 Edel and Powers, 'Henry James and the *Bazar* Letters', p. 55.
11 *Complete Notebooks of Henry James*, pp. 437–8.
12 Roland Barthes, *A Lover's Discourse*, tr. Richard Howard (New York: Hill and Wang, 1978), p. 192.
13 'Mr Henry James Explains Certain Statements Recently Published, his Former Acquaintance with Thomas Carlyle and his Estimation of Alcott and Thoreau', *Boston Sunday Herald*, 24 April 1881, p. 9.
14 John Winthrop, 'Model of Christian Charity', *Winthrop Papers: 1623–1630* (Boston: Massachusetts Historical Society, 1931), p. 294.
15 Quoted in David DeLeon, *The American as Anarchist: Reflections on Indigenous Radicalism* (Baltimore: Johns Hopkins University Press, 1978), p. 22.

16 Orestes Brownson, 'Community System', *United States and Democratic Review* 12 (February 1842), pp. 129–44 (134); Whitman, *Complete Poetry and Collected Prose*, p. 564.

17 Matthew Arnold, *Selected Prose* (Harmondsworth: Penguin, 1987), p. 276.

18 *Tales of Henry James*, III, 59.

19 Charles Sanders Peirce, 'Fallibilism, Continuity, and Evolution', *Collected Papers of Charles Sanders Peirce*, I, 76.

Index